PITT LATIN AMERICAN SERIES PLAS

Urban Politics in Brazil

URBAN POLITICS IN BRAZIL
The Rise of Populism, 1925–1945

☐ Michael L. Conniff

UNIVERSITY OF PITTSBURGH PRESS

Published by the University of Pittsburgh Press, Pittsburgh, Pa. 15260

Feffer and Simons, Inc., London
Manufactured in the United States of America

Library of Congress Cataloging in Publication Data

Conniff, Michael L.
Urban politics in Brazil.

(Pitt Latin American series)
Bibliography: p. 209
Includes index.
1. Rio de Janeiro—Politics and government—Case studies. 2. Municipal government—Brazil—Rio de Janeiro—Case studies. 3. Populism—Brazil—Rio de Janeiro—Case studies. 4. Brazil—Politics and government—1889—1930—Case studies. 5. Brazil—Politics and government—1930–1954—Case studies. I. Title.
F2646.3.C65 320.98153 80–26605
ISBN 0–8229–3438–8

For my parents and Marc, Daniel, and Andrés

Contents

Illustrations

Tables

Abbreviations

ABE	Brazilian Education Association
ABI	Brazilian Press Association
AC-Rio	Commercial Association of Rio de Janeiro
AEC	Commercial Employees Association
AIB	Brazilian Integralist Action
ANC	Constitutional Assembly, 1933–1934
ANL	Alliance for National Liberation
ASA	Archdiocesan Social Association
BOC	Workers and Peasants Bloc
CAP	Retirement and Pension Fund
CFCE	Federal Council on Foreign Commerce
CI	Industrial Center
CLT	Consolidation of Labor Laws
CNT	National Labor Council
CPC	Carioca Proletarian Convention
CRC	Carioca Republican Center
DASP	Departamento Administrativo de Serviço Público (Civil Service)
DIP	Department of Press and Publicity
DOPS	Delegacia de Ordem Política e Social (Political Police)
IAP	Retirement and Pension Institute
IAPI	Retirement and Pension Institute for Industrial Workers
IAS	Social Assistance Institute
IBGE	Instituto Brasileiro de Geografia e Estatística
ILO	International Labor Organization
LEC	Catholic Electoral League

LSN	National Security Act
PADF	Autonomist Party of the Federal District
PCB	Brazilian Communist Party
PD	Democratic Party
PE	Economist Party
PRM	Republican Party of Minas Gerais
PRR	Republican Party of Rio Grande do Sul
PSB	Socialist Party of Brazil
PSB-UPP	Brazilian Socialist Party–Proletarian Political Union
PTB	Brazilian Labor Party
SOS	Social Welfare Service
STM	Supreme Military Tribunal
UDB	Brazilian Democratic Union
UDF	University of the Federal District
UOC	Workers and Peasants Union

Note: For abbreviations of archival collections, consult the Bibliography.

Preface

Understanding populism is essential for the student of modern Brazilian politics, yet scholars have achieved little consensus on what it is. They generally agree that populism involves a mass urban electorate, charismatic leadership, and a balancing of diverse interests in the political arena. Beyond such simple concurrence, however, scholars have formulated the most diverse interpretations of populism. For some, it is opportunistic manipulation of newly enfranchised voters. For others, it is primarily a mechanism of social control for the containment of urban labor. Still others consider it a tool by which newer elements in a ruling elite wrest political influence from older ones. And another group of scholars view populism as an imperfect adaptation of Western democratic procedures to the late-industrializing countries of the Third World. All these interpretations are "true" in that they portray a particular set of historical facts and make them understandable within a familiar theoretical framework. But they are historically unsatisfying because they describe only part of the story—an episode, a movement, a leader, a crisis, or a failure.

This book, although monographic and limited in scope because it concentrates on populist politics in the city of Rio de Janeiro during two decades, aims to be more comprehensive in two ways. First, it defines populism within the larger context of urban history and politics. Second, it studies the circumstances surrounding the rise of populism and then traces its development into a national political phenomenon. Another, though less central, contribution is the book's examination of urban politics not as local but as big-city affairs that interacted with and increasingly shaped national politics in the interwar years. Still, the theoretical treatment of populism contained in the first chapter must remain tentative, an invitation to debate, not a final treatment.

I have attempted to be nonjudgmental in my definition and analysis of populism. I have learned a great deal from sociologists and political scientists who have written on this subject, a debt acknowledged in the notes. Certainly the historian of modern times enjoys the great advantage of being able to share ideas, theories, hypotheses, and data with other social scientists. In the end, however, each scholar must choose individually the truest interpretation of human experience. I have favored the historical approach, stressing long-term trends, antecedent conditions, and inductive treatment of data. I view politics as the way people organize themselves to make collective decisions affecting society as a whole. Most societies make permanent arrangements to delegate decision-making powers to leaders (be they kings, presidents, generals, or saints), giving rise to political life. Leadership in these terms is a neutral phenomenon that can vary in method of election, freedom of decision, tenure, efficiency, mandate, replacement, and representativeness. Populism has been one of the most widespread forms of politics in twentieth-century Latin America and the dominant form in Brazil from the late 1940s until 1964. As such, its origins during the interwar years is a proper subject of monographic research.

I do not believe value-free scholarship is possible, but I do favor dispassionate research and analysis, especially when studying a society foreign to one's own. To the extent that my personal values have crept into the analysis inadvertently, I should state my preferences: representative government, broad discussion of societal decisions, and the greatest good for the greatest number of people. But again, I have tried to keep my judgments in check and to "get inside" populist politics the way a structural anthropologist would, understanding and reconstructing the politics on their own terms, paying special attention to historical manifestations.

A word about geographical terminology is in order. "Rio," "Rio de Janeiro," and the "Federal District" are used interchangeably to designate the city. References to the state will be "Rio state." "São Paulo" always means the state unless the city is specified. All other cities and states mentioned have different names.

Among the many debts incurred in the process of researching and writing this book, the weightiest are owed to colleagues who offered advice and criticism: John D. Wirth, Joseph L. Love, Robert M. Levine, John J. Johnson, Richard M. Morse, Thomas E. Skidmore, and Charles O'Neil. Brazilian intellectuals José Honório Rodrigues, Amaury de Souza, Boris Fausto, Edgard Carone, Simon Schwartzman, Aspásia Camargo, Eulália Lobo, Hélio Silva, and others discussed and offered aid on various aspects of the research. Documentation was greatly facilitated by Jannice

Monte-Mór, Raul Lima, Celina Moreira Franco, and the trustees of the Centro de Pesquisa e Documentação em História Contemporânea. Maria Cecília Velasco e Cruz and Sam Adamo provided valuable research assistance and shared their own findings with me. Among the interviewees, Odilon Baptista and the late Henrique Dodsworth deserve special thanks for patiently recreating for me their city in times past.

Generous financial assistance was given by Stanford University's Center for International Studies, the University of New Mexico Research Allocation Committee, and the American Philosophical Society. Marian Honart, Rocío Brimhall, and Penny Katson kindly typed portions of the manuscript.

Urban Politics in Brazil

1 Introduction

Because the purpose of this chapter is to provide a historical theory of Brazilian populism, a brief working definition at the outset is in order. Populism was an innovative politics in the early twentieth century that attempted to correct abuses of elitist government and accommodate rapid urbanization and industrialization. It was urban, electoral, multiclass, reformist, "popular," nonauthoritarian, and charismatic in leadership. Some of these characteristics, it will be argued, derived from colonial and early nineteenth-century traditions, such as municipal autonomy, elections, holistic social structure, and interventionist local government. Other attributes emerged during the late nineteenth century when municipal self-government was eliminated by what I have called the "metropolitan revolution." A third source of populism was the desire by reformers in the first quarter of this century to help Brazil modernize rapidly without inducing violent upheavals. These contributions to populism, which arose at different times and with differing intensity, began to coalesce in the mid-1920s in Brazil's capital and largest city, Rio de Janeiro.

The colonial legacy of limited self-government helped to legitimate the emergence of populism even though it was of less immediate influence than the "metropolitan revolution" and reformism. Colonial Brazilian cities had enjoyed considerable autonomy from viceregal and imperial authority, a freedom which continued until the mid-nineteenth century. Such autonomy derived from the Portuguese legal tradition that invested the city council *(câmara)* with representation of local citizens, or the third estate. Portuguese law, including that of municipalities, applied in Brazil irrespective of her colonial status. To be sure, Brazilian urban elites rarely influenced imperial policy (the Portuguese *câmaras* had done so before the sixteenth century) but retained almost complete independence in making local policy. Even after the Portuguese Restoration in 1640 under the Braganças, the *câmara* exercised comprehensive judicial and political functions, so that Richard Morse termed it a "miniature audiencia" after the multipurpose judicial bodies in Spanish America.[1] It is worth remembering that the Iberian *municipio* (municipality), descended from Roman times, encompassed sufficient rural land to make the local population self-supporting and made no distinction between township and county, as in the British system. All these characteristics, then, made the city council a powerful authority in colonial affairs, one that could stand up to planters, governors, viceroys, and even kings.[2]

The electoral nature of municipal government was another characteristic of populism which had its foundation in colonialism, in a nearly unbroken tradition from medieval Portugal to nineteenth-century Brazil. The right to elect local officials was a long-standing and jealously guarded tradition in Brazil. The methods of election varied, of course, but in general they stipulated the following steps. Local judges maintained rolls of respectable householders or propertied townspeople, called *homens bons*. These men gathered every three years to elect nominating committees by secret ballot. The committees composed lists of persons best qualified to occupy municipal offices, making sure to screen out relatives or persons susceptible to conflict of interest. The three names most frequently nominated for each post were written on pieces of paper which were rolled up, sealed in wax, and placed in a special bag. Then every year a lottery was conducted, in which a young boy drew the names of those who would serve as councilors. Between elections and lotteries, the bag was kept under lock and key to prevent tampering. Only the presiding judge knew the actual names in the bag, and even he did not know when they would be chosen. All the nominating lists were likewise guarded in the bag to verify the electoral procedures. Cases of fraudulent elections caused great scandals, so we can probably assume that these rules were usually followed. This system was quite unlike that of the Spanish, in which offices were sold and were sometimes even hereditary.[3]

The representativeness of the *câmara* is more difficult to assess on the basis of available research. Most sources agree that sugar planters were the best represented group, a fact which reinforced the *câmara*'s ability to protect local prerogatives. This was so because planters were *homens bons* and nominated their colleagues to municipal offices. The extent of planters' domination varied according to their economic fortunes and their need to hold the reins of power. Without knowing more about the composition of the voter rolls, we are safest in assuming that wealthy persons nearly monopolized big-city *câmaras.* However, the system also provided for representation of artisans and nonvoters by reserving several seats for guildmasters and by the election of a *procurador do povo* (representative at large).[4] As time went on, these nonelite councilors lost influence, but their existence indicated a commitment to broad representation.

Several factors worked to reduce the planters' monopoly on the city council. First, the rise of merchants to respectability during the seventeenth century and their ability to "cleanse" their lineages of non-Christian ancestors brought to the councils a more urban class of men linked to Northern European trading centers. The planters did not relinquish power, to be sure, but rather absorbed up-and-coming burghers into their ranks.[5] Second, the scarcity of white, propertied, and "respectable" men in smaller cities opened the electoral rolls to persons not originally contemplated in the definition of *homen bon:* New Christians, artisans, and racially mixed persons. A reasonable hypothesis would be that over time both ends of the social scale (planters and artisans) probably lost influence in the *câmara,* while the middle ranks (merchants and professionals) gained representation. It is worth remembering that the electoral rolls excluded slaves, former convicts, women, children, and the propertyless.

The ideal of an organic society in which every person had a place and a role in hierarchical fashion was another characteristic of colonial cities later reflected in populism. Society was conceived as holistic, so that all citizens and institutions were theoretically joined in common purposes, especially in the satisfaction of religious, royal, and communal responsibilities. The welfare of the poor and destitute was part of the public responsibility, largely administered by brotherhoods such as the Santa Casa da Misericórdia.[6] Charity was held to be the cement of Catholic solidarity, and frequent religious processions visually reinforced the idea of an organic order. As has long been recognized, even slaves had a place in urban society with their own brotherhoods, churches, and recourse to judicial protection. This organic society depended upon municipal government for its general regulation.

Finally, the interventionist character of the colonial *câmaras* served as a precedent for populism. City officials in Brazil had such broad powers that virtually all aspects of urban activity lay within their jurisdiction. Garcia stresses the multipurpose nature of the *câmara,* with its legislative, fiscal, executive, and judicial roles. And Morse concludes, "the colony was a loose assemblage of villas that exercised sweeping powers by default."[7] The city was a corporate entity, often chartered in foral law, which could receive titles, own slaves, support a militia, raise monies, and in all ways act on behalf of its interests. Its lands were inalienable. City fathers held sacred responsibilities beyond mere physical protection, for they were charged with the creation and support of convents, churches, schools, hospitals, almshouses, and other public institutions. The right to local justice allowed elites to accommodate their interests despite the often stiff intent of imperial code law. Moreover, *câmaras* frequently exceeded their legal charge by conducting war, making peace, annexing land, summoning or even replacing governors, maintaining lobbyists, and convoking citizen assemblies *(juntas gerais).* Thus in the broadest terms, Brazilian cities were nearly states unto themselves, federated in the Portuguese empire.[8]

The city council's ability to regulate business complemented these sweeping powers. Municipal officials protected the quality of life by overseeing free enterprise within city limits. Business could not operate without license, and officials constantly sought to ensure that such concessions served the public interest. This is not to say that capitalism and profiteering were absent from colonial Brazil—the contrary is true—but cities were guarded from the depradations of profit-taking at the expense of the collectivity. It might be termed municipal socialism in a capitalist world. Such municipal powers had been consolidated during the fifteenth and sixteenth centuries, and they continued in force until the nineteenth.[9]

In summary, then, Brazilian urban tradition was electoral and interventionist, it enjoyed considerable independence from higher authority, it sought an organic society, and it was holistic in that it assumed responsibilities for the welfare and prosperity of the entire population. This was a highly adaptable framework based partly on administrative experience from Portugal's far-flung empire, but also one which had evolved along with Brazilian society over three centuries of colonial rule. Therefore, when in the late nineteenth century Brazilian leaders attempted to change the character of urban law and structure, the older traditions could not be eradicated. Out of the disjuncture of the two systems arose twentieth-century populism.

Although urban law had remained largely unchanged in Brazil during most of the nineteenth century, an entirely new legal entity—the nation-state—took jurisdiction over city administration after independence. Within ten years after Pedro II assumed the imperial throne of Brazil in 1841, he constructed a viable, centralized state derived from the French restorationist constitution of 1816 and English parliamentarism. The nineteenth-century Brazilian state concentrated sovereignty in the hands of the monarch and a semirepresentative parliament elected under his supervision. It was also federative, for provinces were allocated control of local justice, some taxes, elections, and municipal administration. The exception to this was Rio de Janeiro, which became a special governmental district (*a corte*, created in 1834).

Initially, cities were not greatly affected by the emergence of the nation-state because municipal government was shaped more by local arrangements between powerful families and burghers than by the Constitution. The cities often rebelled against national encroachments on their autonomy and tended to maintain the traditions of colonial times. But after mid-century, with the onset of a vertiable "metropolitan revolution" in Latin America, Brazilian cities began to grow at accelerating rates and caused leaders to discard the colonial traditions. Demographically, cities grew at unprecedented rates due to in-migration of rural and foreign workers. Societies became far more complex during the late nineteenth and early twentieth centuries, diversifying along class, occupational, residential, and ethnic lines. Economic enterprise shifted from commerce and services toward integrated manufacturing, the delayed onset of the industrial revolution in Latin America. Technological changes such as electric light and power, reinforced concrete and structural steel, potable water, sewage systems, mass rail and automobile transportation, and telephones altered urban life almost beyond imagination. Growing concentrations of people in metropolises also necessitated new forms of social control and accommodation of mass political aspirations. Brazil experienced these changes as much as other major Latin American countries.

Local and national elites in Brazil, faced with the metropolitan revolution, came to regard the older municipal traditions as outmoded, and they began to adopt urban laws then current in Europe and the United States. From the former, Brazilian cities adopted elitist methods for urban development and social control, best exemplified by Georges Haussmann's renewal of Paris during the Second Empire. From the United States, Brazilians borrowed the private tradition of free market determination of services and physical growth. Such influences were not, of course, adopted in an orderly and self-conscious manner; instead, they were taken in haphazard fashion over the space of a generation, roughly from 1880 to 1910. This was the same Brazilian generation that abolished slavery, ended the monarchy, disestablished the church, promulgated a federal republican constitution, and promoted industrialization. It could hardly have done so much without deeply altering the governance of major cities: indeed, the generation of the First Republic (1889–1930) fostered a new approach to urban planning and social control.

A survey of the leading characteristics of "republican urbanism" is indispensable for understanding the populist reaction of the 1920s and 1930s. The new urbanism encouraged institutional privatism by divesting cities of manifold responsibilities inherited from colonial times and by transferring them to private organizations and businesses. During this period major cities were equipped with electricity, gas, water, sewage, modern docks, and transit systems, virtually all of which were privately (often foreign) built. Responding to rapid population growth, private developers opened new suburban districts as well. The provision of meat and food staples, a function closely regulated by the colonial towns, became the domain of big corporations, some international in scope. With regard to business enterprises, cities all but abandoned the old system of licensing and adopted a laissez faire policy. Industry was encouraged by national and state administrations, and it was beyond the scope (or desire) of local officials to regulate manufacturing activities. In all, the new urbanism, coupled with complementary policies at the national level, nearly dismantled the traditions of preceding centuries.[10]

The new urbanism fostered elitist government that no longer cared very much about the poor and downtrodden. French positivism, which deeply infused the governments of this generation, provided a rationale for neglecting the less fortunate. Society would progress, according to positivism, if led correctly by a scientific-minded and determined vanguard. The masses would be pulled along and up if society as a whole progressed. It was wrong to expend scarce resources on the poor, who did not know how to invest in progress. The stick (police repression) predominated over the carrot (better living standards) for imposing social control. For those who found positivism too harsh, there was Spencerianism, a radical version of laissez faire applied to social relations. Also known as "social Darwinism," this approach recommended that the intelligent and talented be encouraged to excel through economic rewards, while the unfit, infirm, dull, and unskilled be allowed to languish and die through natural selection. These two social policies held sway throughout Latin America and especially in Brazil during the period 1880–1910. They provided the sharpest contrast between the old and new urbanism.[11]

Policies sanctioned by positivism and Spencerianism tended to make the rich richer and the poor poorer. Maldistribution of income widened the gap between the classes and diminished interest in an "organic" society. The wealthy began to live and spend ostentatiously in these years, traveling abroad, building sumptuous mansions, and replicating locally the clubs and diversions of the European upper classes. Elegant suburbs sprang up where the wealthy could escape the squalor of downtown and enjoy a version of manor living. Disencumbered of responsibility for the poor, the wealthy enjoyed their station more than at any other time in Brazilian history.

In response to elite disavowal of responsibility for the general welfare of the masses, a great many voluntary associations sprang up in Rio and other Brazilian cities, to provide a modicum of security for the members. Beneficent and mutual aid societies, insurance cooperatives, and medical care groups were formed by the dozens every year after about 1880 as hedges against personal and family catastrophes. The benefit association concept was itself borrowed from Europe and the United States where it had served similar purposes for earlier generations. The social theory of the republican generation required that each person provide for his own welfare, and for the poor and even the middle class this meant banding together. The peak of the associative movement, from 1880 until about 1930, coincided with the abandonment of the colonial urban tradition.[12]

Yet another product of the new urbanism was the "social question," a phrase used widely in Europe and Latin America to describe the problems of indigence, sickness, ignorance, and malaise among the urban masses. The social question had concerned Europeans during the last quarter of the nineteenth century, prompting Bismarck's social security system, Durkheim's treatises on solidarity versus anomie, Leo XIII's encyclical *Rerum novarum,* and many other cures. No sooner did the Brazilian elite abandon the poor to their own devices than some critics charged that the social question had arrived in Brazil. The elite paid little attention to such cries, which merely stated what was generally known. A republican president went so far as to say, "The social question is a matter for the police." As the cities grew and urban unrest became occasionally violent, however, the social question became an insistent indictment of the new urban order; it would be a major ingredient of early populism.

The new urban order in Brazil, dominant from the 1880s until the 1920s, was one of the principal causes for the rise of populism. In particular, inattention to the social question and profiteering from land jobbing and lucrative city contracts produced widespread citizen discontent and eventually voter protest. In the 1920s such reactions were led by politicians, "reformers," who started protopopulist movements. The reformers attacked the undemocratic nature of politics and the plight of the working class, so their platforms demanded the secret ballot, federal supervision of elections, and labor legislation. Yet beyond politics, others sought to improve society or to redeem it from the socially retrograde new urbanism. Lay Catholic leaders in Rio, São Paulo, and the Northeast sought to rejuvenate the church and to give it a mass base. Educators endeavored to turn the *caboclo* (a country "hick") and mulatto into citizens by giving them several years of primary school and the ability to read and write. Modernist artists and writers attacked the wholesale importation of high culture from Europe and challenged their colleagues to choose authentic Brazilian subjects and styles. These and many other reformist stirrings of the early twentieth century were progressive, inspired by a desire to abandon European positivism and to make Brazil into a genuine nation.[13]

The reformers took a great deal from the older urban traditions, wisely arguing that an authentic Brazilian nationality must rest on native foundations. The demand for electoral representation, for example, was largely inspired by municipal autonomy and elections during previous centuries. Church leaders and educators promised strengthened institutions and a holistic society such as those in colonial cities, which they occasionally cited. The modern art movement looked to the Indian, black, and mestizo heritage in its search for the Brazilian identity. Perhaps the most striking undercurrent of the early twentieth century—in view of the official commitment to laissez faire—was the growth of state interventionism. The official ideology of the republican generation was free enterprise capitalism and as little government as practical. Yet Steven Topik has recently demonstrated that republican elites increasingly resorted to public regulation and even ownership of business during this period. Economic crises forced reluctant administrators to intervene in the economy and gradually to undertake planning, totally at odds with laissez faire thinking. The older urban tradition, of course, contained ample precedent for state intervention, and some critics of the government cited it in calling for greater protection of public welfare.[14]

Populism, as it emerged in the 1930s, largely adopted 1920s reform proposals that acted as a bridge between older traditions of local government and the twentieth-century political system. Populism came to favor (among other things) representative elections, interventionism, and an organic social system; it thereby possessed the quality of being both back- and forward-looking. Reformers and populists did not always acknowledge their sources of inspiration, yet colonial precedents certainly lent legitimacy and acceptability to their proposals. Because populism tapped an older heritage, its politics seemed familiar and "right," and it came closer to achieving consensus than did imported ideologies. As will be discussed below, the term "populist" was not utilized by pre-1960 politicians but has been applied to them by later scholars. Since this book attempts to analyze populism in its formative period, it is appropriate not only to apply the term in retrospect but also to define it in more detail at this point.

Populism was a political movement that arose in response to the metropolitan revolution and against the elitist urban policies that had accompanied it. Populism promised to restore the holistic society and self-government abandoned in the late nineteenth century. Populism stood for a society in which all persons had a place and in which classes were indistinct. Rather than a laissez faire competitive system which could be exploited by the wealthy, populism called for an interventionist state (or city government) which would look after all persons, regulate economic relations, promote the well-being of the downtrodden, and bring about social justice for all. The strength of populism came from the fact that it revived a tradition not yet forgotten in folklore and popular memory.[15]

Populist politics could not re-create the colonial city in the twentieth century; rather, its proponents assembled a program out of those elements that could be adapted to the big city, thereby avoiding anachronisms. They combined a patrimonial order (authority delegated by the king or president) with the more ancient tradition of municipal autonomy. Thus, populism promised restoration of sovereignty to the people and harmonious relations with national authorities. Populism was difficult to categorize ideologically precisely because it addressed a tradition which was understood by most people without full articulation. By the same token, the populist retained the faith of his followers even when his programs failed because of the implicit promise to restore a lost heritage.[16]

Because Brazilian populism addressed issues of the new versus the old city, it was always urban. Occasionally rural movements, especially messianic ones, would arise in response to local conditions, but they were not populist. Nor were attempts by later politicians to mobilize peasants a manifestation of "rural populism." The peasant leagues of the early 1960s were merely a transfer of populist recruitment methods into the countryside, where they failed because no electoral, organic, self-governing tradition existed. Even the Rio Grande do Sul chapter of Getúlio Vargas's Brazilian Labor Party was not populist, although it regularly gave him large voter turnouts. This vote was based upon small town machine politics. The populist mode of politics in Brazil derived from the colonial urban tradition and could thrive only in big cities.

The electoral nature of Brazilian populism has already been discussed, but several additional points need to be made. Whereas colonial elections were indirect and limited to respectable householders, populism stood for direct elections and a broader franchise, especially including the lower class. Here the colonial tradition was enlarged by eighteenth-century democratic notions. Women and eighteen-year-olds were enfranchised, and enormous expansion in voter participation occurred during the decades after 1930. A second important change was the desire by populists to see honest elections prevail in the countryside. The city was now seen within a national context and as having suffered under the rural-based *coronel* system, based on electoral fraud and violence. Populists believed that, as the urban electorate grew relative to the total electorate, cities should have more influence in national affairs, which could only occur if rural elections were honest. Therefore, they favored universal application of democratic procedures.

In actual operation, populist politics were not purely democratic. In the decades before mass media penetrated lower-class neighborhoods, any politician had to maintain a staff of precinct workers to recruit new voters and instruct them in balloting. These staffs were supported on the public payroll and in other ways, and they distributed favors in poor neighborhoods in order to maintain the loyalty of their followers. Thus, populism often utilized clientelistic recruitment methods. In addition, interest groups arose in this period to represent the more homogeneous nuclei of citizens, and they too became important in electoral recruitment. Populists often established mutual relationships with such organizations in exchange for votes. Pluralist politics were fully compatible with populism. Finally, the charismatic nature of leadership, discussed below, eroded the representativeness of populism by evoking unwarranted faith in the leader. But despite these democratic shortcomings, populism did advance participatory politics considerably.

The ideal of an organic, holistic society in colonial cities contributed to the multiclass nature of populism. If government was to be responsible for all sectors of society, it should elicit support from as broad a constituency as possible. Therefore, populists claimed to represent "the people" and sought to recruit from all social strata. Populist movements were always coalitions. The importance of this multiclass approach was twofold: it promised to strengthen the organic society, and it allowed the populist a great advantage over narrowly based parties or movements. Because of its multiclass aims, populism deemphasized class structure and conflicting interests in society. Indeed, populists ideally generated and managed consensus decision making. In practice, of course, consensus is unattainable, but it was a populist mandate which daily shaped political choices and gave populism a distinctive character.[17]

Multiclass also implied incorporation of the lower classes into the institutions of society, or "social integration."[18] One of the reformers' major complaints against the republican generation was its inattention to the social question and to marginal classes in large cities. Too many migrants and poor people, reformers held, were not effective citizens who participated in society. To integrate them became the goal of reformers and populists in the decades following World War I. In Brazil, social integration had specific meanings: acquisition of skills and education for employment in industry and large organizations; exercise of the rights and duties of citizenship; membership in local and professional associations;

familiarity with the city and nation; internalization of the cultural values of urbanites, including consumption patterns; and relinquishment of rural or foreign ways. Social integration along these lines became the charge of populist movements. It should be noted, however, that definitions of the dominant culture were being expanded by artists and intellectuals to include many folkways previously looked down upon, a change which lent populism its "popular" character.

The very term "populist" came from the political style of appealing to the masses (*povo* or *classes populares*); hence populism was a "people's movement." Just who the "people" were depended upon time, place, and observer, but their existence was crucial for the populist's legitimacy. Partly for this reason, considerable attention focused on popular culture and folklore during the interwar years. Intellectuals looked inward, searching for the national character and the roots of nationality. A new racial and cultural history (largely the work of Gilberto Freyre) defined the quintessential Brazilian as a mixture of Portuguese, Indian, and Negro. With this search for the true "people" came greater interest in the poor and unlettered, in whose simple lives might exist the key to understanding the very complex nature of metropolitan society. Populism was a political manifestation of this search for national character, and the temporal coincidence of the two was not accidental.[19]

Another important feature of Brazilian populism, shared by other Latin American movements, was its charismatic leadership. Charisma is, according to Max Weber, a source of authority derived from exceptional personal qualities that generally arises when traditional rule has failed, that is, rule based on religious or hereditary rights. That such a failure had occurred in Brazil was abundantly clear by World War I, for the monarchy had been overthrown, the church disestablished, and leaders were unable to make republican government function correctly. The metropolitan revolution exacerbated what became by the 1920s a republican crisis of legitimacy and a general disaffection with the political system. Under these circumstances, people looked to unusual leaders, men endowed with special qualities that gave them the right to govern, qualities such as integrity, courage, morality, devotion to the poor, patriotism, and protection of traditional values. When disaffection reached the pitch of a reform crusade in the 1920s, leaders depended upon the special moral authority provided by their personalities.[20]

The charismatic leader should be distinguished from the messianic one. The messiah derives his authority from the ability to lead his followers to some promised land, to give them a state of grace unattainable on earth. The messiah devises religious teachings to fabricate a desirable other world. Followers often commit their faith to the messiah without any palpable rewards in this world.[21] On the other hand, the relationship based on charismatic authority is one of *exchange,* wherein votes and support are given to the leader for rewards in this world, either psychological or material. Unlike the messianic leader, the charismatic politician behaved in ways formally prescribed by society, or he changed them with the consent of the governed. That is, he invoked man's law rather than God's. The principal areas of congruence between messianic and charismatic leadership are condemnation of existing states as corrupt or immoral and need for dynamism and constant renewal of the leaders' legitimacy. In the case of messianism, progress has to be made toward the promised land, whereas populism requires continual expansion and incorporation of the people into the campaign.

Populism is sometimes associated with authoritarianism and fascism, a mistaken idea in light of this book's findings. To be sure, the authoritarian tradition is strong in Brazil and appears in some populist administrations, but it is not a necessary, much less a logical, combination. This observation flows from our definition of populism as urban, electoral, multiclass, popular, and reformist in the sense of seeking to integrate the poor into mass society. In the case studied in this book, authoritarian forces mobilized in the mid-1930s to suppress populist ones, and out of that confrontation arose a dialectic which still influenced Brazilian politics a generation later. This is not to say that populism is always opposed to authoritarianism or that they are mutually exclusive forms of governance. Rather, the conclusion to be drawn from this case study of the origins of Brazilian populism is that the two derive from distinct historical roots in colonial times.[22]

The colonial city possessed two different and potentially conflicting legal traditions, the patrimonial and the municipal. The former delegated authority to local officials to rule on the king's behalf, in territories "owned" by the king. The latter, derived from Visigothic times, invested sovereignty in village elders, who might ally themselves with a king through a *foro,* or contract. Many of the attributes of colonial cities discussed above were standard in foral law. It was common for patrimonial and municipal traditions to create a tension between imperial and local sovereignties, with royal officials often on the side of colonial subjects.[23] In times of crisis, this latent clash could flare up, as occurred sporadically during colonial times and the Regency period, when cities frequently declared themselves in revolt against higher authorities. The details of these uprisings are not important for this discussion, only the general observation that the two distinct legacies—patrimonial versus municipal—continued in the popular culture. Populist stirrings in the 1920s clearly drew upon municipal tradition when they opposed the elitist, unrepresentative government instituted under the First Republic.

Not long after the appearance of populism in Rio de Janeiro, however, an authoritarian tendency surfaced again, to become dominant from 1937 to 1945, and after 1964. From the standpoint of urban governance, authoritarianism can be traced to patrimonialism. Briefly, the king was sovereign and could impose his will upon towns and cities, even when it contradicted the wishes of the citizens. One of the best reasons for imperial intervention was the assurance of peace and harmony, as during a civil disturbance or foreign invasion. More self-interested royal actions, such as tax increases, trade regulation, or withdrawal of privileges, required more finesse on the part of crown officials, and on many occasions the colonial burghers successfully blocked such moves. The point to be stressed is that higher rule could only be imposed over local desires under certain circumstances, mostly having to do with resolution of crises and with physical preservation of the colonies.[24]

Authoritarianism as it appeared in the 1930s closely fits the description of imperial intervention. It was exercised chiefly by the army, which had appropriated the emperor's "moderating power" of the nineteenth century and justified its actions on the basis of imminent civil conflict and subversion. The endangerment of social peace was used to justify the suspension of constitutional guarantees and elimination of Rio's populist movement. Elections were postponed indefinitely, other forms of popular representation (e.g., independent unionism) were curtailed, and many progressive reforms eliminated. Charismatic leaders were removed from the political arena, now monopolized by Vargas. The systematic eradication of populism by the authoritarian-minded leaders of the late 1930s was no accident; it was necessary to legitimate their own powers.[25]

The authoritarian viewpoint was not unjustifiable in the troubled 1930s. The metropolitan revolution had brought hundreds of thousands of rural migrants to the cities, some of whom were ill prepared to assume full citizenship in mass society. Industrial and clerical employment was new to many migrants, raising the specter of mass anomie or social malaise. Since the turn of the century radicals had attempted to organize a proletarian revolution, and their successes during the years from 1917 to 1919 sobered members of the middle and upper classes. By the early 1930s communism appeared capable of creating a movement to threaten the social order. The authoritarians wished to stem these radical forces, yet they did not desire solely to return to the status quo ante: they accepted the processes of the metropolitan revolution as beneficial. They disagreed with the populists over the means for integrating the poor and rural migrants, as well as what constituted tolerable levels of debate and social conflict. In all fairness, it must be said that each side had considerable evidence supporting its position. And, as it turned out, the patrimonial tradition prevailed over the municipal in the 1930s.

The dialectical nature of the conflict between populism and authoritarianism, then, derives from the two legal traditions of colonial cities. The perilous international climate of the 1930s and world-wide ideological conflict (especially between communism and fascism) certainly heightened the sense of emergency, but the real struggle was between these two indigenous tendencies. As urbanites responded to the metropolitan revolution and to the suppression of centuries-old legal rights, disorientation and confrontation were unavoidable. Both populism and authoritarianism were adaptive but not reactionary solutions to the crisis. Populism, in fact, had progressive features. Together they represented the resurgence of colonial legacies in twentieth-century garb.

Out of the confrontation of the 1930s emerged a symbiotic relationship which I call the "populist-authoritarian counterpoint." This relationship of mutual antagonism has endured for over a generation now, and it is likely that, until it is broken, Brazilian politics will continue to experience abrupt shifts in trajectory accompanied by violence and dissipation of public energies. This is not to say that populism and authoritarianism have remained unchanged, however. Both have evolved with the progression of the metropolitan revolution. Following the Estado Novo (1937–45), populism moved beyond social integration and electoral democracy to economic developmentalism, the form that characterized the second Vargas presidency (1951–54). It could have radical overtones, as in the Quadros-Goulart-Brizola variants of the 1960s. What tied these later phases to early populism was continued stress on the colonial urban traditions of elections, social solidarity, and interventionist government. During the 1950s, a new brand of authoritarianism also evolved under the aegis of the military. Its principal doctrine was "national security" in the broad interpretation fostered by the Superior War College. It too could become radical in its campaign to save the nation from the depredations of the populist "demagogues." To emphasize a major finding again, populism and authoritarianism are distinct political phenomena, both derived from colonial urban roots.

Very few social scientists and historians have studied Brazilian populism and authoritarianism as coherent political forms in their own right. Rather, they have interpreted them as derivatives of some other process, for example, the "bourgeois revolution," "dependent industrialization," "modernization," "massification," or a "hegemonic crisis." The larger phenomenon determines the character assigned to populism and authoritarianism. This book argues that these are historically rooted political forms responding to the challenges and opportunities of urbanization in the twentieth century. They cannot be understood as mere byproducts or "dependent variables." A brief review of the literature on

Brazilian populism will emphasize the revisionist nature of this interpretation.

The term "populist" was probably first used in Brazil in the 1950s. An early reference occurred in an unsigned 1954 article, "Que é o Adhemarismo?"[26] Populism as practiced by Adhemar de Barros was described as reactionary and fascist, and it was said to draw upon both urban and rural voters. Preconditions cited were massification of society (i.e., rapid growth of cities without the development of class identity) and diminished representativeness of the dominant groups. Also noted were charismatic leadership and lack of ideology. Several late-1950s articles in the prestigious *Revista brasileira de estudos políticos* also mentioned populism, though without definition or analysis. It was a concept whose time had not yet come.

The first serious interpretation of populism came in 1963 in an article by Francisco C. Weffort, a political scientist at the University of São Paulo. Weffort defined populism somewhat vaguely, stressing its urban habitat and recruitment of the masses. He noted populist expansion of state intervention in comparison with its laissez faire predecessor, and he described it as "the state through its leader putting itself in contact with individual [citizens], formed into masses." He claimed that populism betrayed the masses, for it constituted a "politics of transition leading inevitably (through capitalist development) to a crushing of the petit bourgeoisie by large-scale capital." He discussed the myth of the "people-community" in which class does not exist.[27]

In subsequent articles, Weffort developed his concept of the *estado de compromiso,* or regime in which no single sector of society is hegemonic, necessitating a popular, bonapartist leader who can create a mass base for remaining in power. Therefore, populism "was a certain concrete manner of manipulation of popular classes but also a means of expressing their frustrations." He went on: "It was a structuring of power for the dominant groups and a principal form of expression of popular emergence in the process of industrial and urban development. It was one of the mechanisms by which the dominant groups exercised control but also one of the ways that control was threatened." The masses were not altogether inert, for they could from time to time exert spontaneous pressures. Weffort's later writings continued the search for a coherent theory of populism, looking especially to the labor movements of the 1940s and 1950s.[28]

Octávio Ianni, a São Paulo sociologist, began to employ the term populist in the late 1960s, especially in his book on the 1964 coup, *O colapso do populismo no Brasil.* Ianni's interpretation stressed the structural causes of populism, which were modernization in the social, economic, and political realms. He viewed populism as democratic and positive, a legitimate expression of the will of the masses. As he summed up, "Brazilian populist democracy was a political form adopted by mass society in the country."[29] The 1964 coup ended the progressive stage, replacing it with "associated dependent development," suppression of the people's voice, and a variety of other ills. Dependence on the leading industrialist countries was incompatible with populist democracy, and the latter succumbed.

In the early 1970s Ianni extended his interpretation of populism to all of Latin America, especially in *A formação do estado populista na América Latina.* Rapid changes in the world economy during the early twentieth century sparked processes of modernization throughout the region. These developments eventually came into conflict with the requirements of international capitalism, for they promised nothing less than true independence. Populism, no longer a dynamic, autonomous political form, became for Ianni another of the "contradictions between social progress and economic dependency" and a bonapartist intermezzo in the bourgeois revolution.[30]

A common interpretation among social scientists is that populism is a product of dependent capitalist development in Latin America, a view best exemplified in chapter 5 of the book by Fernando Henrique Cardoso and Enzo Faletto, *Dependency and Development in Latin America.*[31] In their view, populism derived from the growing difficulty of governing urban industrial society in the twentieth century, a process over which the Latin American nations themselves had little control because it had been shaped by the dominant industrial powers. As the urban working class gained strength, it had to be co-opted into the system, which was usually accomplished with corporatist labor federations and police controls. The populist leader, in this interpretation, was little more than an agent of the dominant class, aiding the manipulation of the masses. The dominant class, in turn, was beholden to and dependent upon power brokers in the industrial countries. In the end, then, the populist was the tool of international capitalism, working through the national bourgeoisie.

Kenneth Erickson employed empirical evidence to link "dependency theory" and populism in his book on Brazilian labor and more boldly in an article entitled, "Populism and Political Control of the Working Class in Brazil."[32] Erickson's thesis, approximately that of Cardoso and Faletto, is supported by his study of labor manipulation by the Goulart government in the year just prior to the military takeover of 1964. Generalizing backward in time, Erickson concludes that populism betrays the working class and thwarts its historic impulse to improve its standard of living and have a voice in government. Populism, in short, is an instrument for the suppression of the proletariat.

This brief review of the literature on Brazilian populism provides a sampling of the social science approaches utilized in the past, not an exhaustive catalogue. Other works on populism, in Brazil and Latin America, are mentioned in the text and notes of this book. It needs stressing that populism, a topic central to the history of modern Brazil, is complexly related to a variety of subjects, such as authoritarianism, corporatism, military civilian relations, urban history, and social relations. Therefore, this book is not a definitive statement; rather, it breaks new ground by offering a historical theory of populism which stresses its roots in the urban past. It focuses on protopopulist reformers in the 1920s and on the first genuine populist movement in Brazil, which arose in Rio in the mid-1930s. These years, analyzed in some detail, are seen as the formative period of urban politics in Brazil. The final chapters trace the connections between 1930s populism and the national movements which emerged in the late 1940s.

Because I have argued that populism grew out of the urban past, I begin with a description of Rio de Janeiro in the 1920s. The physical and social setting, while not entirely unique, contained features which set it apart and help explain more intimate aspects of its political life. Thus, the second chapter is a "tour" of the physical city that sets the stage for analyses of populist preconditions in society and politics during the 1920s (chapters 3 and 4).

2 □ *Cidade Maravilhosa*

A major goal of the metropolitan revolution was the modernization of Brazil's cities, especially the federal capital of Rio de Janeiro. Municipal officials consciously eradicated vestiges of the colonial cities, just as they hoped to erase the mental heritage that went with them. The physical accomplishments of the republican generation were prodigious and to a great extent gave shape to the metropolises of today. Skyscrapers arose, boulevards were blasted through old tenement zones, business districts were remodeled, and pristine suburbs appeared around the edges of the old cities. In the early years of this century, residents of Rio began calling themselves "Cariocas" to be distinguished from the rural inhabitants of the surrounding province, the Fluminenses. They also gave Rio the epithet, *cidade maravilhosa*, or marvelous city, which is still used today. A newly created tourist department extolled the beauties of the city to Europeans and Americans, part of a broad effort to raise Brazil's standing in the eyes of the outside world. Yet despite the remarkable facelift and publicity, much of the colonial city remained, in poor districts, behind buildings' facades, and of course in the people's mentality. The tension between the modern and the colonial was best seen in the disinclination of planners to deal with slums and shantytowns, a responsibility they would have taken on several generations earlier.

Rio's natural setting was as beautiful as tourist brochures said, though Europeans found it too hot in the summer (December to February). Subtropical in latitude, Rio was warmed and bathed by the predominant northeasterly trade winds and currents. In the winter months (June to August), cyclonic weather systems brought cool air and rain from the south. The city possessed one of the best harbors in the world, Guanabara

Bay, a submerged river valley capable of receiving deep draft ships. Knobby granitic mountains draped with tropical foliage created pleasing contrasts with the city, bay, and oceanfront beaches.[1] Cariocas enjoyed showing off the natural wonders of Rio, often quipping that God should not be held responsible for the city the Brazilians had wrought on His marvelous site.

Rio's growing fame as a metropolis in the tropics was of recent origin. During the nineteenth century the city had been a crowded, unhealthy port, subject to frequent quarantines and peopled largely by petty aristocrats and Negro and mulatto masses. For European habitation Rio was decidedly inferior to Buenos Aires, the self-styled "Paris of South America."[2] Rio's center had grown dense by accretion until it nearly strangled itself with shops, pedestrians, and handcart traffic. The best business locations had been along the narrow streets running west from the wharves, such as Ouvidor and Alfândega, but even there the squalor of the alleys was depressing. Virtually all buildings were of the *sobrado* type: a store or shopfront some five to eight meters across, open onto the narrow street; a counter, office, or stockroom in the rear; and living quarters in a loft or a second story overhead. Most clerks and shopkeepers (predominantly Portuguese) lived on the premises, adding to the density and sanitation problems. The center was a walking city, moreover, because most people lived in or near their workplaces. In 1906, two hundred sixty thousand persons (32 percent of total population) resided downtown. Streetcars, introduced in the late nineteenth century, could not easily penetrate the dense city center. They served largely to decongest the periphery and to facilitate weekend excursions to the beaches, botanical gardens, and other outlying attractions. Turn-of-the-century Rio, then, was a city whose standard of living was seriously threatened.

Beginning in about 1902, federal and local authorities undertook to remodel and sanitize the downtown area, inspired in part by the successful renewal of Paris carried out a generation earlier by Georges Haussmann. The city center was opened to traffic and sea breezes by means of a wide boulevard, the Avenida Central (later Rio Branco, or simply the Avenue), which served as a grand axis for new projects. Soon it was flanked by modern buildings of three to five stories, where the best businesses in town relocated. A site there, which might cost up to $100,000, was an excellent real estate and prestige investment. At the south end of the Avenue, a monumental quadrangle of new public buildings was formed by the National Library, the Municipal Theater, the Fine Arts Museum, and the Monroe Senate Building. Adjoining this area to the west lay a zone dedicated to movie houses and cafes, soon known as Cinelândia. Other major arteries helped prepare the city for the age of the

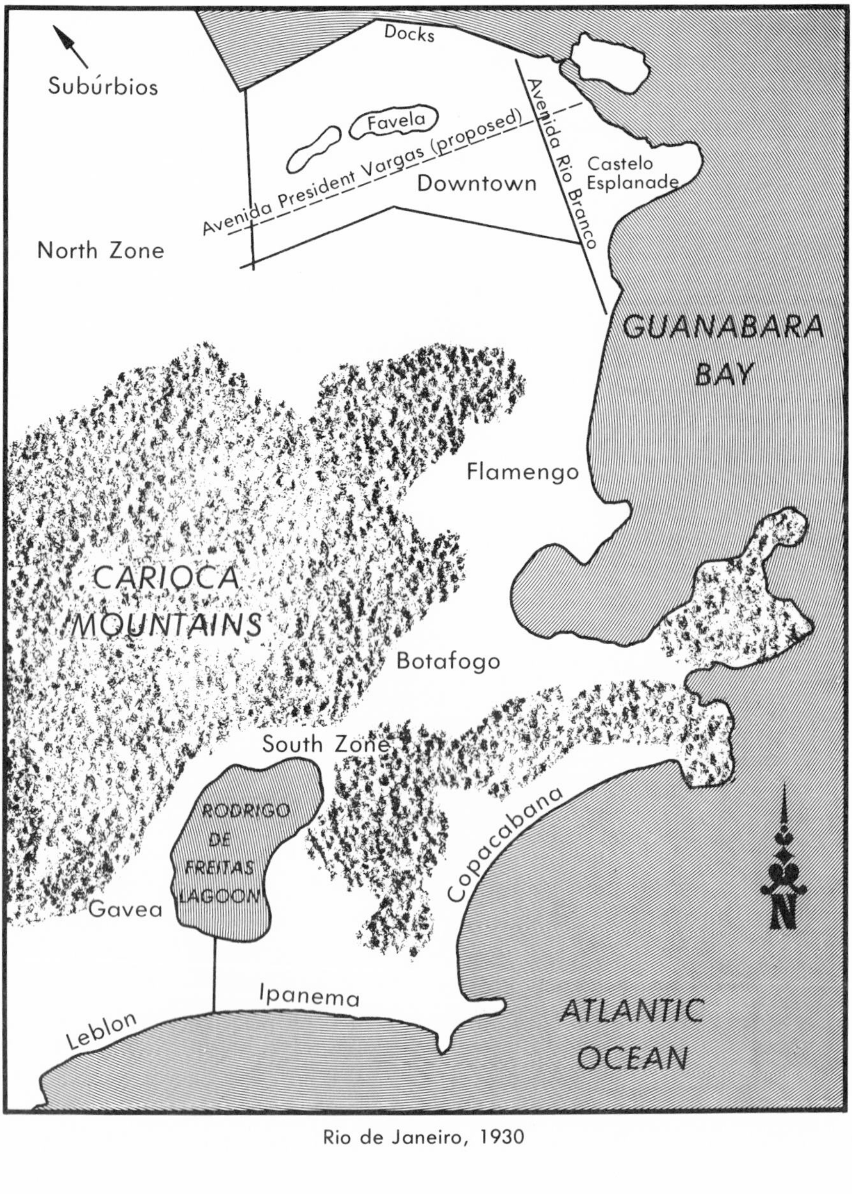

Rio de Janeiro, 1930

automobile, just entering into vogue, by destroying strategic slums and providing egress from downtown.[3]

Complementary developments further enhanced the lifestyle of the capital. Yellow fever had been eradicated within a few years through new techniques of mosquito control applied by Dr. Adolfo Cruz, head of the federal health service. The Foreign Ministry commissioned books by internationally known writers to encourage tourists to visit the capital. In 1906 the city was put on its best behavior for the Third International Conference of the American States (the first two having been held in Washington and Mexico City). The 1908 National Exposition likewise presented Rio at its best and occasioned the erection of special exhibit halls by Brazil's leading trade partners. The bid for recognition paid off, for by 1910 England, France, the United States, and the Vatican had raised their missions in Rio to ambassadorial rank. In these and other ways Rio was self-consciously remodeled and given a new image: it was to embody the finest Brazil had to offer the world.[4]

By the 1920s Rio rivaled Buenos Aires in physical beauty and cosmopolitanism, and the republican generation pledged to continue modernizing their city. Most believed this commitment meant Europeanization with a tropical flavor; some believed it could be achieved by simply importing the accouterments of civilization from abroad. This was true to some extent, for all manner of modern goods, technology, and fashions were unloaded directly from the holds of ships or were brought indirectly through magazines and films. These foreign ways offered an attractive new style of life, and the Cariocas led the country in accelerated adoption of new trends. Among the fads of the 1920s were downtown skyscrapers, private clubs, automobiles, single-family homes in suburbs, horse racing, art nouveau architecture, the Charleston, and jazz music. The motion picture was an important source of behavioral innovations. By the late 1920s Cinelândia underwent a skyscraper boom, with twelve-story buildings establishing a new height standard for the Avenue; sidewalk cafes and movie marquees at the ground level created an atmosphere of gaity. In 1928 the city boasted seventy-seven movie theaters, which featured such celluloid heroes as Rudolph Valentino, Douglas Fairbanks, Jr., Buster Keaton, Mary Pickford, George O'Brian, Charlie Chaplin, Lon Chaney, and Hoot Gibson. So pervasive was this foreign borrowing that even poor people learned to snap their fingers to jazz and to say a few words in French and English.[5]

The exuberant embrace of things novel and foreign was perhaps nowhere as evident as in the widespread enthusiasm for aviation. The airplane seemed the perfect form of transportation for Brazil. Appropriately, every schoolboy learned that the Brazilian inventor Alberto Santos

Avenida Rio Branco, ca. 1920, showing the tower of the *Jornal do Brasil* building.

Dumont had been the first man to fly a heavier-than-air craft (1906) while experimenting in Paris. When Santos Dumont returned to Rio in 1928 he was given a state reception as the "Father of Aviation." Meanwhile, a crew of five local aviators (including one Negro) flew the seaplane JAHU from Genoa to Santos, completing the first Brazilian transatlantic flight. Their reception in Rio was understandably more glorious than that accorded a similar Portuguese flight three months earlier. The experimental became routine as Rio became interconnected with other cities by regular air service in the late 1920s. In fact, authorities were beset by active competition for route clearances: it seemed that Rio was to be center of South America's air transport network. In anticipation the city began building a modern airfield on landfill adjacent to downtown.[6]

City officials continued rebuilding Rio during the 1920s, employing explosive, hydraulic, concrete, and pneumatic techniques borrowed from the industrial countries. The noise and havoc of widespread demolition muffled appeals to spare historic sites and old but serviceable housing. The city's leading paper, *Jornal do Brasil,* underlined the infatuation with renewal in an article entitled "The Tumultuous City," in which it claimed that urban noise enlivened and cheered the populace.[7] Moreover, a weakness for the grandiose was never missing; in 1920 the city borrowed $20 million to convert the commuter lines of the Central do Brasil railroad to electric power. But instead of investing the money in the much-needed project, the mayor decided to employ it razing Castelo Hill, the historic site of Rio's founding in 1565. Located between the south end of the Avenue and the old docks, the hill was regarded by the mayor and his engineers as an eyesore and an obstacle to expansion. Therefore, they removed it with hydraulic mining equipment and employed the debris as landfill. The project was sufficiently advanced in 1922 to utilize some of the reclaimed land for the National Centenary Exposition, a trade and commemorative fair which again attracted foreign visitors. Gradually the land was platted and offered for sale, but to the chagrin of city officials, no bids were made. The area, renamed Castelo Esplanade, remained mostly bare until the mid-1930s, when it was taken over by government buildings and parking lots.[8] This project demonstrated the flair for grand undertakings which inspired officials of the *cidade maravilhosa,* but it also created a preference by mid-decade for general city planning by revealing the dangers of such improvisation.

One reason for the city's inability to sell Castelo lots in the late 1920s was the simultaneous suburban boom; most real estate development was taking place in outlying residential zones. Rio underwent a rather haphazard suburban expansion because of topography. The land is broken and treacherous, strewn with swamps, mountains, and sandy flats that even today vex city engineers.[9] No clear-cut preferences on the part of each socioeconomic sector guided a more orderly occupation. The upshot was a disorderly growth outward from the business district into fairly heterogeneous suburbs, spurred in the 1920s by rapid growth of streetcar, bus, and taxi systems.[10]

The oldest suburbs were located in the areas known as the North Zone and Flamengo-Botafogo, occupying a half circle with a radius of some seven kilometers, running from the northwest edge of the city clockwise to the south shore of the bay. The North Zone, comprising the neighborhoods of São Cristóvão, Tijuca, Vila Isabel, and Engenho Velho, had originally been settled in the nineteenth century after swamp drainage and all-weather roads made it habitable. Table 1 shows that by the time of the 1920 census, two hundred forty-six thousand persons resided there, or about 21 percent of the total population. To the south of downtown, on the narrow shore of the bay, lay other old neighborhoods, notably Lapa, Glória, Flamengo, Botafogo, and Santa Teresa. The latter, built up the side of Carioca Mountain, enjoyed fresh breezes and a fine view of the city and bays, but its steep roads proved difficult for most vehicles. Like the other old suburbs, it was no longer very fashionable for well-to-do families. Some one hundred thirty-four thousand people (12 percent of the city) lived in the Flamengo-Botafogo area. These older neighborhoods, containing about a third of the urban population in 1920, had become transitional zones penetrated by slums, night club districts, and factories and had been abandoned by affluent residents.[11]

Beyond the North Zone lay the Subúrbios, a score of new neighbor-

TABLE 1: Population of Rio de Janeiro (in 000s)

	1890	%	1906	%	1920	%	1940	%	1950
City Total	523	*2.8*	811	*2.6*	1158	*2.1*	1764	*3.0*	2378
Downtown	261	—	260	*1.4*	316	*−2.7*	184	*−2.2*	148
North Zone	87	*3.0*	139	*4.1*	246	*2.6*	410	*2.2*	509
Flamengo-Botafogo	73	*2.4*	107	*1.6*	134	*1.4*	178	*1.8*	214
South Zone	5	*6.5*	13	*8.1*	38	*6.3*	130	*5.3*	218
Subúrbios	93	*4.4*	186	*5.9*	414	*3.6*	858	*4.2*	1287

Sources: Brasil, *Recenseamento do Rio de Janeiro (Distrito Federal) realizado em 20 de setembro de 1906* (Rio: Oficina de Estatística, 1907), p. 23 (hereafter censuses will be abbreviated *Recenseamento 1906*, etc.); *Recenseamento 1920*, vol. 2, pt. 1, p. 3; *Recenseamento 1940*, pt. 16, p. 51; *Recenseamento 1950*, vol. 24, pt. 1, p. 64.

Note: Some inconsistency between zone boundaries exists, and columns do not add due to rounding and to inclusion of transient population in the total. Growth rates (in italics) are average annual cumulative.

hoods that underwent a remarkable expansion in the 1910s and 1920s. Unlike their American counterparts, the Carioca Subúrbios have acquired a disagreeable image, one of provincialism, isolation, and low status, but in the early twentieth century many recent arrivals to the city saw the Subúrbios as up-and-coming neighborhoods that in time would become respectable and attractive. The unpleasant connotation they have today resulted from the failure of those hopes to be realized.

The boom in the Subúrbios had been made possible by the provision of commuter trains along the four principal rail lines fanning out of Rio to the northwest. Land was cheap, having been reclaimed through drainage and mosquito control. Speculators followed the lead of lucrative suburban developments in other cities and bought up tracts of land near train stations for subdivision and sale. These subdivisions, known as *loteamentos*, sometimes had a full complement of services—paved streets, sewers, water, gas, schools, and so on—but many had been left undeveloped for subsequent owners to complete. As might be expected, the model tracts nearest the stations enjoyed more services and rose in value, while those farther away (often served by secondary streetcars) remained unimproved. By 1920 some four hundred fourteen thousand persons lived in the Subúrbios, the population having risen by a phenomenal 5.9 percent a year over the preceding decade.

Despite financial and demographic success, the Subúrbios by 1920 faced serious problems, not the least of which was the disenchantment of many residents. The dream of Garden City faded, and the rail-oriented, linear settlements sank into isolation, separated from one another by hills and farms and often without transport or services at night. Each subúrbio developed its own parochial identity depending on its age, the class of people, and the nature of local enterprise. Unlike the pattern in most major cities, land values and quality of life decreased with distance from downtown. In remote areas land was cheaper, utilities scantier, contact with the city more tenuous, and dependence on agrarian vocations more common. There was a poignancy about the Subúrbios, and by the late 1920s the "plight of the Subúrbios" was widely discussed.[12]

The principal reason for the deterioration of the Subúrbios was the diversion of public investment to other parts of the city—in essence, the city never had provided sufficient services for such a large population. Commuter trains, streets, utility grids, schools, clinics, and the like were either forgotten or allowed to languish. Particularly irksome was the poor condition of the government-owned Central do Brasil railroad, much of whose equipment dated from the previous century; the beds were uneven, the rolling stock slow and unsafe, and the trains insufficient to carry peak traffic. As noted above, the $20 million borrowed in 1920 to electrify the lines had been diverted for the Castelo Hill project. The scandalous condition of the Central was responsible for nearly an accident a day by 1926, causing the popular daily *Correio da Manhã* to dub it the "road of death."[13] Frequent breakdowns and accidents drove commuters to despair and occasionally to riot, at which time trains usually would be set on fire. The diversion of monies from the Central was doubly unpopular among Cariocas: first, because it was for a project of dubious value; and second, because it condemned tens of thousands of persons to isolation and deteriorating quality of life. Similar broken promises, though less public, took place daily, affecting schools, health care, services, and so on.

But where was the money being diverted, and who benefited? Basically, city fathers invested heavily in the South Zone, a brand new elite residential area along the ocean beaches of Copacabana and Ipanema. Until the late nineteenth century, these beaches had been avoided, on the theory that sea breezes caused respiratory ailments. When seaside resorts came into vogue in Europe, however, the elite quickly recognized the value of their own nearby beaches. Two streetcar access tunnels to Copacabana (built in 1892 and 1902) were widened to accommodate automobiles, and by the 1920s much of the narrow beach was platted and occupied. Living in the South Zone had the added advantage of allowing residents to dispense with summer homes in Petrópolis, the mountain resort where the nineteenth-century nobility had vacationed to escape the summer heat of Rio. Clearly it was an unbusinesslike and antiquated custom to abandon the city for three months out of the year; a home in Copacabana would permit year-round occupancy. All of a sudden Copacabana became the place for up-and-coming Cariocas to live, and land values climbed as much as a thousand times in the 1920s.[14] In 1920 there were thirty-eight thousand persons residing along the beach, and for the next twenty years this area was the fastest growing in the city (6.3 percent per annum).

The style of life in the South Zone fit the cosmopolitan mood of the 1920s. Single-family houses with yards and access to the beach became indispensable to those who wished to live well. The automobile was nearly as important, to provide a leisurely drive downtown. Studebaker was the most popular car in the 1920s, but Ford campaigned hard to gain a foothold in the burgeoning market. The Automobile and Touring Clubs (the names were in English), formed about this time to promote the motor age in Brazil, offered their members talks by specialists from other capitals of the world. The general consensus was that the auto would accomplish for the city what the airplane would for the country: cut distances and mobilize population and resources for a modern nation. A major event of the period was the 1928 inauguration of the Rio–São Paulo highway, linking Brazil's two main metropolises. Some had reservations about the automobile—the *Correio da Manhã*, for example, ran a series entitled "Our Urban Traffic Problem"—but even the skeptical were disarmed by the novelty of driving. Between 1903 and 1930, the number of automobiles registered in the city rose from five to nearly seventeen thousand.[15] And of course proponents pointed to London, Paris, and New York as cities that charted the future for Rio.

The crowning moment of the South Zone was the 1923 inauguration of the Copacabana Palace Hotel, owned by the wealthy Guinle family. The new hotel boasted dozens of rooms overlooking the beach, as well as an enclosed swimming pool, a casino, and the most glamorous dining salon in the city. The Copacabana Palace immediately became the select place for elite weddings, luncheons, and social gatherings, and its casino was crowded with gamblers and the more adventurous members of the upper class. By the end of the 1920s the Copacabana Palace had become the elegant pacesetter for the whole city.

South Zone development required far more substantial public investment than the Subúrbios, yet it was underwritten with alacrity because it brought recognition from foreigners and benefited the elite. Landfill and tunnels, tidewalls, new utilities, macadamized roads, parks, and beach facilities took up a majority of the funds available in the city budget during the 1920s. Indeed, a tourism department was created for the purpose of publicizing abroad the beauties of Rio's beaches. And as more tourists flocked to Rio, the South Zone became more popular among affluent Cariocas.

The rise of the South Zone caused the eclipse of the North Zone, which could not compete for real estate investment and lacked the elegant symbols of the beachside communities. Representative of the trajectories of the two zones was the competition between the horse-racing societies, the Derby and the Jockey Clubs. The former had built its track in São Cristóvão and drew its members from the best families in the North Zone. The Jockey was newer, had a track on the edge of the Botanical Garden in the South Zone, and represented the elite of the new beach communities. In the 1920s the two clubs built luxurious quarters side-by-side on the Avenue, where members who worked downtown could dine in the early afternoon and place bets. Yet, despite the nearly identical facilities of the two, the Jockey emerged as the more desirable of the two clubs. Its track was more popular and its members likelier to occupy positions of leadership in the city.[16] In the same way, the South Zone overtook the North Zone as the preferred residential area, and it gained the lion's share of public investments.

Housing in the growing edges of the city, both north and south, was largely financed by family savings and hence accommodated only those whose income was steady and above subsistence. Even though a substantial amount of housing for the poor was being built beyond the view of tax authorities, the property tax rolls clearly show the trend was for more middle and upper income housing. Table 2 presents the number of housing units assessed by the city, according to rental value (estimated in the case of owner-occupied dwellings). Symptomatic of the general trend was a rise in the average assessed rental value from $36 to $38 per month between 1925 and 1929. A general decline in the cost of living index during the last years of that decade did not affect the rising assessments, clearly showing the preference for construction of higher income units at the relative neglect of low-cost housing. Middle-income units experienced the largest growth over the five-year period, constituting about 70 percent of all new units on the tax rolls. Upper-income housing expanded rapidly also: fifty-two hundred units were added to the rolls, making up nearly a quarter of new assessments. In contrast, low-income housing considered legal by the city grew scarcely at all, failing to keep up with the general population growth. Suburbanization, then, did not benefit everyone equally: it encouraged middle- and upper-income housing expansion and channeled public works investments into the most affluent zones.

Where did poor and working class families live, those whose incomes did not permit expenditures of $25 a month on rent? A comparison of the

TABLE 2: Housing Assessments in Rio, 1925–29

Income Group	1925	%	1927	%	1929	%	New Assessments	%
Low (rental value less than $25/mo.)	71,300	*66*	71,700	*60*	72,900	*55*	1,600	*7*
Middle (rental value $25–84/mo.)	28,900	*27*	37,100	*31*	45,200	*34*	16,300	*70*
High (rental value $25–84/mo.)	8,200	*7*	10,000	*9*	13,400	*11*	5,200	*23*
Total	108,400	*100*	118,800	*100*	131,500	*100*	23,100	*100*

Sources and methods: The number of units assessed by rental value was reported in the city's official bulletin, the *Jornal do Brasil,* 10 Apr. 1931, p. 19. Income groupings are arbitrary, employing natural breaks in the distribution that correspond to prevailing income levels in the city. For example, the highest paid tradesman earned about $78 per month, while a middle-class family of seven was estimated to have paid $72 per month on rent. An average exchange rate of $117 U.S. per *conto* was utilized.

city population (about one and a half million) and numbers of houses assessed shows that if the average household consisted of five persons, more than half the population of Rio was left unaccounted for. Basically, there were three housing alternatives for the poor: *casas de cômodos,* old manor houses abandoned by the elite and subdivided into rooms; unimproved *loteamentos* in the Subúrbios; and favelas, squatter settlements on hillsides and inhospitable terrain. All these forms of cheap housing—on the rise in the 1920s due to rural migration—are important for understanding the quality of life of the urban masses.[17]

The *casas de cômodos* were large houses or run-down apartment buildings, generally located in the older suburbs, that had been converted by former owners or slum landlords into high-density cheap housing. Many times former owners had sold out in order to move to the more fashionable South Zone. These tenements became quite numerous after the turn of the century, at which time it is estimated they housed some seventy-eight thousand persons, or nearly 10 percent of the urban population. The advantage of *casas de cômodos* for the poor lay in their low cost and proximity to downtown, allowing one to walk to work or look for casual employment. Although single immigrant men had predominated in the tenements, by the 1920s internal migrants also became numerous. Two related types of working-class housing were the *cortiço* (beehive) and *cabeça de porco* (hogshead), exceedingly small and dismal quarters which had been built specifically for workers and their families. Aluísio de Azevedo's novel *O cortiço* (1896) portrays the squalor of life in such tenements at the end of the last century, and conditions had improved little by the 1920s.[18] Inner-city slums were not uncommon in the large cities of the world, of course, and often they offered temporary refuge for migrants who would soon establish families and modest homes in more respectable neighborhoods.

At the outer edges of the Subúrbios, unimproved *loteamentos* provided some escape from the city slums, though as indicated above the scarcity of services made these areas less attractive in the long run. Even though the tax records used for table 2 reveal little low-cost construction, a fairly rapid rate of growth of new units in the Subúrbios is indicated by two housing surveys conducted in 1920 and 1933, showing some fifty-five hundred new units per year.[19] These houses were small and lacked even rudimentary services such as piped water and sewage, and many of the residents were employed in farming, railroad maintenance, or in the cattle fattening and slaughter yards some forty kilometers to the west.[20] These semirural zones were unlikely to afford means for self-improvement, much less eventual escape into better neighborhoods. Probably the most poignant account of the erosive effects of isolated life in the Subúrbios in Assis Barbosa's *A vida de Lima Barreto* (Rio: Civilização

Brasileira, 1952), which recounts the tragedy of the famous mulatto author who lived in Engenho Novo until his death in 1921. For the upwardly mobile, these neighborhoods were dead-end streets; for the alienated, like Lima Barreto, they were "cemeteries of the living."

The last, and as it turned out most successful, low-cost housing alternative was the favela, or squatter settlement on unused land near densely occupied zones. Having begun as small clusters of shacks on hillsides or beaches where conventional building was impeded, in time they grew up near factories, construction sites, transport terminals, or upper-income neighborhoods where work was available. The first favela had been erected on Providência Hill near the Ministry of War in 1897 by disabled soldiers mustered out after the Canudos expedition. By 1920 the original favela occupied the entire hill (by then called Favela) and comprised some twenty-five hundred shanties according to the census. The site was ideal for the working poor because it was near the docks, rail stations, and factory and warehouse zones. From downtown the favelas spread rapidly, even becoming entrenched on the hills behind Copacabana and Botafogo.[21]

The mushrooming of favelas and tenements in the 1920s constituted a social problem in the eyes of planners and politicians. Between the 1920 and 1933 housing surveys, the number of favela shacks in Rio sextupled, growing at an average annual rate of 14 percent. By the latter date, some seventy thousand persons lived in favelas. There are no figures available on parallel tenement growth, but the expansion of South Zone construction suggests that older areas were rapidly transformed into slums. Congress created a special commission in 1925 to study low-cost housing, eliciting a number of plans to deal with the problem. With the exception of slum removal, though, nothing was done to restrain the free market, and the question of low-cost housing remained for future planners.[22]

Two important notions regarding urban growth and design emerged in the 1920s: that planning could no longer be carried out piecemeal by engineers, and that the selection and siting of public works could help to alleviate social problems. An editorial in the *Correio da Manhã* in mid-1926 articulated these ideas. It began by criticizing the engineer-mayor who had razed Castelo Hill during the early 1920s, calling him the "Ferdinand Lesseps of Rio's mountains" and thereby facetiously comparing his feat to the building of the Suez Canal and the formation of the Panama Canal Company. Just when the city needed schools and hospitals for the working-class population, the mayor had favored showy projects such as Castelo Hill and the construction of hotels and restaurants. Engineers tended to be carried away with huge undertakings that left the city deep in debt and did nothing to solve pressing human problems. The next mayor, the *Correio* continued, had been a hack politican who reduced all expenditures and limited his functions to state receptions for distinguished visitors. The city now needed a mayor who could strike a balance in administration by building schools, hospitals, and paved roads into the Subúrbios so that outlying districts would have access to vital services.[23] These sentiments reflected a broader concern on the part of socially minded persons, which will be discussed in the next chapter. It is worth stressing here that the physical planning of the city by the 1920s had become complexly linked to the well-being of the poor, an idea directly descended from colonial urbanism.

As if in response to the suggestions of the *Correio da Manhã*, the incoming mayor in 1926, Antônio Prado Júnior, announced that he would contract a French urban specialist, Alfred Agache, to devise Rio's first general plan. Agache arrived in July 1927 and gave a series of lectures to educate the public and prepare local aides for the tasks ahead. During the next several years he coordinated teams of city employees in the detailed work, which ranged from sewage grids to architectural codes.[24] Published in Paris in 1930, the Agache plan was the first comprehensive attempt to manage the metropolitan revolution. The principal features of the plan were a rapid transit system, removal of the docks and railhead farther northwest, and construction of an imposing capitol complex on the Castelo Esplanade. Agache argued that the capitol would confirm Rio as the administrative center of the vast Brazilian hinterland, as well as impress visitors with Rio's premier standing among Latin American cities.[25]

The Agache plan was European in that it assumed full powers to remake the entire city; it was the heir of Haussmann's designs for Paris. The main thrust was to provide transportation and utilities to all the outlying workers neighborhoods to the northwest of Rio. Basic services would satisfy the poor and give them the means for self-improvement. Agache stopped short of recommending remedial action for social problems, clearly beyond his mandate from Brazil's government. City engineers did, however, take Agache to the top of Favela Hill to solicit his opinion: he suggested relocation of the squatters to government-built housing in the Subúrbios.[26] Prado complied by offering free building rights for favelados willing to relocate, but when that failed he ordered the favelas razed. In early 1928 hundreds of shacks were torn down, their residents obliged to find new homes. The removal coincided with Carnival, prompting several groups to protest through samba verses. An example was the Pierrots':

> Beneath the blows of the pick and of urban progress
> Disappears the mocking face of tradition and malevolence

With the razing of the Favela and the scattering of its ruffians.
Now where will they fight for "her," where will they show off?
It is a tradition dying, humbled [Agache-ada] before a prejudice,
A vague hope of renewal by the mayor.
And the cans, boxes, boards, parrots, puppies,
All rolled together without pretentions will be lost along the road![27]

This popular protest revealed that poor housing was felt to be merely a symptom of larger social problems, ones created by the metropolitan revolution itself.

The Agache plan sought to be comprehensive but really only suggested technical solutions. While the plan admitted that the city had some responsibility toward the working class and linked physical design and social welfare, its creator was a product of the same school of urbanism as the Brazilian elite and therefore failed to draw upon the strong urban legacy that survived in the popular mind. The generation that took over in the 1930s, especially the populists, simply ignored Agache's work.

3 □ Social Structure and Reformism in the 1920s

Much of the appeal the colonial urban tradition held for 1920s reformers was its promise to reintegrate society into an organic whole in which every person and group had a secure place. Although few persons actually spoke of such tradition, the holistic city nonetheless lay at the heart of their efforts. The metropolitan revolution had altered Rio's social structure, expanding the diversity of people and roles while simultaneously sorting them into several strata. Differentiation of roles and jobs enriched urban life, multiplying the influences each person experienced in a lifetime. It helped fulfill new ambitions, for mobility through education, training, talent, physical relocation, and chance opportunity was greater than at any time in the city's history. Those located at intermediate levels in society, whom John J. Johnson termed the "middle sectors," were especially mobile.[1]

Despite the enhanced opportunities of urban life, many people were discontented. Material deprivation cursed those at the bottom of the social scale. In addition, a certain amount of genuine anomie was caused by industrial employment, the rootlessness of city life, the decline of traditional institutions, and, of course, the abandonment of the organic urban ideal itself. In response, a variety of reform movements appeared during the 1920s, each with its own program but most within the older holistic tradition. Their goal was to incorporate "marginal" groups into society, be they the poor, the disenfranchised, or the illiterate. Identifying the problem was a major step toward the political solution, which turned out to be populism.

Social Stratification

Rio's society in the 1920s contained four horizontal strata or classes, in the sense that non-Marxist sociologists use the latter term: the elite, the middle sectors, the working class, and the lower class. Since these strata had meaning to contemporaries, they were recognized and referred to in newspapers and in scholarly works. The criteria for belonging to one or another level were family background, wealth, education, and membership in clubs and associations. More rigorous conditions were attached to the upper levels of society, so that the whole structure was pyramidal, the lower class being numerically the largest. No methodology will allow exact delimitation of Rio's strata, for Brazilian censuses of that era produced only limited information. Therefore, much of the analysis that follows is based on evidence from the press, scholarly books, biographies, and fictional literature, with additional attention devoted to associations and interest groups, on which there is a mass of information available in the daily press, special reports, annals, and magazines.[2] Certain characteristics of voluntary organizations are especially relevant to reformism and the growing participation in politics witnessed in the late 1920s; group membership, because it could be a criterion for belonging to a particular stratum, could act as a socializing force on group values and behavior and provide an effective means of interest expression. Therefore voluntary associations provide important information concerning social structure.

Rio's upper class was composed largely of families that had inherited wealth and standing. Many descended from the elite of the nineteenth century who had ruled in the country's capital; others were descended from patriarchal clans in the provinces, which had established branches in Rio for the purpose of conducting family business and politics. Of more recent origin were foreign industrialists, financiers, and merchants who, due to economic success and polished manners, were welcomed into elite clubs and eventually into families. Members of Rio's upper class were urbane, cosmopolitan, and generally accustomed since childhood to assuming leadership roles. The formality of the nineteenth-century city, whose life centered on the court, had given way in the twentieth to a more relaxed intermingling of elites from the political, social, economic, and cultural spheres. Aristocratic usage, for example, had almost disappeared, except for an occasional provincial or foreigner who purchased a title from the Vatican. No impenetrable barriers separated the elite from the middle or working classes because leadership required direct, albeit paternalistic, contact with persons of all rank.[3] Besides, the progressive spirit of the 1920s favored social democratization, at least rhetorically.

Upper-class clubs, however, were anything but democratic. High society belonged to a dozen or so such groups, in which membership was exclusive and by invitation only. The Derby and Jockey were prominent, as were the Yacht Club in Botafogo, the Automobile and Touring Clubs, the Country Club in Ipanema, and the Gávea Golf Club.[4] The behavior of members in these organizations might be relaxed and even casual, as befit the mood of the 1920s, or members might not even participate; but belonging itself was essential for upper-class status, and memberships were passed on from father to son. In a rapidly growing and changing city, such apparently frivolous clubs were in fact the stabilizers and meeting grounds of the leading families.

The business of the elite, nonetheless, was principally business, and specialized organizations watched over the production, exchange, and sale of goods and services in the city. Private enterprise was a mixture of traditional and modern—big corporations with substantial foreign participation were generally joint stock companies, while the all-Brazilian firms tended to be family or partnership ventures. Few stocks were sold, no stock market existed, and most bonds were those of the government. New capital, in other words, came from family assets or abroad.

While a preference for personal and family networks dominated business dealings, many of the regulatory and market functions of modern corporate affairs were performed by businessmen's associations. By the late 1920s, business organizations constituted a major category of voluntary associations (see table 3). Some fifty-five existed, their activities noted in the daily newspapers and in published reports. The oldest and most prestigious was the Commercial Association of Rio de Janeiro (AC-Rio, 1834–), which had become a national peak association by 1930. In that year, twenty-four business associations were federated with the AC-Rio, in addition to 440 firms and 600 individuals. Fifteen commercial associations in the states were members of the AC-Rio, which acted on their behalf in financial and government dealings, and many foreign businessmen's groups also belonged. The venerable newspaper, *Jornal do Comércio*, served as the semiofficial organ for the AC-Rio. Businessmen generally referred to themselves as the "conservative" or "productive" classes, and they were the sector best represented by interest groups.[5]

A broad range of issues concerned the AC-Rio and its member associations. A perusal of the daily press and the annals of such organizations reveals that their attention was dominated by tariffs, trade regulation, government budgets, prices, labor relations, expositions, taxes, port maintenance, and communications. Though consensus was not always reached, widespread agreement emerged during the AC-Rio's First Congress of Commercial Associations of Brazil, held in 1922. The congress

TABLE 3: Voluntary Associations in Rio

Class	No. Reported in Municipal Canvass, 1921	Members Reported, 1921	No. Mentioned in Newspapers and Trade Magazines, 1926–30
Businessmen	*15*	*3,084*	*55*
Professions	*25*	*5,274*	*33*
Civil Servants	*67*	*37,127*	*39*
Govt. employees	42	22,664	22
Military, police	18	11,405	13
Day laborers	7	3,058	4
Skilled, clerical employees	*23*	*7,497*	*33*
Labor	*89*	*62,648*	*91*
Stevedores, seamen	22	10,896	25
Railroads	13	13,842	15
Public utilities	3	NA	2
Factory workers	8	NA	13
Store clerks	7	32,715	4
Hotel, restaurants	3	NA	6
Self-employed	13	2,373	14
Unskilled	20	2,822	12
Mutual aid and service	*241*	*87,150*	*87*
Mutual aid	183	68,525	63
Brotherhoods	58	18,625	24
Total	*460*	*202,780*[a]	*338*

Sources: See ch. 2, n. 2, for the 1921 data base. New observations were gathered from the daily press and trade magazines. Tabulation was by the Statistical Package for the Social Sciences.

NA = not available.

a. For only 180 reporting associations.

hammered out a statement on government policy which generally was acceptable to businessmen as well as to politicians. The type of state preferred was laissez faire on the British model, under which it was the government's primary responsibility to assure a good climate for private enterprise. This entailed preserving economic stability and enforcing business-sanctioned rules of commerce.[6] Among the things most opposed by businessmen were income, interstate, and high export taxes; inefficiency on the government-owned and subsidized Lloyd Brasileiro steamship line and Central do Brasil railroad; currency fluctuations and resultant price instability; and government regulation generally.

The presidents of the AC-Rio and other major business federations were of course members of Rio's elite and enjoyed access to all levels of government. They plied elected officials with banquets and receptions, and they sponsored public meetings between government and business leaders.[7] Such events might take place in the AC-Rio's "Palace of Commerce" on the Avenue or in one of the prominent social clubs. For example, five hundred of Rio's leading citizens, calling themselves the Conservative Classes, sponsored a formal banquet in the Automobile Club for President-elect Washington Luís in October 1926. In the keynote address, the president of the AC-Rio cautioned against policies which might prolong the economic instability of the previous two years: "There is no way to plan ahead. The laborer, despite his assurance of finding work, feels uneasy, not knowing if his wages today will allow him to purchase basic necessities tomorrow; the middle classes, with the same uneasiness, cannot afford the normal comforts of life; the farmer, the merchant, the industrialist all experience serious uncertainty." The event was designed to assure the president-elect the support of the elite in exchange for his pursuit of an economic stabilization program.[8]

A second national peak organization for business was the Industrial Center of Brazil (CI, 1904–), which changed its name to the Industrial Federation in 1931. The CI aggregated manufacturing firms and associations, as well as those merchant houses which contributed some value-added to their products. There was rarely disagreement between the AC-Rio and the CI, and indeed their boards were partially interlocking. The fact is that industry had arisen out of commerce, and few policy differences separated them. Most manufacturing firms had simply begun to produce merchandise they formerly imported, while continuing to import other lines as well as intermediate goods. The CI met every two weeks, and its members actively debated the progress of industry and problems it faced. The president of the CI through most of the 1920s and 1930s was Francisco de Oliveira Passos, an industrialist himself, son of the mayor who remodeled the city twenty years earlier, and a leader in the Rio chapter of Rotary International.[9]

Another businessmen's peak association that warrants mention is the Portuguese Chamber of Commerce and Industry (1912–). The Portuguese had always dominated Rio business, able to withstand occasional nationalist campaigns against them. The AC-Rio for that reason refused to divulge the nationalities of its members, but among the associations that did report, over 60 percent were foreigners, mostly Portuguese. The daily newspaper *A Pátria* carried much news of interest to the Portuguese community and devoted a full page to its association activities; several newspapers were owned by Portuguese businessmen. The Portuguese Chamber had some six hundred member firms in 1920, most of which traded with Portugal, and it represented three other Portuguese chambers in other cities. Though the Portuguese Chamber stopped publishing figures, it is likely that membership declined during the 1920s as firms switched to the AC-Rio or other associations not so openly foreign. Most other foreign chambers (British, American, French, Spanish, etc.) belonged to the AC-Rio, whose genealogy if not membership was 100 percent Brazilian. Indeed, an important role of business associations was to help well-to-do foreigners become integrated into the elite. Foreigners had considerable advantages over natives for upward mobility, especially with a business association "passport." The Portuguese Chamber apparently languished because it could offer little aid to its members vis-à-vis the Brazilian elite, especially during times of economic trouble and heightened nationalism.[10]

Smaller business organizations flourished in the 1920s, following the outward expansion and diversification of the city. Among those mentioned frequently in the press were the Suburban Commercial Association (1916–), which operated beyond the North Zone; the Hotel Proprietors Center (1911–); the Drygoods Retailers Society (1880–); the National Agricultural Society, a peak organization for groups in the nearby states of Rio and Minas Gerais; the Cotton Textile and Thread Manufacturers Center, whose members experienced marketing problems after 1926; and the Commercial League, made up of leading import-export houses.[11] In terms of number and effectiveness, there is no doubt that business associations representing the elite as well as owners of medium-sized enterprises grew and prospered in the 1920s. As instruments of the elite they performed crucial functions of economic regulation and interest aggregation.

It may be useful here to sketch in the career of a successful businessman from the 1920s as illustrative of the elite. Ernesto Pereira Carneiro (1877–1953) was the son of a wealthy merchant in Recife. He was sent to Paris, Lisbon, and London for schooling, and upon graduation he became a partner in the family business. In 1914 he moved to Rio de Janeiro where he established his own import-export house, the Commerce and Navigation Company, that had several ocean-going ships. During the First World War he defied German submarines to supply England with textiles and food, at great personal profit. At the end of the war Pereira Carneiro purchased the *Jornal do Brasil,* Rio's leading newspaper, as well as the title of count from the Vatican. He also added a shipyard, a salt refinery, and a cement factory to his enterprises. By the 1920s Pereira Carneiro was one of Rio's most successful businessmen, a member of the AC-Rio, the CI, and the National Agricultural Society. In 1927 he was a delegate to the Pan American Trade Conference in Washington, where he attempted to attract foreign capital by publicizing the good business climate in Brazil. A crowning moment of his career was his election to the presidency of the AC-Rio in 1930.[12] Perhaps Pereira Carneiro pursued status symbols more than most members of the elite, but his case illustrates the upper-class orientation to business and the propensity to diversify.

One manifestation of the social change and mobility of the 1920s was the appearance of a younger, more progressive elite associated with the beach communities of Copacabana and Ipanema. Here one found nouveau riche industrialists, doctors and lawyers whose fortunes had been made, and aggressive immigrants who wished to partake of the most up-to-date living. Tradition and family were not as important to these people as was the urge to assume leadership in modernizing the country. They traveled to Europe with more frequency. This new elite was sympathetic to the current reform movements, and they were poised to take command from the old guard should the need or opportunity arise. They were the patrons of the Chapel of Copacabana, which dispensed charity among the favela poor, for example, and they attended public masses for out-of-favor revolutionaries. It would be wrong to attribute too great a significance to this new elite, but it was from their ranks that reform efforts gained support in the late 1920s and leadership for the populist movement emerged in the 1930s.

Rio's middle sectors, while developing identities of their own by the 1920s, still took most of their cues from the upper class. Dozens of social and sporting clubs were formed after the beginning of the century, in imitation of those of high society. Most of the purely status-seeking groups proved ephemeral, but the recreation clubs, by drawing continually on enthusiastic youth, became firmly established. Soccer, rowing, scouting, cycling, and gymnastics all got their start in Brazil in this way. Even today, these clubs continue to provide multiple leisure activities for families on weekends.[13]

Middle-sector occupations were crucial in the daily life of Rio in the 1920s. The leading professions were law, medicine, and engineering, and they were prestigious enough to be careers for the elite. These professions had existed since colonial times, associated with the higher status of university-trained bureaucrats from abroad. Most lawyers, doctors, and engineers by the 1920s were educated in local universities, but the mystique persisted due to extended training, accreditation, and ethical commitments. Membership in the Order of Lawyers Institute carried much prestige as well as permission to practice in the city's courts. The National Academy of Medicine afforded similar prerogatives to doctors. The academy's journal was designed to publicize the latest advances in medicine, and its monthly meetings often featured lectures by foreign specialists.[14] Finally, the Engineering Club (1880–), while less guildlike, conferred prestige on its members. The club sought to certify its members for public bidding and to keep watch over urban problems of an engineering nature. From 1887, the club published a journal that transcribed communications from members and important correspondence. Paulo de Frontin, a towering figure in Rio during the 1920s, was closely associated with the club, of which he had been president since 1903.[15] These traditional professions were critical to the well-being of the city, for they allowed the elite to influence the other strata of society and provided services essential for daily life.

Within the leading middle-sector occupations, such as law, many levels of income and status existed, ranging from near-elite to the margins of the working class. At the top of the profession a lawyer had access to the intimate affairs of the wealthy, both family and financial, and for obvious reasons such a man was paid well. As in most western societies, lawyers in Rio were sophisticated mediators and agents whose careers were tied closely to those of their clients. Law practice could in fact serve as an entree into the elite through marriage or a business partnership. At the bottom of the law profession, on the other hand, were the *rábulas,* law students, clerks, or expeditors who helped settle legal problems without formally appearing in court. *Rábulas* were especially common among the voluntary associations of the middle and working classes, serving as group legal counselors. Some were shysters, to be sure, but many were dedicated to fair pursuance of their clients' rights and were esteemed by their more respectable colleagues. Labor lawyer Evaristo de Moraes (1871–1939) is a good example: for many years a *rábula* for unions, he was appointed chief counsel to the minister of labor in 1931, where he enjoyed great prestige.[16] The disparity of status levels within the professions inhibited the formation of a broader middle-class identity, but a few values—public service, professional ethics, and education, for example—can be attributed to the middle sectors as a whole.

Many new middle-status vocations had arisen since the late nineteenth century, becoming the leading edge of socioeconomic diversification. Among the most numerous were teaching, health and welfare services, public security, and journalism (see table 4). A common attribute of these roles was "intellectual" or supervisory activity, however routine, instead of manual labor, which automatically categorized the working class. Moreover, some accreditation and secondary education were required for middle-sector jobs. Unlike the traditional professions, these new occupations did not approach the elite, and at the bottom they overlapped with the better paid organized workers. Indeed, salaries and status of many middle-sector employees were precarious, and hence great value was attached to job stability.[17]

TABLE 4: Occupational Structure of Rio (in 000s)

Category	1906	1920	1940	1950
Primary (agriculture, livestock, mining, etc.)	*26*	*30*	*23*	*24*
Secondary	*116*	*156*	*156*	*251*
Manufacturing	84[a]	56	123	
Small shop production		74	2	251[b]
Construction	32	26	31	
Tertiary	*245*	*291*	*496*	*679*
Finance	1	3	12	26
Transportation, communication, warehousing	23	44	64	90
Health, education, welfare	10	23	75	72
Civil service	12	25	52	46
Police, military	17	25	46	79
Commerce	62	85	109	123
Liberal professions, clergy	2	14	17	13
General services	118	72	121	230
Total employed	*387*	*477*	*675*	*954*

Sources: Recenseamento 1906, p. 104; *Recenseamento 1920,* vol. 2, pt. 1, pp. 514–15; *Recenseamento 1940,* part 16, pp. 20–23; *Recenseamento 1950,* vol. 24, pt. 1, pp. 26–29. The figures have been considerably reworked and occasionally supplemented from other sources to gain comparability, but slight errors remain.

a. Includes manufacturing and small shop production.

b. Breakdown not available.

Middle-sector occupational groups numbered a little over 100, judging from table 3. Civil servants, military and police officers, the professions, and skilled and clerical employees accounted for 108 groups in 1921 and 100 in the late 1920s. Not all members of the middle sectors belonged to occupational associations, to be sure—many remained in brotherhoods and mutual aid societies—but it is likely that they were among the best represented by interest groups.[18] The slight decline in total number of middle-sector associations over the 1920s may not be significant and may have been offset by larger memberships. Certainly the occupations on which they drew were the fastest growing in the city. Impressionistic evidence strongly supports the view of healthy, well-organized associations among the middle sectors.

Rio's newspapers devoted considerable space to the activities of middle-sector associations, corroborating the view that they were prospering. Government employees were by far the most vocal. The Naval and Military Clubs (1884–, 1887–), for example, promoted their professional interests through meetings, monthly publications, and direct pressure on the government.[19] The civil servants were active as well. The Municipal Employees Beneficent Society, claiming to be the largest of its kind, secured discounts for members in stores and provided disability and retirement benefits.[20] More militant were members of the Civil Servants Club (1916–), who numbered over a thousand and showed an attraction to politics. One of the ways civil servants brought pressure to bear on the administration was by allying with government workers. For example, beginning in 1926 they fomented demonstrations on the part of the City Workers Circle and the City Workers Beneficent Center (1911–) in order to gain pay raises. This agitation, coupled with electioneering (to be examined in the next chapter), led to a substantial $10 million raise in December 1928.[21] In all, civil servants and government workers comprised several dozen associations that spoke for tens of thousands of members. It is not surprising, then, that they were a major element in Rio society.

In nongovernmental areas, middle-sector professional associations were also numerous. The Brazilian Accountants Guild (1926–) pressed for official recognition by which to certify its members. Intellectuals and school administrators belonged to several groups, the most influential of which was the Brazilian Education Association (ABE, 1924–).[22] Newspaper reporters and employees had exceptionally active associations, among them the Brazilian Press Association (ABI, 1908—), the Press Circle (1922–), and the Press Association of Brazil (1927–).[23] Many middle-sector groups published magazines or journals for their members as a means of keeping them abreast of current developments. Examples could be multiplied, but the foregoing illustrate how voluntary professional associations promoted the interests of their members and propagated values more broadly than their immediate membership alone would suggest. The complexity of their activities will become clearer when we turn to middle-sector reform efforts of the 1920s, an important antecedent of populism.

The working class was the city's largest social component and in many ways its most heterogeneous. The rapid growth of the city had drawn in persons from many areas and from many walks of life, some of whom urban society was ill equipped to socialize rapidly. Therefore more traces of foreign, rural, and traditional culture remained at the lower levels of society. "Foreign" among the working class did not have the favorable connotation it did for the elite because it implied poor immigrant and even African rather than modern European. Rural, of course, always carried negative overtones in Luso-Brazilian usage. Consonant with the foregoing analysis, a primary division in the working class was between those who belonged to unions and workmen's mutual aid groups and those who did not. Before taking up that division, however, some demographic background is needed.

The 1920 census showed that native Cariocas slightly exceeded outsiders (52–48 percent), a proportion which likely held for the working class as well. Among non-Cariocas, most were from the states of Center-South Brazil, especially Rio de Janeiro and Minas Gerais. Foreigners constituted 21 percent of the urban population. Of the migrants from other states, most were single women in search of jobs in domestic service or factories. Nearly always the shorter the distance traveled, the higher the proportion of female, unmarried, and young people.[24] The census failed to gather data on race, but it is certain that many migrants were mulatto and *caboclo*. A 1927 report on army draftees throws more light on the kind of male migrant who might end up in provincial capitals or Rio. Of thirty-nine thousand recruits between the ages of twenty and twenty three, most were of "good constitution," and some 70 percent were classed literate. The average height was 1.66 meters, weight 58.2 kilograms. Racially, whites predominated with 59 percent, mixed were 30 percent, and blacks 10 percent.[25] The large proportion of whites probably resulted from the fact that most army recruits were from the south of Brazil, which was settled by European peasants. Among foreign immigrants in Rio, finally, the Portuguese were most numerous, followed by Italians and Spaniards. Their origins in Europe were usually modest.

An occupational profile of the Carioca working class may be obtained from the 1920 census, shown above in table 4. Manufacturing, commerce, and domestic service accounted for some 60 percent of the economically active population. As might be expected, these sectors paid meager wages and demanded long hours. Unions and workmen's aid groups had the lowest density among these laborers, with the exception of retail commerce. At the top of the working-class occupational scale, on the other hand, were skilled tradesmen, transportation employees, and warehousemen, who were especially well organized. Their control over critical trade functions in the city certainly enhanced their standing.

Wages among Rio's working classes depended upon market forces, protective measures enacted by the government, and the bargaining power of unions. As for market forces, labor was generally plentiful, which allowed employers to set low scales despite protestations to the contrary by business associations. Immigration was encouraged and even subsidized, and by the late 1920s the onset of the Depression caused unemployment and forced out migration from major cities. The exception to labor abundance was the highly skilled tradesman who earned wages comparable to the lower levels of the middle sectors. Table 5 displays some of the wage data compiled by the U.S. embassy in Rio for 1927. The

TABLE 5: Wages in Rio, 1927 (dollars per day)

Occupation	High	Low	Monthly Average[a]
Electrician (master)	$4.20	1.80	$78
Carpenter	3.60	1.80	70
Mechanic	3.00	1.80	62
Bricklayer	3.00	1.44	58
Factory worker (male)	3.00	.96	51
Chauffeur	2.40	1.80	55
Streetcar motorman	2.40	1.44	50
Stevedore	1.80		47
Electrician (apprentice)	1.68	1.20	37
Factory worker (female)	1.68	.84	33
Cook	1.50	.75	27
Maid	1.00	.50	18
Waiter	.90	.50	17
Day laborer	.84	.36	16
Factory worker (child)	.76	.36	15
Agricultural worker	.75		19

Sources: Internal Affairs of Brazil, 832.504/22, 25 Aug. 1927.
a. Assumes 26 workdays per month.

cost-of-living index had declined somewhat after peaking in 1925, but prices still stood at 20 percent over 1920–23 levels. Therefore, even the highest paid workers could barely qualify for middle-income rents analyzed in chapter 1, assuming that housing should not constitute over a quarter of family earnings. Most persons who joined the labor force in the 1920s, then, earned low wages and were forced to choose one of the low-cost housing alternatives. The embassy report commented that many working-class families survived by eating black beans and squatting in favelas.[26]

Government legislation during the 1920s did help raise the standard of living slightly, at least for organized workers able to avail themselves of such protection. Most urban employees were entitled to accident indemnification (1919), federal mediation of conflicts by the National Labor Council (CNT, 1923–), and two weeks of paid vacation per year (1925). In addition, transportation workers were covered by federally supervised Retirement and Pension Funds (CAPs, private railroads 1923, public railroads and shipping companies 1928).[27] But little of this legislation was in full operation, and the CNT, the mediation board appointed by the president and imbued with public powers for arbitrating labor conflicts, was at best a toothless, smiling agency favorable to business. Critics sometimes referred to it as the Ataulfo de Paiva Foundation, due to its president's penchant for hiring cronies with the $75,000 provided by pension fund contributors. It lacked authority with union leaders and avoided pressing business for compliance. Needless to say, none of the more progressive measures—eight-hour-day, prohibition of child labor, collective bargaining rules, workplace safety—were contemplated by the CNT, and by 1930 public opinion favored the enactment of a complete labor code, comparable to those that existed for commercial and civil law.[28]

Labor unions themselves probably did the most to raise wages and improve working conditions for their members. The labor movement had a late and faltering start in Brazil, compared to her southern neighbors, due to the smaller numbers of Europeans and their relative quiescence. The militant phase of trade unionism in Brazil culminated in the 1917–19 general strikes in Rio and São Paulo, after which the radical leaders were silenced and the unions tamed through a variety of means, constitutional and otherwise. Repression is well documented for the years 1920–24, a time when strikes were brutally put down and unions infiltrated by police.[29] Since all but wildcat strikes were impossible, workers' organizations concentrated on building monetary reserves and member loyalty.

The 1920s were not a time of union expansion, then, but of consolidation. Most new unions and workmen's aid groups were formed among the skilled and better paid who could afford the luxury of paying dues. Examples were the Ship Caulkers Beneficent Union (1924–), the Garage Workers Association (1928–), and the Railroad Workers Beneficent Center (1929–). The latter helped sponsor the publication of the *Railroaders Magazine,* which was addressed also to stevedores and merchant seamen. Older unions that survived the government repression of the early 1920s were in the best position, of course. A specialist's assessment of the major unions in 1929 listed the following: the Drivers Resistance Association (1906–), the Stevedores Union (1903–), the Transporters Social and Beneficent Center (1916–), the Stokers Union (1903–), the City Workers Beneficent Center (cited above), the Marine Pilots Society, the Coal Workers Association (1905–), the Handcart Operators Protective Union (1919–), the Blacksmiths Union (1926–), and the Foundry Workers Syndicate.[30] Many of these unions would be converted into retirement institutes during the 1930s as part of the corporatist strategy of social integration.

If unions could not go on strike (with isolated exceptions), what functions did they perform? The more established defended their members in relations with management, covering the full gamut of issues. Mixed opinions exist as to their effectiveness: leftist critics argued that they only sought accommodation, while businessmen claimed that unions extracted every possible benefit. The truth seems to be in between. For example, a representative of the International Labor Organization (ILO) visited Rio in mid-1925, and after speaking with knowledgeable persons he concluded that the country was backward in its social legislation. He urged government initiative and more independence on the part of labor organizations. The U.S. ambassador privately concurred: "I do not foresee that Brazilian labor will obtain an opportunity to organize. . . . The Government keeps a directing hand on all labor organizations and does not allow them to express their aspirations unchecked."[31] Clearly under these circumstances, skilled tradesmen and employees of the transportation sectors were in the best position to improve their income levels.

Perhaps just as important a function of Carioca unions was promotion of brotherhood and solidarity among workers. Most unions met frequently and created a sense of participation and belonging for members. Virtually every group purchased its own building during the 1920s as a symbol of stability and union hall loyalty. Meetings generally were held between 7 P.M. and 9 P.M. on weekdays, and the minutes of many were summarized in the press. Most big dailies carried a section for labor news, and on special dates, such as general assemblies and anniversaries, they often ran articles of up to five columns, with historical background on the group. Labor Day (May 1) celebrations received extra attention in most papers.[32] Such coverage probably sold newspapers, but it also contributed to the identity of the worker as union member and citizen. Furthermore, unions sponsored festivals and dances to raise money and promote membership. A typical union *festa* would include a live jazz band, dancing, and dramatic routines. Finally, a broad range of medical and disability benefits was available to union members. Larger groups owned out patient clinics, held doctors' consulting hours, and provided loans and travel expenses for rest and therapy. The well-endowed Commercial Employees Association (AEC, 1880–), for example, spent nearly twenty thousand dollars in 1927 on medicine, family support, funeral expenses, and retirement and disability pensions.[33] The foregoing strongly indicates that unions socialized their members to an organized labor identity, in addition to providing family security and leisure activities. The importance of these functions is greater when it is recalled that in 1912, 27 percent of workers' association members were foreign born, and a larger portion was from other states.

A third major role of workingmen's associations was politicization. Union elections were often heated affairs that brought out the rank and file. One of the largest turnouts noted in the press was twelve hundred stevedores in August 1926, and union votes of several hundred were common.[34] Union democracy, although not universal by any means, was a goal fostered and partly achieved by Carioca labor. Members could become leaders, they could speak up in meetings, and they could read about their activities in the morning paper. As we will see in chapter 4, by the late 1920s unions had become a potent force in local politics as well.

Union participation also promoted a broader vision of working-class problems. Many groups, for example, published or contributed to labor newspapers and magazines. Larger unions occasionally sent observers to national and international labor conferences, such as those of the ILO. By maintaining formal and informal ties with sister unions and confederations elsewhere, unions helped create labor cosmopolitanism. An example was the 1927 joint telegram sent by Carioca unions to Calvin Coolidge to protest the executions of Sacco and Vanzetti.[35] In these and other ways, then, Rio's workingmen's associations promoted worker participation in local and national affairs. This was an essential condition for the emergence of prepopulist labor coalitions in the late 1920s.

Not all workers belonged to unions, of course, and we must turn now to the last major component of Rio's society in the 1920s, the lower class. Little has been written about this sector, which in Brazilian usage is termed the "masses" or the *povo* (people), but some information has been gathered by cultural anthropologists.[36] The lower class was only a generation removed from the slaves of the 1880s, and much of their behavior and mentality derived from that earlier system. Racially, they were mostly black and mulatto, with some admixture of *caboclo*. They were uneducated and functionally illiterate. The masses had, as did their slave predecessors, broadly defined roles, especially personal service and physical work. They were maids, cooks, street cleaners, porters, and manual laborers. Not all blacks performed these tasks, but virtually all menial labor was done by blacks. The well-to-do harbored a certain paternalistic admiration for the *povo*, especially for its ability to adapt and mold itself to the needs of the larger society without losing its folkloric qualities. This feeling may be perceived in Gilberto Freyre's classic, *The Masters and the Slaves*, published in 1933. Freyre marveled at the maleability of the black culture, which became intermingled with the Portuguese and Indian heritages. Freyre's book concerned seventeenth-century society, of course, but his outlook toward the black is revealing. Whether or not racial and cultural democracy could ever exist in Brazil, Freyre's book, as well as other studies in this genre, struck a sympathetic chord in thousands of Carioca readers.[37] It was a myth whose time had come.

Great prowess was attributed to the masses in certain realms other than physical labor. Blacks, it was held, had a better developed sense of rhythm, and they were credited with the invention of the samba for which Brazil is famous. With the samba came dance and Carnival. Blacks also, according to popular belief, had a special sensitivity to other-worldly spirits, and persons of all social levels consulted the practitioners of spiritualism and Afro-Brazilian *macumba* (an illegal religion which featured communication with spirits and magic spells). Their physical capability, it was thought, gave rise to heightened sexuality, as attested in the myth of the *mulatta quente*, or sensual mulatta.[38] Such ethnic beliefs about the *povo* could be multiplied, but the point is simple: the "people" in 1920s Rio was an elastic concept about a readily identifiable class of unorganized workers who, far from constituting a threat to the established order, were a productive and benign part of society. Uplift and integration to a higher level, therefore, would become the strategy of social reformers who wished to help the masses.

Rio society was growing and becoming differentiated rapidly in the 1920s, which meant that the interrelationships between groups and sectors were constantly changing. The overall impression, nonetheless, is of peaceful evolution and successful adaptation to metropolitan life. Tension was for the most part contained.[39] One reason was the upper class's sense of noblesse oblige or duty to promote social well-being. Then too, the process of diversification created opportunities everywhere for the upwardly mobile, so that it was possible to get ahead, especially while the economy was expanding. Finally, associations greatly facilitated interaction between the various socioeconomic levels.

Brazilian society operated with a strongly hierarchical orientation, inherited from colonial times and still at work in the 1920s. The transition from plantation life to the city during the nineteenth century had not, according to Gilberto Freyre's *The Mansions and the Shanties*, undermined the overall verticality of social relations. The paternalism of the upper class and the mediating action of the traditional professions allowed city life to adopt plantation manners. Clearly, though, changes in the patriarchal system were in order for Rio of the 1920s, which now required complex relationships and the flexibility to accommodate expanding business enterprise, government, and middle-sector professions. Voluntary associations provided the social cement, as it were, to hold men together in viable numbers through structural changes. For example, if a businessman closed a store and opened a factory, he needed to fire clerks and hire mechanics, a difficult transition in a patriarchal order. With unions and businessmen's associations to locate jobs and find new workers, caring for their families in the interim, the shift was no longer so traumatic. Multiplied thousands of times, such cushioning action by unions and mutual aid groups allowed the city to grow rapidly without explosive social tension.

Voluntary associations had another great advantage over patriarchal family networks and traditional institutions: their ability to change from vertical to horizontal orientation. Most of the time businessmen's groups, civil servants' societies, and unions operated hierarchically, taking their cues from the elite and the government and passing orders, as it were, downward to clerks and workers. In most Western nations such organization had proved to be the most efficient. Sometimes, however, business and the government could not reach agreement, and the former coalesced into a broad front to oppose the latter. Businessmen could put aside day-to-day differences among themselves in order to unite against perceived threats from above (or below, for that matter). A good example was their reaction to the government's decision to stabilize the exchange rate in 1926 and return to the gold standard. Rio business groups protested the low rate chosen, calling it deflationary and harmful to their interests.[40] This was an effective manner of economic adjustment and tension management.

Workers' groups too could unite horizontally against employers, despite government curbs on strikes. When in 1926 the textile industry found itself overstocked and forced to cut production, the Union of Textile Factory Workers convoked a series of meetings with other unions to protest layoffs. A wildcat strike a few months earlier served warning that broader labor action might follow. The situation improved and the confrontation was averted.[41] The actions of civil servants' associations to extract salary increases from the administration have already been mentioned. The matter of labor alignment was, of course, part of the universal debate of the era over trade (vertical) versus industrial (horizontal) unionism, and the issue was far from settled in Rio in the 1920s.[42]

More permanent horizontal alignments existed, to be sure: the AC-Rio and the CI were both cross-sectional and hence potentially united for defense above and below. Labor unions, though not as advanced, also attempted to form permanent confederations. The principal stimulus for union federation was labor legislation already on the books but not enacted, especially the Vacations Law of 1925. In mid-1926, for example, a national labor congress was held to determine how to implement the law. Enabling legislation was signed in October 1926, but throughout 1927 unions found it difficult to obtain vacations for their members. In December 1927 another labor congress was held for the purpose of publicizing widespread noncompliance by employers.[43] Eventually most workers were given vacations, but as late as 1929 the Union of Textile Factory Workers filed suit for three years back vacations. By then, however, federation had progressed much farther, and a powerful labor congress, with the help of the ILO, drafted a full labor code, the main outlines of which were accepted by both presidential candidates that year.[44] Such horizontal federation of unions, designed at first to gain legislative support from the government, led directly to the formation of labor parties, to be discussed in the next chapter.

Voluntary associations, then, by reacting quickly and flexibly to complex problems, managed to avoid or at least ameliorate adverse effects of change on their members. Temporary shifts from vertical to horizontal alignment, while in the short run conflictive, actually achieved substantial reduction in social tension. The positive roles played by voluntary associations were generally acknowledged by observant Cariocas. Newspaper coverage given to meetings and activities was one form of recognition. Even lower-class Carnival clubs—*blocos, ranchos, bandas,* etc.—were reported in the months prior to the main event. The *Jornal do Brasil,* noting the formation of the Brazilian Teachers Association, commented approvingly: "Brazil is a land in which all sectors [*classes*] tend to form their associations."[45] It would be naive to suggest that all voluntary associations were "beneficent," as so many of their names proclaimed, but certainly they were effective agents of conflict resolution and bargaining in the socioeconomic diversification of the 1920s. As we will see in the next chapter, they also became the constituent parts for the populist movement, at first tentatively in the 1920s and then permanently in the 1930s, making the transition from pluralist to coalition politics.

Voluntary associations could not, however, resolve two more serious challenges to business-as-usual, which as it turned out became triggers for the emergence of populism. These challenges were a perceived lengthening of extremes in standards of living and an extended economic recession which pitched into the Depression of 1929. Without more data at hand it is impossible to determine whether the distribution of income was actually becoming more unequal during the 1920s, but the flow of migrants into the city and the increased contact between different levels of society fostered the impression that the "rich were getting richer and the poor poorer."[46] In general terms, this was one meaning of the term "social question" so talked about since the early twentieth century. Migration to the city brought rural folk and ethnic groups whose ways denoted poverty and cultural backwardness. They were of course visible in growing numbers on city streets. The concentration of wealthy people in Copacabana and surrounding neighborhoods, contrasted with the decline of the North Zone and the Subúrbios beyond, also gave an impression of growing disparities. Most noticeable of all, of course, was the mushrooming of slums and the favelas on hillsides downtown or in well-to-do neighborhoods. The discomfort such visible poverty caused was conveyed in the Rotary Club request of 1926 for the city to "defavelize" its hillsides.[47] Here, perhaps, was an unspoken goal of city planners' designs to "do something" about favelas: put the poor and recent migrants into their own neighborhoods and reduce unstructured contact with them.

The Social Question and Reformism

The perceived inequalities of income in the 1920s sparked two reactions. First, politicians and labor leaders formed alliances which sought to capture power through elections and redress income disparities. These leftist labor factions will be examined below. Second, a number of reformist groups emerged within the professional middle sectors and new elite, whose general goal was to lessen poverty, uplift the masses, and thereby reduce the distance between the wealthy and the poor. Without this broad concern for social reform populism could not have arisen.

Since the turn of the century, the so-called "social question" had emerged as a general desire throughout the western world to improve the living and working conditions of the masses, mostly through protective legislation, agencies of socialization, and even government mediation of industrial relations.[48] The decade of the 1910s had witnessed major political and social upheavals around the world, with concomitant labor unrest. Brazil, as noted above, had experienced labor mobilization between 1917 and 1919 and had effectively repressed it. Many Brazilians, however, believed that the government had overreacted and should instead address the social question directly in order to maintain the pace of modernization. In this respect Brazil was far behind her Latin American neighbors.[49] Uruguay had long been a leader in social reform, and in the 1920s a number of new measures provided protection for the urban worker. The 1916 accession of the Radical Civic Union in Argentina promised major social initiatives as well. Mexico had promulgated the remarkably progressive Constitution of 1917, which contained several chapters devoted to the social question. Finally, in Chile, Arturo Alessandri had come to power at the head of a broad coalition in 1920, which by 1925 had given the country one of Latin America's most advanced labor codes.[50] Brazil itself had pledged such reforms when signing the Treaty of Versailles, but little had been accomplished prior to 1929. The social question in Rio, in fact, revealed the limits of pluralist interest group action and spurred more direct approaches.

The ILO was the foremost source of Brazilian goals in social legislation. Besides signing the Versailles Treaty, Brazil had ratified many ILO conventions, only to find Congress unwilling to enact them. Even business-oriented newspapers such as the *Jornal do Brasil* and *O Globo* chided the government for not fulfilling its humane duty to the working class. The more popular *Correio da Manhã* made the social question a moral crusade. President Washington Luís (1926–30) had endorsed some labor legislation prior to his unchallenged election but had set that promise aside once in office. The statement "The social question is a matter for the police" was attributed to Washington Luís, who indeed did little to further the cause of the working class.[51] Pressure mounted by 1929 when the ILO "package" included the following measures: work accident prevention and compensation; job safety and hygiene; reduced workload for pregnant women; protection for women and adolescents; elimination of labor by children under fourteen; strike and lockout prevention through mediation; labor courts; expanded retirement and disability systems; the eight-hour-day; Sunday rest; and government inspection of work conditions.[52] Many Brazilians believed that such measures were just and had to be implemented directly by the government.

A little known measure passed in 1928, called the Getúlio Vargas Law, was among the boldest and foreshadowed social policy after Vargas's accession to power. Originally proposed in 1924 as an addendum to the Civil Law Code, it governed contracts between theatrical groups and impresarios. Among the advantages for actors were provisions for thirty days' pay for broken contracts, travel expenses, accident compensation, and protection of authors' copyrights. Because the measure became civil law, the artists' unions could go directly to court instead of the CNT.[53] It was therefore an important step toward Vargas's federalization of labor relations in the 1930s, analyzed in chapter 7.

Education was held to be nearly as important as labor reform for dealing with poverty and the social question. The Brazilian Education Association (ABE) was at the front lines demanding more legislation and support for schools. The ABE was a national organization with its major constituents among educators in Rio and São Paulo, especially the group which later was known as the Pioneers, led by well-to-do intellectuals Fernando de Azevedo, Carneiro Leão, Lourenço Filho, and Anísio Teixeira. The ABE worked on multiple fronts: weekly meetings by educators proselytized members; articles in the press won over the public; special courses and seminars brought in fresh ideas; three National Educational Conferences in the late 1920s propagated goals; and the leaders themselves, many of them directors of education in the larger states, implemented their approaches as vigorously as possible.[54] One of the ABE's more sensational moves was to recruit aviation pioneer Santos Dumont to their cause on his return from Paris in 1928. Tragedy marred the effort, however, when a plane filled with well-wishers crashed during the reception, killing several brilliant young reformers. Afterward Santos Dumont donated patent rights on his inventions to the ABE, which hoped to equate the ideas of aviation progress and education in the public mind.[55]

Fernando de Azevedo, who as Rio's Director of Education between 1927 and 1930 conducted a major school reform, was perhaps the most articulate of the ABE pioneers. Having grown up in the manufacturing center of São Paulo, Azevedo believed that the future of Brazil lay in continued urbanization and industrialization. Education was the key to preparing the masses for citizenship in the new society. In his voluminous *Brazilian Culture*, first published in 1933, Azevedo stated that middle-class Brazilians had developed a responsibility toward the poor and were committed to remaking society along modern European or North American lines. The ABE approach stressed total overhaul of the school system, from buildings to curricula. It launched a vigorous assault on scholasticism, elitism, and unprofessionalism, promising instead to provide a democratic and pragmatic education for all. Even in the capital city, Azevedo and the others exclaimed, education was woefully neglected. A census of school-age children revealed that only 58 percent were attending classes.[56] The battle was joined and nothing less than the future citizenry of the nation was at stake.

Not all allies in the struggle for education were agreed on strategy, however. Another movement underway in the state of Minas Gerais sought a return to Catholic values. Led by lawyer-politician Francisco Campos, this wing used the schools to inculcate values of patriotism, hierarchy, discipline, and religiosity in the populace, while at the same time drawing the church into league with the state in the common effort to create a strong nation. Campos began such a program in Minas, and later, as first Minister of Education after 1930, he would impose a similar design on national policy.[57]

Campos's effort was itself part of a larger movement to reform Brazilian society, known as the Catholic Revitalization. Disestablished in 1889, the church had languished from lack of patronage and declining vocations, and by 1920 its leaders had perceived a veritable religious crisis in the country. The church was weakest in the city, for it was clear that secularization followed urbanization. Rio displayed the symptoms prominently: there were only a thousand priests for a city of over a million persons, and Protestantism and African religions had made deep inroads among the inhabitants. Brotherhoods, the mainstays of secular church influence since colonial times, were declining rapidly: the last had been formed in 1916, and the last Third Order in 1910.[58] Membership size had also slipped, for Cariocas now preferred associations based on occupation. Revitalization was a loosely constructed movement to regain lost influence and win back the fallen. Led by Archbishop Sebastião Leme (cardinal of Brazil between 1928 and 1942), the efforts ranged from proselytization among well-to-do youth, through the Dom Vital Center (1922–), to re-establishment of the church. The revitalization strategy was elitist: convert the leaders and the masses will follow.[59] In the confused years following the 1930 Revolution, a strong push was made to implement these plans, though it would be ideologically opposed to the populist mainstream.

Apart from these major currents of educational and moral reform, other movements existed, some long lasting and some ephemeral. The fact is, reformism was in the air in the 1920s, infecting everyone but especially mobilizing the new elite and the middle sectors. There was the National Defense League (literacy), the Brazilian League for Mental Hygiene (prohibition of liquor), and the Brazilian Association for Social Hygiene. Some of the catchwords of the 1920s reflect the reform spirit: justice, literacy, free press, effective suffrage, health, nationalism, citizenship, progress.[60]

One group which especially drew the attention of the reform-minded was the *tenentes*. This movement, so-called because of the predominance of lieutenant cadets and junior officers in its ranks, was really a series of military rebellions between 1922 and 1927. The movement mobilized dissent from the backward Northeast to Rio Grande do Sul and provoked a nationwide state of siege. At its peak the tenentes comprised several thousand men, and the government was unable to do more than chase them over the countryside. The actual program of the movement was vague, yet urban reformers, especially in Rio, lionized the tenentes anyway. The press followed their exploits and created a mythical doctrine called *tenentismo*, for which the rebels supposedly fought. Actually tenentismo became nearly anything reformers wished it to be; amnesty for the tenentes and enactment of reforms became a cause célèbre in the late 1920s. However, the government refused to consider amnesty, and most of the tenentes were forced into exile or languished in jail. Many of these famous rebels would join the populist movement in Rio after 1930.[61]

Feminism was another reform current growing in strength in the 1920s. A number of professional women from Brazil attended the 1922 Panamerican Feminist Conference, and later that year they held Brazil's first women's meeting. They formed the Brazilian Federation for Feminine Progress, which constituted a network of feminist advocates in the major cities. Surprisingly, they made most headway in the backward state of Rio Grande do Norte where in 1928 women were first enfranchised in state elections. A driving force in the movement was Rio's Bertha Lutz, scientist and daughter of Adolfo Lutz, the public health pioneer from São Paulo. She and her colleagues found themselves bored by ordinary activities reserved for well-to-do women, such as charity and education. They saw politics as the most effective way to give women a voice in public affairs, and they would use politics to broaden their civic rights in the 1930s within the populist movement.[62]

Economic Decline in the Late 1920s

These and other reform movements operated in an environment of optimism until 1926, after which economic recession and insecurity began to plague the city. (See the speech by the president of the AC-Rio quoted earlier.) Instability brought layoffs and unemployment, bankruptcies, and increased socioeconomic tension. Reform efforts were redoubled to meet the anxiety of the times, and proposed solutions gradually became bolder. The downturn was not consistent until the onset of the 1929 Depression, and although 1927 and 1928 were good years in production terms, some sectors experienced continued difficulties for a variety of reasons. The social and political developments of the last years of the decade grew in part out of the poor business climate that began in 1926.

That year saw a severe recession in Rio and São Paulo, referred to in the press as an "industrial crisis." Textile output for the second year in a row was down to 80 percent of the 1922–24 level, and imports gained increasing shares of the market. Many factories cut back to a four-day production week, and three strikes followed in quick succession (see table 6). Government policy was partly to blame for the situation: since 1924 credit had been restricted to curb inflation, and interest rates had soared. This produced a wave of bankruptcies in 1925 and 1926 that further restricted credit by creating distrust among businessmen.[63] This situation lasted until mid-1927, when a decline in the exchange rate afforded some protection for local producers. In the third quarter of 1928 the government again restricted means of payment, and the results were similar: textile overproduction, shortage of credit, high interest rates, production cuts, layoffs, and bankruptcies. In the first four months of 1929 more than two hundred bankruptcies and one hundred out-of-court settlements were executed, for a total value of nearly $25 million. By the end of the year, 686 companies with aggregate liabilities of $155 million had gone out of business. Thus an intentional recession preceded and led into the Depression of the 1930s.[64]

From 1925 to 1930 there had been only fleeting periods of prosperity, and Rio businessmen held the president responsible. In his message to Congress in 1930, Washington Luís acknowledged that 1929 had been: "a difficult year indeed; the [yellow fever] crisis arose . . . as did the indus-

TABLE 6: Socioeconomic Indicators of Unrest

Year	Federal & City Fiscal Deficit (−) or Surplus (+) (millions)	Rio Industrial Production Subject to Consumer Tax (millions)	Per Capita Brazilian GNP, 1939	Foreign Currency Reserve Changes (millions)	Foreign Deportees from Brazil	Labor Strikes	
						Rio	São Paulo City
1925	−5.4	96.4	58	56	3	—	—
1926	−26.0	111.5	57	143	11	3	1
1927	−1.8	111.5	58	99	102	1	2
1928	+14.8	135.7	67	66	130	5	5
1929	+11.1	106.9	66	−33	167	3	6
1930	−93.5	85.0	59	52	141	—	11

Sources: Federal deficit and per capita income, Annibal Villanova Villela and Wilson Suzigan, *Política do governo e crescimento da economia brasileira, 1889–1945* (Rio: IPEA/INPES, 1973), pp. 156, 185, 436; industrial production, foreigners deported, *Anuário 1939–1940,* pp. 1320, 1428; Rio budget, *Rio, Distrito Federal,* pp. 52–53; changes in currency stock, Marcelo de Paiva Abreu, "A missão Niemeyer," *Revista de administração de empresas* 14 (1974):8; strikes, from Rio daily press and Simão, *Sindicato e estado,* pp. 137,140.

Note: money is expressed in U.S. dollars.

trial overproduction crisis, the agricultural crisis of falling prices (especially for coffee), and the political crisis, which both drew upon and exacerbated the others." The businessmen's *Jornal do Comércio* bitterly replied that if 1929 had been bad, 1930 was going to be far worse, given the Wall Street crash. Signs of trouble were unmistakable: to survive many of the unemployed took to begging and petty crime, and newspapers wrote of the "vagabond problem." [65] Thus on the eve of the Depression, business was bad and a definite malaise had set in.

Bad business also meant hard times for labor, and the late 1920s saw a sharp increase in union strife. In September 1928 a major strike broke out in the Guanabara shipyards, followed by two more, one in a shoe store and another in a textile factory. The shipyard strike, joined by a number of unions but opposed by the police, lasted for over a month. In December two more strikes erupted, in the enormous Brahma Brewery and in a hotel. During the first half of 1929, three more strikes occurred, all of them sanctioned by one or more unions. Factory workers who walked off the job in January were represented by the Union of Textile Factory Workers, which reached a settlement. The Bakery Workers Union went on strike in April and stayed off for a month, finally achieving most of its demands. The same month construction workers staged a wildcat strike, which was soon sanctioned by the Regional Union for Civil Construction. Lasting only a few days, it too was successful.[66] Thus in a very short period the peaceful labor relations in Rio had disappeared and a new militancy took hold of the working class.

The business difficulties and strikes of the late 1920s did not, however, mean that labor and management were about to declare war. On the contrary, they looked to the government to bring back prosperity. After mid-1929 no more strikes occurred, but both labor and business turned their attention to the presidential election of March 1930. The two paramount issues from their points of view were a labor code and an end to coffee price support programs which drained off credit; from early in the campaign both candidates agreed to these positions. A hiatus in industrial strife ensued, therefore, as associations threw themselves into politics to an unprecedented degree.

The events of 1929 and 1930 demonstrated beyond a doubt the efficacy of Rio's metropolitan social structure, especially its ability to mediate industrial conflict. But for many observers the pluralist world of small groups competing in an open marketplace was deeply dissatisfying. Why couldn't industrial society recapture the solidarity of an earlier time, in which guilds united workers and managers in common purpose? What if the strata should rigidify into classes that could then organize politically or spawn revolution? And how to incorporate the lower class, the *povo*, whose clubs and associations were not even in the marketplace, so to speak? These and other questions lay behind the reformers' search for an organic society whose very structure would eliminate conflict among men. In some sense, their goal was the restoration of the colonial urban tradition. Political reform was central to that task, so many of the reform-minded set out to expand the electorate and to arm politicians with bolder mandates. Therein was born the push toward mass politics and populism.

4 □ Toward Mass Politics

Social reformism and the tensions caused by economic instability in the late 1920s gave rise to a new politics which challenged the clientelistic system of the city. The number of voters in Rio and other large cities grew rapidly, pointing the way to mass politics. Although the full impact of the urban vote would not be felt until after World War II, in the 1920s its influence created a competitive atmosphere conducive to experimentation with leadership styles and coalitions. The emergence of an autonomous urban politics began an inexorable transfer of power from the countryside to the cities and from bosses to populists.

The indicators of political change were far more visible than underlying social transformations. The number of persons voting tripled, from twenty-one thousand in 1919 to over sixty-four thousand in 1930. Reform politics spawned the city's only genuine party, the Democrático (PD) in 1927, and from then on leading associations set up campaign funds and committees for active participation in elections. Indeed, coalitions of interest groups emerged, mobilizing memberships in the pursuit of larger goals. To some extent the rapid politicization of Cariocas was a reflection of national trends, especially the inability of the major states to choose a single candidate in two of the three presidential elections of the 1920s. But even more it was due to the internal workings of society and the interplay of local interests. Politicization in Rio paralleled and surpassed national developments, forecasting urban political trends for the next generation.[1]

Before analyzing urban politics of the 1920s, a brief description of Rio's administration is necessary to set the stage. Governance of the city was complex and multifaceted, divided among a score of federal and local agencies. For this reason pressures upon the administration came from all quarters, from local to international. The result was intentional ambiguity in decision making that blurred responsibility and benefited those at the top. Issues such as large public utility concessions or regulation of transportation cut across various levels of power. The more money or voters affected, the higher the issue was likely to go for resolution. Even purely local affairs such as urban zoning might merit federal scrutiny if the interests of out-of-state or foreign elites were at stake.[2] The fluidity of decision making, originally for the convenience of the highest authorities, tended to make politics in Rio complex, which was reflected in city government.

For reasons of presidential security, the mayor was a direct appointee of the chief executive. He was often a member of the elite from the president's state—for instance, Alaor Prata under Artur Bernardes (1922–26) and Antônio Prado Júnior under Washington Luís (1926–30). The mayor's personal friends, who often hailed from the president's home state also, were appointed to high posts or received preferential treatment in city contracts. Federal regulation of most urban services, from sanitation to local police and courts, further interlinked national and city affairs. For these reasons, the presidential circle (to which the mayor belonged) was the highest domain of city politics.

The mayor worked loosely with the city's twenty-four elected councilmen, over whom he had considerable influence though less statutory power. The 1892 Federal District Charter authorized the mayor to veto City Council legislation, which could then be reversed by the federal Senate. This power was extended in 1926 to include a line-item veto over the Council-drafted budget, giving the mayor de facto control of much local patronage. For example, in 1928 the Council created a subsidy for Carnival groups, obviously to win sympathy among poor constituents, but the mayor vetoed it and allocated the money instead to foreign tourist promotion.[3]

Rio voters also elected three senators and ten deputies to the federal Congress. The principal function of these representatives was to secure legislation advantageous to the city as well as to mediate between federal authorities and local constituents. They did not sit on major committees, but in compensation they could work the halls of government for special favors, at which some became quite adept. Elected officials could overrule even the mayor if their vital interests were threatened. For example, the mayor began vetoing expenditures savagely on the eve of an election in 1928. The Senate reinstated many items, including one which raised councilmen's salaries to nearly $5,000 per year.[4] After the election, however, things returned to normal, which meant collaboration and mutual support between the mayor and elected representatives.

Over the years, the intermixing of presidential and local governance created an informal though viable political system. Most presidents, dedicated to beautifying the city and providing orderly administration, disbursed federal funds far in excess of what was collected locally in taxes. Moreover, because political trouble could be amplified out of proportion by the capital's active press, they tried to get along with the Carioca populace. This was not always easy, as Artur Bernardes discovered: he became so hated that his mere presence in the city after the end of his term caused riots and necessitated armed guards. But again, the norm was mutual cooperation. Presidents preferred friendly, pliable politicians in local office, and they were willing to open public coffers to assure their election. For their part, Rio leaders needed more patronage around election time and tried to maintain working relationships with federal authorities.[5]

The police played an important part in local administration and politics as well. They were divided into the military and civilian branches, respectively under the Ministries of War and Justice. The uniformed military police, created in 1809, patrolled the streets by day and managed traffic; they were the most visible and the least political arm of the law.[6] The civilian police wore no uniforms and were responsible for the security of the government, enforcement of laws, and liaison with state police and foreign intelligence agencies. Especially powerful was the Quarta Delegacia de Ordem Política e Social (DOPS), charged with intelligence, labor relations, and censorship. The civilian police chief, traditionally a lawyer, often bypassed his minister to report directly to the president, an indication of the political sensitivity of the job. He was unlikely to last through a succession, therefore, and 1926 was no exception: the old chief was fired for permitting excessive graft, and a new one—trusted by the president—was appointed in December. Under Washington Luís the police were given broadened arrest powers to offset any libertarian tendencies after the end of the state of siege in Rio. In 1927, amid growing electoral unrest, they were authorized to close any organization or newspaper which disturbed the peace (Lei Toledo). And of course many techniques of questionable legality were used to spy on politicians and labor leaders. Some commentators believed that police excesses actually provoked rather than calmed trouble, an observation which seemed true given the rise of labor militancy.[7]

Newspapers were the prime medium of politics in the 1920s, carrying intimate details about candidates and deals, reporting on elections, and occasionally discussing long-term changes. During the early 1920s the press had generally been at odds with the government—some papers had been so combative that the police imposed censorship and jailed newsmen under the hated Press Decree of 31 October 1923. In 1926 censorship was lifted and relations between the press and government improved, even though the decree remained on the books as a threat. Most editors adopted a circumspect attitude toward the government, while the conciliatory nature of politics generally overcame militancy. The possibility of censorship, plus the habit of secretly subsidizing friendly papers, assured that some of the press was progovernment most of the time. Table 7 lists the major newspapers.[8]

TABLE 7: Major Newspapers in Rio

Title	Date Founded	Circulation	Owner (nationality other than Brazilian)
Jornal do Comércio	1826	25,000[a]	Oscar Rodrigues da Costa and Leandro Martins
O Paiz	1883	40,000	João Souza Lage (Port.)
Jornal do Brasil	1891	75,000[a]	Ernesto Pereira Carneiro
Correio da Manhã	1901	90,000[a]	Edmundo Bittencourt (Port.)
O Imparcial	1911	NA	Henrique Lage
A Noite	1911	NA	NA
O Jornal	1919	45,000	Assis Chateaubriand–Diários Associados[b]
A Pátria	1920	NA	Francisco Valadares
O Globo	1925	30,000	Irineu Marinho
A Manhã	1925	10,000	Mário Rodrigues Filho
O Brazil	—	15,000	NA

Source: See ch. 3, n. 8.
NA = not available.
a. Estimated.
b. Alfredo Pujol and Guinle family major stockholders.

The oldest daily was the *Jornal do Comércio,* whose makeup and content were conservative by 1920s standards. Its circulation was small, for it was read mostly by businessmen. It was in some ways the *Wall Street Journal* of Brazil. In order to compensate for low sales, the presses were kept busy with outside work, especially printing the magazines and annals of businessmen's associations like the AC-Rio. Purchased in 1923 by two wealthy men and managed by Felix Pacheco, the foreign minister under Bernandes, it was the most openly progovernment. Ernesto Pereira Carneiro's *Jornal do Brasil* was the most successful in the country, with the second largest circulation and sound management. In its back pages the paper carried decrees and notices from the city government, which were later compiled into official publications, providing steady work and income. In addition, its more attractive format, popular classified section in the front pages, and well-known writers gave it a huge readership, both in Rio and in the states. These two papers constituted the "established press" of Rio.

Most popular, however, was the *Correio da Manhã,* an opposition paper which invariably sought unusual stories and editorial slants. It was owned by Edmundo Bittencourt, a combative Portuguese lawyer-journalist who, among other things, spent several years in jail for helping incite tenente revolts in the early 1920s. Bittencourt pioneered sensationalism in the Rio press, and it paid off: the *Correio* had a circulation of some ninety thousand. Bittencourt's hatred of Bernardes (who had ordered him imprisoned) knew no bounds, but the fiery editor was also unfriendly toward all traditional politicians. For example, he refused to endorse any candidates in the 1926 local elections but voiced general approval of labor nominees as more authentic representatives. The *Correio* specialized in news of the tenentes throughout the late 1920s and often had a correspondent on the scene of their great march of 1924–27.[9] It was natural for the *Correio* to favor reform causes and politicians because they provided ammunition against constituted authorities and made good copy as well. Bittencourt's success undoubtedly convinced other newspaper publishers to flirt with opposition journalism.

Many other dailies in Rio, too numerous to mention, were sustained by a combination of sales, advertising, and subsidies. Few were financially independent, and most changed hands frequently. The government itself was not above pressuring, buying, or silencing a paper it disliked, and the 1920s saw a high rate of turnover and many new papers founded. Symptomatic of this turbulence was the appearance of new and more combative newsmen's associations in the late 1920s. Thus, while on the surface good relations prevailed between the government and the press, the growth of a new politics contributed to diversification of the city's press.[10]

It should come as no surprise that politics had a strong hierarchical orientation, given the nature of social relations sketched in chapter 3. The citizen naturally looked to the patriarch for guidance, and the leader expected compliance from his followers. In the more modern setting of 1920s Rio, the politician replaced the patriarch, but the patron-client axis remained. The profession of politician, like law and medicine, had a diversity of ranks along which the individual might progress. Likewise, it could be an entree into the elite, for at the pinnacle of a career one could pose as "statesman" and be admitted to the highest circles. At the bottom, of course, little money or status attached to the job. Surveying the political system from top to bottom, four traditional leaders can be discerned: grand figures, *chefes, cabos,* and reformers. Brief examinations of these personae will demonstrate the vertical, clientelistic nature of politics in Rio.

The grand figures *(figurões)* were those who had risen to the top of the pile, who were therefore bonafide members of the elite, and who had access to the presidential circle. Only two or three could exist at any time, cordial rivals for preeminence in city affairs. Because the presidency and mayoralty were usually reserved for outsiders, the office of senator was the highest in Rio politics and the final plateau for a *figurão*. City-wide senatorial elections were held every three years to fill nine-year overlapping terms. Although the Senate was not as active as the Chamber of Deputies, it enjoyed far more prestige and with the Chamber approved the budget. Because the government spent enormous sums on salaries, purchases, and services in Rio itself, senators from Rio played a major role in gaining favors for special groups of employees and businessmen. Indeed, it was the stock-in-trade of the *figurão* to protect federal and municipal constituents. In 1927 it required over seventeen thousand votes to be elected senator and twice that many in 1930.

Paulo de Frontin (1860–1933) was unquestionably a grand figure in 1920s Rio. A famous engineer and entrepreneur in his own right, Frontin entered electoral politics by being voted directly into the Senate in 1917. In 1919 he served a lame-duck term as mayor, during which he favored city employees with incredible liberality and thus cemented his position in Rio politics. After a brief term in the Chamber, he was elected to the Senate again in 1921, and was reelected in 1930, the year his mandate was canceled by the revolution. His role in scrutinizing the annual budget became so important that one colleague called him the "de facto manager" of the purse strings. With that role went the overall coordination of Rio politics. Frontin's constituency could not be narrowly defined, of course, for he had to represent city and federal employees, businessmen's associations, major labor unions, and a wide variety of personal and professional associates. Generally speaking, though, he best served the interests of downtown, the now-populous inner suburbs (North Zone and Flamengo-Botafogo), and the developers at work along the South Zone beaches. As mayor, in fact, he promoted the growth of the South Zone. It required all his considerable skills to keep such constituencies satisfied.[11]

The fluidity of political life in the capital prevented the existence of parties such as those which dominated the major states of Brazil. Rather, shifting alliances led by *figurões* predominated. Frontin, for example, who headed the Carioca Republican Center (CRC), tried to form a party in 1926 but soon desisted. The reason cited by the *Jornal do Brasil* was that any attempt to write a platform would make shambles of his fragile following. So the CRC remained a floating assemblage of all those politicians who believed that their careers would, at any given moment, benefit from association with Frontin. The usual way to signal alliance with a *figurão* was to attend (and be noticed at) one of his frequent receptions, birthday celebrations, or bon voyage parties.[12] Whether or not to ally with Frontin, however, became an increasingly difficult choice, for Rio's other *figurão* (Frontin's chief competitor) grew in stature and popularity in the late 1920s.

Irineu Machado fought his way to the top by usually joining every antigovernment movement which came along and by frequently employing unconventional means of combat. He was a lawyer specialized in labor affairs, but he had worked in the Ministry of the Navy, the Central do Brasil Railroad, and the University of Rio de Janeiro, gaining large and loyal followings every place he went. He was through-and-through a politician, equally at home on a soapbox and on the floor of Congress. A flamboyant and winning orator in the days before mass communications, Irineu posed as a man of the people and a defender of the working class against the rich and powerful. Since most of his constituents were federal employees, he was able to reward them throughout his many terms in Congress (deputy 1912–, senator 1916–) with special retirement systems, raises, and job stability. When he could not convince his colleagues to go along, he would filibuster the budget until they gave in, to the delight of the general public.[13]

Having led a trenchant campaign against Artur Bernardes in 1922, Irineu was fraudulently denied reelection to the Senate in 1924, after winning more than two-thirds of the North Zone vote. After spending three years in Europe he returned and ran again, swamping his opponent (supported by Frontin and the other senator) with 61 percent of the vote. Although Irineu's support had originally come from the North Zone and Subúrbios, in 1927 his margin was equally wide in all zones. Upon being seated in the Senate, he addressed the senator who had taken his seat (after helping in the purge) as "that fellow who has been renting my seat." According to one awed observer, two coffins would be required for Irineu's funeral, one for the body and another for the tongue.[14]

To everyone's surprise, Irineu decided to back the government candidate in 1930, and it was openly rumored that the government had either bribed him with $150,000 or blackmailed him with some personal scandal.[15] Whatever the truth of the rumors, it was a mistaken choice, because the upheaval of that year terminated his career. Nonetheless, Irineu had by that time helped to revolutionize Rio politics by moving away from narrow clientelistic representation to a broad coalition of forces and by using charismatic qualities and preaching (insincerely, it turned out) social reform. He was, therefore, a model for other reformers as well as a precurser of populism in the 1930s. Frontin and Irineu were the genuine grand figures of the decade. (Rio's other senator was little more than an administration placeman.) These two made the decisions, struck the bargains, and created the alliances that guided the rest of the politicians.

The next level of leadership was that of the *chefes políticos* (bosses) who ruled zones of the city, occupied most seats in the Chamber, distributed the bulk of the patronage given out, managed elections, and oversaw the daily working of government on behalf of their constituents. To some extent *chefes* were the urban analogues of the *coronéis*, small town and rural bosses who dominated public life in much of the interior; they, like the *coronéis*, exchanged local votes for assorted government favors, such as jobs, contracts, and public works. The principal difference between *chefes* and *coronéis* was that the former could not commit fraud or violence with the ease of the latter. This meant, among other things, that urban politics were more honest and representative, and less coercive, than those in the countryside.[16]

Chefes políticos were usually lawyers or doctors, less frequently professors, teachers, and journalists. They tended to have long-standing residence and practice in their districts, which meant they were more numerous downtown and in the older suburbs. The *chefe* was an intermediary between the grand figure and the precinct captain, and his social status was middle-sector. The *chefe* associated paternalistically with his voters in public ceremonies and in personal consultation, and though he left the daily chores of politics to his aides, he frequently gave free professional services to needy constituents. His role was as close to that of patriarch as any in the city, but that too was changing with the shift from clientelism to interest politics. In order to defray the costs of public life and reward his followers, the *chefe* needed government favors to distribute, such as roads, drainage canals, jobs, and so forth. Therefore, he was nearly always an elected official or an administrative head.[17]

When they chose to run, *chefes* could usually win election to the Chamber, which required between one and three thousand voters. All adult literate Brazilian males could qualify to vote, but the procedures for registering were complicated. Politicians often spoke of "their" voters, by which they meant persons they had registered and who were loyal to them. At election time each voter cast a ballot *(chapa)* with the names of four candidates for deputy (eight for councilmen). Each candidate distributed his own ballots before the election, with his name printed at the top and three printed below (seven for councilmen). The inclusion of other names on the ballot occasioned considerable bargaining. For example, candidate A might choose to put B's name on his list if B reciprocated, wherein each would receive the votes of the other. If A and B had nearly equal electorates, each would double his total. Between candidates with unequal followings, deals might affect only a stipulated number of ballots. Some agreements embraced three or more candidates, with complicated formulae for exchanges of votes. A *chefe* whose election was assured might give positions on his ballot to a protégé or someone to whom he was in debt. Of course fraud and double-dealing occurred, so each *chefe* had a network of informants to make sure that agreements were honored.

When two or more elections coincided (such as for president, senator, and deputies in 1930) the complexity reached amazing proportions. The *Jornal do Brasil* observed: "Politics in the Federal District are surely the most difficult in the country. Infinitely fragmented, without a leader who has sufficient support to be elected on his own merits, local politics live off of agreements, counterbalances, and unstable combinations which, like bubbles, appear and disappear with ease."[18] Thus a period of intricate bargaining, usually directed by the *chefes*, preceded elections. Such alliances commonly dissolved after the election.

Rio's best known *chefe político*, virtually an ideal type, was Dr. Júlio Cesário de Melo, a physician from the semirural precincts of Campo Grande, Santa Cruz, and Guaratiba at the western edge of the Federal District, an area also known as the Carioca Triangle. Cesário delivered jobs, public works, and services for the constituents of his backward area in exchange for their votes. In 1915 he built his own medical clinic, where he often gave free treatment to his followers. His main source of city jobs was the slaughterhouse, the processing center for all fresh beef for the city. Cesário's many favors to the district earned him the title of "King of the Triangle." Cesário usually supported incumbent governments in order to keep patronage flowing, but he was also free to bargain with the opposition if it suited his needs. He could count on about 80 percent of the four thousand votes cast in the Triangle by the late 1920s, one of the largest voting blocks in the city. Reform politicians from the North Zone and Subúrbios in the late 1920s sought to prevent Cesário's election because he typified the traditional paternalistic boss.[19]

The *cabo eleitoral,* or precinct captain, worked the grass roots of Rio politics in the 1920s. He recruited from several dozen to as many as a thousand voters and provided local services in exchange for their loyalty. The *cabo* allied with a *chefe* the way the *chefe* did with a *figurão,* creating a triadic relationship which moved patronage down and votes up.[20] Mutual assistance and protection bound the actors together, at least temporarily. The *cabo* dealt in small favors—a paved street, a sidewalk, a job on a road gang, or protection against vandalism—but his importance was enhanced by his constant availability to the local populace. He was usually a long-time resident and a community leader, acquainted with all on a first-name basis. As elections approached, he carefully reviewed his constituents' registration papers and provided new ones when necessary. Voter registration was complicated, and if the *cabo* himself was not a notary public, he was the close friend of one. Occasionally a prospective voter would be illiterate and would have to be taught to sign his name to qualify. When the campaign heated up, the *cabo* established a political center and distributed printed material, including his *chefe's* ballots. He took his people to campaign speeches and sponsored rallies or luncheons for local notables. Typically candidates would promise all sorts of local improvements in order to enthuse the crowds. Finally, on election day the *cabo* was responsible for getting out the voters and verifying that their ballots were cast properly. In repayment, the *cabo* received a cash payment at election time and in addition was protected in a well-paying government job.[21]

The *cabos* had such varied careers that few could be considered typical. Nonetheless, some generalization is possible. Their social standing was middle-sector because of their public employment, but they could never aspire to elite status. If they wished to be in the spotlight, they could run for the City Council, election to which required a minimum of about six hundred voters. Through training and financial success *cabos* might eventually become *chefes*, especially if they began their careers in densely populated downtown or North Zone districts. No matter how high they eventually rose, though, *cabos* kept their feet firmly planted in their home precincts.[22]

Reformers were the last major category of leader in 1920s Rio. They were politicians who opposed the established order and called for major changes in Carioca life. In the broadest sense, they led the reaction against the elitist "new urbanism" of the republican generation. They also, though more selectively, championed some of the social reforms outlined in chapter 3, especially those favoring workers. Yet the reformers were, above all, working politicians: rather than seek a philosophically coherent world, they recruited large numbers of voters who saw themselves as effectively disenfranchised by the existing system. Thousands of these people had in fact stopped participating in politics, believing that change from within was impossible. The reformer convinced them otherwise and hewed a career out of the rough timber of citizen alienation.

Reform politics went back some time in Rio. In the 1880s Cariocas had led the national movement for abolition of slavery. In the 1890s they had fought to obtain a republican form of government under civilian control. In 1910 and 1919 they had favored Rui Barbosa's *civilista* campaign, as had urban voters from other states. And in 1922 they had voted against the official candidate Artur Bernardes. Not all "opposition" votes were cast solely according to conscience, of course, but enough to assure the success of some reform politicians in every election. Therefore, they had become traditional figures in the system that they consistently opposed.

The Carioca sympathy for reformers contributed to the complexity of Rio politics, for even established figures occasionally had to oppose the government to retain the loyalty of their constituents. The case of Irineu has been described: it was said that local *chefes* and *cabos* had to fall in with him just to keep their voters in line. Frontin, too, was for a time a member of the opposition and was regarded an upstart for his favors to municipal workers. His nephew and protégé, Henrique Dodsworth, bourgeois to the core, often voted with the opposition and won great popularity by sponsoring the Vacation Law in 1925.[23] Some degree of reformism was simply good politics, especially early in one's career. Reformers carried on such activity consistently. The general sympathy for the opposition also fostered ideological flexibility, for all manner of foreign philosophical strains flourished among educated Cariocas. But these foreign strains seldom lasted with a politician, because his relation to the government and to his immediate superior in the clientelistic triad was the prime determinant of his stance on a particular issue. This was not true of reformers; their ideologies had to be constant to be believed. Most stood to the left of classic liberalism.

Reformers in the 1920s came from the North Zone and drew their votes from working-class neighborhoods and older suburbs. Their issues were usually civil service benefits, labor legislation, transportation and utilities for the Subúrbios, and a return to moral values in politics. This did not mean that reform was not popular in the South Zone but that the division of the city into two electoral zones made it difficult to be elected from the new beach communities. District one comprised the business area, Flamengo-Botafogo, and the South Zone, in which traditional *chefes* usually carried elections with their large downtown electorates. District two comprised the North Zone and Subúrbios, where the electorate was more accessible. The reformers' style was well suited there, for they tended to be good orators and militants who thrived on campaign tours of factories, railroad yards, and Subúrbio train stations. This was certainly true of the outstanding reformers of the 1920s, Maurício de Lacerda, Azevedo Lima, and Adolfo Bergamini.

Maurício de Lacerda was a leading reformer and among the most popular men in Rio during the 1920s. Scion of a decadent Vassouras coffee clan and a dedicated socialist, Lacerda had gained a large following among the residents of the North Zone. His truculent independence and honesty made him a legend, and he was also a fierce advocate of social legislation. While still in jail for complicity in a tenente revolt in 1924, Lacerda was registered as a candidate for the Council in 1926 and elected on the strength of colleagues' ballots. His appeal came in large measure from his disdain for patronage politics and his courage in attacking the evils of the government. Lacerda used the Council in the late 1920s as a "fragile but daring forum . . . against infringements on freedoms, against laws of repression, and for our election campaigns."[24] João Baptista de Azevedo Lima was a protégé of Irineu and a firm ally of Lacerda. Son of a wealthy physician in São Cristóvão, Azevedo Lima took up his father's profession and inherited the family clinic. Attracted by socialist politics, he became a spokesman for industrial labor unions in his area and represented them in the Chamber throughout the decade. In 1928 he helped form the Workers and Peasants Bloc (BOC), a front for the fledgling Communist party.[25] A third major reformer was Adolfo Bergamini, a lawyer who represented Central do Brasil Railroad workers in the Subúrbios where he himself lived. Son of an educated Italian immigrant, Bergamini had worked his way through law school as a reporter for various Carioca newspapers. Assured by his railroad voters of a seat in the Chamber after 1921, Bergamini developed a bold and critical style of parliamentary repartee which pleased his constituents and gained him notoriety among older politicians. For example, his first speech in Congress was a memorable harangue about police harassment of his campaign. When another deputy officiously asked if his presence was not proof that the elections had been honest, Bergamini shot back, "And your presence, Sir, is proof that they were *not!*"[26] It was easy to see Irineu's influence, but these reformers were more dedicated to political and social change than their mentor.

These and about a half dozen other reformers were known in the press as the Parliamentary Left, referring to the socialist leanings of many. The reformers were too few and individualistic to create a real party, but they worked together much as did the *chefes* under Frontin or Irineu. They collaborated with opposition groups in other states; they ran Lacerda for the Council in 1926 and exiled tenente leader Luís Carlos Prestes for the Chamber in 1927 (he lost); they continually pressed for tenente amnesty; and they exchanged ballot positions among themselves. They found it difficult to agree on a program, just as did the other factions, so they cultivated personalist followings with their flamboyant style.[27] Only in 1927 would most join the new Democratic party, when the opportunities for middle sector and elite recruitment became clear.

Despite the occasional excitement of a reformist speech or a fight on the floor of Congress, Rio politics was not a popular activity until after 1926. Prior elections had been in general orderly, honest, and poorly attended. The clientelistic organization of traditional politics made it difficult for innovators to break into public life. The system would tolerate a handful of reformers—indeed it needed them to provide legitimacy—but the rule for most was slow progression up the ranks. The system of registration discouraged widespread participation by voters as well because it cost time and money (usually a cabo's) to get on the electoral rolls. In short, patronage politics kept the electorate small and disciplined. That was to change in the late 1920s because social diversification required a more adaptable, effective system.

The principal failing of the *chefe* and *cabo* system was its unresponsiveness to differentiation in urban society. *Chefes* and *cabos* were rooted in the local affairs of older neighborhoods, whereas the city was fast becoming a metropolis with varied new interests to be met. The proliferation of associations, newspapers, and middle-sector occupations signaled the changes, to which patronage politics were becoming irrelevant. Businessmen had little faith in the financial judgment or probity of elected officials whose debts to parochial interests and to one another were well known. The new elite associated with the South Zone despaired of achieving urban renovation as long as politicians from older neighborhoods dominated local government. The middle sectors realized that *chefes* and *cabos* could never form the vanguard of a nationalist movement which would endow citizenship on the masses. In short, the *chefe* and *cabo* system had become an obstacle rather than a means to progress. Therefore, a new brand of politics emerged in the late 1920s, characterized by new methods of recruitment and representation.

The new politics of the late 1920s no longer depended upon neighborhood *cabos* and voting centers for support but rather drew upon interest groups. The groups themselves provided the cohesion formerly supplied by the *cabo*, and because their interests were better defined it was easier to achieve them through political means. Moreover, a larger electoral following was possible working through organizations, several of which could be represented simultaneously. The new politics did not please everybody: as one critic said some years later, "The secret ballot converts individual corruption into that of groups, classes, and special interests."[28] The superimposition of interest group over traditional neighborhood politics was largely responsible for the huge rise in voting between 1926 and 1930 (see table 8).

Labor unions were a natural field for new voter recruitment after 1926 because of rising competitiveness and low turnouts. For example, 130 candidates filed for the twenty-four Council seats in that year, but only twenty-eight thousand persons voted, slightly more than in 1922. Sensing the new opportunities, some unions took the lead. The powerful Commercial Employees Union (1908–) formed a "party" to recommend candidates to its fifteen thousand members, and the Construction Workers

TABLE 8: Rio Voter Turnout, 1919–30

Year	Month	Voters	Offices
1919	Apr.	21,000	President
1922	Mar.	25,000	President
1926	Mar.	28,000	President, councilmen
1927	Feb.	39,000	Senator, deputies
1928	Oct.	42,000	Councilmen
1930	Mar.	64,000	President, senator, deputies

Sources: Jornal do Comércio, 2–22 Mar. 1922, passim; *Correio da Manhã,* 3 Mar. 1926, p. 1; *Jornal do Brasil,* 26 Feb. 1927, p. 8; 3 Mar. 1930, p. 8; *O Jornal,* 1 Nov. 1928, p. 4.

Beneficent Center also summoned its members to discuss voting strategies. But because no labor leaders themselves were candidates, the *Correio da Manhã* concluded that workers were exploited *(cavalgado)* by traditional politicians who did not deserve labor's support.[29] While that may have occurred before 1926, soon after the election unions took the initiative.

The next elections were held in February 1927, by which time labor had become far more assertive. In August 1926 a *chefe* in the waterfront district of Gamboa formed the Labor party to back his candidates for Congress. A special election in September to fill a vacant Council seat showed that Frontin's group was being severely challenged by Irineu's forces in North Zone labor circles. Throughout late 1926 voter registration went on at a rapid pace. For example, the Commercial Employees Union registered five hundred voters; an industrialist newcomer signed up eleven hundred persons; and the AC-Rio set up a registration service for clerks employed by its member firms. On the eve of the election, the Municipal Workers Union formed a campaign committee to get its members to the polls. The upshot was a 40 percent increase in voters over a ten month period that largely benefited candidates favorable to labor.[30] The push toward mass politics had begun.

Recruitment of labor and intensification of interest group politics continued for the October 1928 Council elections, even though no federal seats were at stake. On 15 November feminist leader Bertha Lutz addressed a large labor meeting, pressing for extension of voting rights to women. Azevedo Lima, now a leader in the Communist party and the BOC, campaigned the hardest, registering voters throughout the North Zone. The AC-Rio kept its voter registration services, as did numerous union election committees. On May 1 (Labor Day) the signs of labor politicization were clear. Three competing labor rallies were held: the BOC's at the waterfront; anticommunist unions downtown; and the reform politicians' near the Bangu textile factory in the Triangle.[31] The BOC, the most disciplined and challenging of the labor fronts, met with the growing police harassment as the election neared, which only hardened its leaders' resolve and generated public sympathy. Another ephemeral Labor party appeared, seeking to win support from both business and labor in the second district. The Commercial Employees Union party was said to have twenty thousand voters, an exaggeration suggestive of the general optimism of labor organizers in the late 1920s.[32]

Reform and political experimentation were in the air, and Rio's new elite and middle sectors mobilized for elections with nearly the same enthusiasm as did unions. Inspired by the success of a similar group in São Paulo, two dozen political hopefuls founded the Democratic party (PD) on 17 May 1927. Meeting in the offices of the Brazilian Association for Social Hygiene, the organizers announced that the PD was to stand for the "destiny of Brazil in the hands of her sons." The main planks of its platform were: liberalism under the 1891 Constitution; independence of the judiciary; expansion of primary education; strengthening of technical and professional high schools; advanced social legislation; extreme moral rectitude in public office; and creation and guidance of responsible public opinion. That was a strong indictment of the republican system coming from persons who had not been treated badly by it; also revealed was the extent of middle-sector and professional alienation. Among the founding members of the party were nine businessmen, seven professors of medicine and engineering, five professionals, and two civil servants. Many were members of the Brazilian Education Association and all were well known in professional circles but newcomers to politics. Adolfo Bergamini, representing the Parliamentary Left, was present at the ceremony.[33]

Within a short time the PD seemed on its way to becoming a viable party. In a week two thousand new members signed up, mostly employees of the founders. Their professions were store clerk (40 percent), student (21 percent), civil servant (11 percent), engineer (6 percent), and a smattering of other professionals, workers, and military officers. Students were active in recruiting new members.[34] Their precinct captains were a far cry from old-style *cabos*—in Copacabana they included a general, a priest, and several physicians; and in the North Zone intellectuals like Jacobina Lacombe, Miguel Calmon, Roberto Macedo, and Cumplido de Santana. Their goals, however, did not become much clearer. Claiming that the PD was neither a class-based nor revolutionary party, leaders explained that it represented intellectual circles and tomorrow's generation, meaning mostly the technical and professional schools. They sought to "moralize politics, clean up elections, and awaken the slumbering conscience of the nation." The *Jornal do Brasil* noted a few months later that the PD was only spouting "democratic superstitions" and was unlikely to achieve a significant program. Contrary to its sister party in the city of São Paulo, the PD in Rio lacked a firm base and competed with legitimate opposition forces, that is the Parliamentary Left. The criticisms were valid.[35]

For their part, the reformers were divided over how to deal with the PD. Bergamini joined the new party wholeheartedly and became a leader, along with several of his colleagues. Lacerda, always independent, tentatively sided with the PD while warning that it needed to cut ties with the PD of São Paulo, which represented mostly businessmen and planters.[36] Azevedo Lima, deeply committed to communist politics, denounced the PD as bourgeois, a view not difficult to sustain. Indeed, on Labor Day 1928 the PD sponsored a rally at the Bangu factory in the Triangle, at which the principal speaker had the noteworthy pseudonym León Bourgeois. An excerpt from his speech: "Each one of us feels that he is a link in an immense chain, that stretches out in space, across the surface of the earth, wherever there is a worker . . . a chain that extends through time . . . aristocracy exists no more on earth, not of blood, nor spirit, nor birth, nor profession. All occupations become one, bound together in the duty to be useful . . . the cult of eternal beauty."[37] Whatever its failings, the Parliamentary Left could never commit such idiocy on the soapbox.

With the exception of Azevedo Lima, the reformers did join the PD in the hope of tapping what appeared to be a large new elite and middle-sector electorate. The PD signed up thousands of members and registered them to vote: in December 1927 they claimed fourteen thousand members and in May 1928, fifteen thousand. If true, the PD was approaching the threshold of senatorial politics. Yet on the eve of the municipal election they proved naive and inept. They denounced fraud long before the voting but were unprepared to man the tables. At the last minute they decided to work the neighborhood organizations (Centros Pro-Melhoramentos) in the hope of drawing off *chefe* and *cabo* votes, without seeking to reconcile such patronage promises with their philosophical goals.[38]

The results of the Council election of 1928 were disappointing but instructive to both the labor and the PD leaders. Out of twenty-four seats, the BOC and the PD each won two. None of Bergamini's candidates were elected nor were those of the Labor party, although to some extent they gained publicity from the campaign.[39] The reasons for the poor showing of the new politics were several. First, they had insufficient time to train leaders and recruit voters, as their many mistakes showed. The PD effectively tapped the new elite and middle-sector reform groups but as yet had no viable platform to offer such an amorphous constituency. They took satisfaction from the fact that the city election had gotten out forty-two thousand voters, six thousand of whom were members of the PD. Second, the *chefe* and *cabo* politics were by no means indefensible to the PD and labor attack. Old politicos saw the threat and mobilized thousands of voters themselves through registration and deals with one another.[40] They also helped push up the total turnout. Third, reformers found themselves in an awkward position straddling labor and reform constituents whose interests far from coincided. Symptomatic was the fact that the PD's main newspaper, *O Jornal,* was the only major daily with no labor page. Finally, labor unions as yet had no working politicians to run on their own tickets. Even the BOC candidates chosen by Azevedo Lima and the communists, billed as worker-intellectuals, were poor politicians.[41] Therefore the only alternative for noncommunist unions was to bargain with traditional *chefes* and assert their influence among other competing interests. It was at best an unsatisfying compromise.

Both the PD and the labor factions profited from the lessons of 1928, for there was no doubt that in the long run they would gain more power. The PD continued registering voters as a civic duty but lost one of the councilmen in a plane crash shortly after the election. The BOC was harassed by the police who continued to break up their meetings, sometimes with gunfire.[42] But despite these setbacks, they looked ahead to the 1930 presidential race as a great opportunity to push the new politics to their limit. It was already a contested election and would prove to be the climax of the system of government Brazil had known under the republican generation. The 1930 revolution and its impact on Rio politics are the subject of the next chapter.

Populism, it will be recalled, was a reaction against the republican generation and its abandonment of Rio's centuries-old urban heritage. In order to restore that tradition, populists needed to assert local municipal autonomy over the patrimonial authority. Opposition politics in Rio were a clear manifestation of this desire for Carioca autonomy. The social question and the reform politics to which it gave rise also constituted preconditions for populism, which promised to incorporate the poor into mass industrial society. The franchise had to be extended to the masses in order to validate local autonomy, a tendency clearly present in 1920s Rio. Finally, populism was a campaign whose mission was not merely day-to-day governance but restoration of an ancient order, and hence it required charismatic leadership. Irineu, Lacerda, and Bergamini certainly elicited deep loyalty from their followers, based on the perception of their superior qualities. Their repudiation of patronage politics challenged the legitimacy of the *chefes* and *cabos* and helped undermine the republican system itself.

In short, most of the elements of populism were present in late 1920s Rio, but they had yet to be assembled into a workable political movement. The reformers were on the track and would probably have succeeded eventually, for they were intelligent, resourceful men. But the incumbent system was tough, and as yet none of the reformers had found a way to reconcile the two new strains of politics, middle-class and labor. Bergamini made the most concerted effort to amalgamate the two by expanding his electoral base from the North Zone to the PD, but he failed. He would continue to try for the next three years without success. As it turned out, populism came from an entirely different source—it was imposed from above by the generation that accompanied Getúlio Vargas to power in 1930. Nevertheless, the experimental politics of the 1920s were crucial to the success of the populists in the 1930s.

5 □ Election, Revolution, and Depression in Rio

Although Brazil, like the rest of the world, endured great turmoil during 1930 in the form of economic hardship and political unrest, the revolution of that year was not simply a response to the international crisis. It had roots deep in Brazil's regionalist politics and in the discontent felt by educated people for the poor national administration. For this reason, 1930 was a major break with the past that released pressures for change built up during the preceding generation. Most of the reform currents of the post–1930 period can be traced to developments in the cities during the 1920s or before. That is not to say that the revolution was an urban-rural conflict but that new leaders, drawing on the frustrations of new elites and middle sectors, took over and sponsored change from above, change meant to address these frustrations and to contain labor unrest. These efforts led national politics toward populism; the first experiment was Pedro Ernesto Baptista's Autonomist party in Rio. Leaving aside national events, a fairly direct line of causality can be traced in Rio from sociopolitical reform movements in the late 1920s to the revolution of 1930 and to populism of the mid-1930s.

From early 1929 the pace for local and national politics was set by the presidential election scheduled for March 1930. The central dynamic of the contest was Getúlio Vargas's challenge of the official candidacy of Júlio Prestes; Prestes, like President Washington Luís who had nominated him, was from the state of São Paulo. Vargas's campaign, called the Liberal Alliance, brought together the Republican parties of Rio Grande do Sul (PRR) and of Minas Gerais (PRM) as well as reformist leaders in major cities. Vargas was not well known, his only federal posts having been deputy and minister of finance (1926–28), and for a time Vargas vacillated, hoping to be won over by a conciliatory offer from the government. But the offer never came, and by mid-1929 Vargas was committed to a campaign that would severely tax PRR and PRM resources and would surely break all voting records. Managers in Rio Grande and Minas began recruitment drives and pledged state monies to the election, and since these two states were the first and third in number of registered voters, the campaign had some hope of success. An important element in the strategy was the use of Rio politics to generate antigovernment publicity as well as issues attractive to urban voters elsewhere.[1]

Rio played a far more important part in national affairs than its small share of the electorate (5 percent) would suggest because it was the forum for political debate in Congress, the press, and interest associations. The Liberal Alliance strategy called for heavy denunciation in Congress of the government and its candidate, which would be picked up and broadcast nationwide by the Rio press. The Alliance platform would stress reforms favored by educated urban voters and thereby gather support from the Democratic parties of Rio and São Paulo and similar factions in other cities. In the city of São Paulo voter turnouts had climbed from eight thousand to twenty-seven thousand between 1922 and 1928. The urban voter campaign, combined with the massive drives in Rio Grande and Minas, might have put the Alliance over the top, but the ten largest cities accounted for only one hundred thirty-three thousand votes (7.3 percent of national total), and the distribution held some unpleasant surprises for the reformers.

The Liberal Alliance program was tailored to urban reform sentiment of the 1920s. The party convention, held in Rio in September 1929, approved such planks as electoral reform and the secret ballot; freedom of unionization, the eight-hour-day, a minimum wage, and protection for women and children on the job; amnesty for the tenentes; and autonomy for the Federal District. The latter promise was especially popular in Rio where reformers had for years demanded local election of the mayor and greater control over city services.[2] A leading architect of the Alliance platform was the thirty-nine-year-old journalist Lindolfo Color, a Gaúcho (native of Rio Grande do Sul) and protégé of the regional boss Borges de Medeiros. An exceptionally energetic man, Color took over *A Pátria* and, after making it the Alliance paper, coaxed other editors into supporting Vargas. He drafted the convention platform, wrote voluminously for other papers, and managed to keep up his congressional duties. He acquainted himself with International Labor Organization standards, of which he became a proponent in Brazil. By the end of the campaign he had pushed Vargas toward a more comprehensive position on the social question.[3]

The race reached its climax when Vargas (breaking a promise to Washington Luís not to campaign outside of the state of Rio Grande do Sul) spoke in Rio on 2 January 1930. Because of police refusal to authorize a hall for his appearance, the local managers mounted a stage with microphones on the Castelo Esplanade. This setting was doubly symbolic: first, symbolic of government mismanagement of urban renewal and second, symbolic of denial of politicial rights to the candidate. Vargas's speech was directed largely to the Cariocas:

> Experience . . . has amply demonstrated the inefficacy of the mixed administration to which the capital has been subjected . . . yet even leaving aside the unworkable nature of the caretaker municipality, it would be appropriate now to recognize the political and administrative maturity of the city . . . by choosing their own mayor the Cariocas may keep close watch over local affairs and hold him directly accountable, the essence of republican institutions. Finally, it is neither just nor reasonable that we fail to recognize the local administrative abilities of this largest and most advanced city of Brazil, a capability which is attributed to all other states, even to the most backward and undeveloped.[4]

Vargas's labor promises went beyond the convention platform, calling for a comprehensive labor code covering the welfare and working conditions of urban and rural laborers. The code would frankly address the social question by legislating on additional issues such as education, hygiene, housing, nutrition, social security, and even sports and cultural activities. These new proposals were well received by the crowds, which surpassed the expectations of the local coordinators. At that point it seemed certain that Vargas could carry the capital.

Reform politicians in Rio, recovering from a disappointing showing in the 1928 municipal elections, decided to join the Liberal Alliance bandwagon and to push coalition tactics as hard as possible. Bergamini and Lacerda led the Rio Alliance group, which comprised Francisco Sales Filho (representing civil servants); Evaristo de Moraes; the two BOC councilmen; some university professors, newsmen, and writers; and J. J. Seabra and Cândido Pessôa, displaced Northeastern politicians who had been elected to office in Rio.[5] The overall goal of the group was to elect Vargas to the presidency and Seabra to Frontin's seat in the Senate while holding their four congressional places in the Chamber. They believed that Vargas would be a popular candidate and, if elected, would reward them handsomely for their aid. Their most optimistic hope was to gain control of an autonomous Rio government. Bergamini was the most active

Alliance organizer, attempting again to build the labor and middle-sector coalition that had eluded him in 1928.

The defection of Bergamini and Lacerda to the Vargas camp and the loss of several other leaders condemned the PD to extinction. For a few months it registered voters but dropped out of the news in early 1929 and failed to make a showing in the election. Some PD members supported Vargas as a reform candidate while others—seeing the contest as a mere split in the old guard—abandoned the party. In September, after the PD and its sister party in São Paulo had supported Vargas, the U.S. ambassador described the various PDs as "small and fragmentary groups, principally in São Paulo and Rio de Janeiro, having neither national cohesion nor significance. Its platform consists of vague generalities with no appeal to a politically immature electorate."[6] Not until 1933 would the PD be revived, ironically in competition with the populist movement. Its importance in 1928, however, was in mobilizing members of the upper and middle strata previously too pessimistic to take part in politics.

The increasingly enthusiastic campaign for Vargas in Rio met with a late but formidable effort by the administration to win the city's votes for its candidate, Júlio Prestes. Everyone from the president down took part, and Frontin's Carioca Republican Center (CRC) was the local sponsor. The special attention to Rio politics resulted from Washington Luís's desire to vindicate his own choice for successor and to prevent the election of opponents in the capital. Luís himself visited the Commercial Employees Association in order to win their support for the official ticket.[7] Prestes's platform did not differ substantially from Vargas's, for both candidates recognized the appeal of reformism. The government's planks most attractive to Cariocas, announced in an Automobile Club banquet in December, consisted of continued financial stabilization, improved transportation and communication, voting reform, electrification of the Central do Brasil commuter lines, construction of an airport on the Esplanade, improved education and hygiene, and a labor code up to ILO standards.[8] The main thrust was not toward issues, however, but toward winning the backing of Rio's working politicians.

Frontin coordinated the intense effort to bring all the *chefes* and *cabos* into line, using the powerful logic that Prestes would be elected no matter what they did and that the administration truly cared this time. The considerable economic hardship the country experienced in late 1929 and early 1930 certainly raised the stakes—in prosperous times one could survive without government favors but not during a depression. As a result of Frontin's efforts, nearly all the city's *chefes* and *cabos* decided to support the official ticket in 1930. Even Irineu and Azevedo Lima did so, a remarkable change given their uncompromising opposition in previous years. We cannot be sure why Irineu chose to back Prestes, but it must have been in exchange for a substantial favor. Azevedo Lima apparently made his decision based on personal friendship with Prestes, whom he had known in the Chamber. For whatever reasons, Frontin's recruitment efforts paid off remarkably well.[9]

Organized labor was left in a quandary by the CRC success. Ordinarily, most unions would have followed the lead of the reformers in the second district, now irretrievably split with Bergamini and Lacerda for Vargas and Irineu and Azevedo Lima for Prestes. Worse, the BOC was itself rudderless and unable to follow the government candidate. It backed Vargas for a time, but finally decided to run its own Communist party candidate for president, alienating itself from labor's ranks.[10] Since no genuine labor leader or party had emerged throughout the politicization of 1926–28, it is not difficult to understand why unions and interest groups chose to support the government ticket. With a minimal amount of leadership labor might have maintained independence, but without it (and facing economic trouble with the onset of the Depression) most unions chose the cautious path of supporting the official candidate.

In the month before the election the progovernment *Jornal do Brasil* carried notices of forty-six labor and neighborhood organizations which supported the Prestes-Frontin slate. They included three railroad workers groups, many dockworkers and maritime unions, the Drivers Resistance Association, two favela associations, and numerous neighborhood groups from the North Zone. After the election the *Railroaders Magazine* claimed that the railroad vote had put Prestes over the top in Rio. Election results demonstrate that the official ticket received the bulk of its support from the rank and file of Rio's associations.

The presidential contest drew a record turnout of sixty-four thousand votes in Rio and toppled national records. To the surprise of most observers, who had expected Cariocas to follow their tradition of opposition, Prestes won with a 51 percent majority. Frontin beat Seabra by a similar margin, and independent-thinking Lacerda was the only opposition candidate to run well. Bergamini and Pessôa were barely reelected, and Sales Filho lost his seat in the Chamber.[11] Analysis of the returns by district, controlling for several socioeconomic variables, supports the view that organized labor saved the official ticket. Table 9, although flawed by the ecological fallacy,[12] provides evidence that working-class neighborhoods favored Prestes and suggests that the middle-sector districts (liberal professionals, the well-off, and civil servants) favored Vargas as a reform candidate. To the extent that the correlations in table 9 are significant, they demonstrate that organized labor and the middle sectors played identifiable roles in electoral politics outside the *chefe* and *cabo* system.

The positive association between the vote for Vargas and districts with

TABLE 9: Correlations of Voting for Vargas with Family Background of Public School Children, by District, 1930

	Workers	Poor	Civil Servants	Factory Workers & Clerks	Middle Sectors	Liberal Professions
Pearson's r	−.56	−.27	.23	.29	.29	.30
Regression coefficient (slope)	−.61	−.26	.35	.44	.28	1.69

Sources and methods: Election returns are from *Jornal do Brasil*, 3 Mar. 1930, p. 5, and school children classified by family background from ibid., 4 Sept. 1930, p. 21. These figures are subject to the ecological fallacy and should not be interpreted as individual voting patterns. See n. 12 for further qualifications.

many commercial and factory workers requires special note. These people were among the least paid and most poorly organized in the working class, between unionized labor and the lower class. That they favored Vargas suggests that they were not closely policed by the *chefes* and *cabos* and were thus available for recruitment at large. This conclusion is bolstered by impressionistic analysis of the election returns. Gávea and Engenho Velho, where many textile factories and workers districts were located and which were not centers of union activity, gave Vargas about two-thirds of their votes. Santa Rita, Gamboa, and Engenho Velho, on the other hand, where dock and railroad workers lived, all gave comfortable margins to Prestes. Much evidence suggests, then, that organized labor could effectively get out the vote but that untapped middle sectors and poorly organized workers were available to nontraditional politicians. The trick would be to form such a coalition strong enough to win an election.

Bergamini was desolated by the 1930 election failure. He received 12,800 votes in the congressional race as compared to *chefe político* Cesário de Melo's 16,600 in the same race. He had consciously tried to run an "American-style" campaign on his and Vargas's behalf, addressing rallies and picnics but neglecting grass roots deals with *cabos*. From all appearances he had hoped to win votes from the reform-minded middle sector, from his working-class constituents, and from the poor in general. To what extent he did cannot be determined, but his showing was not voluminous enough to constitute a breakthrough in coalition politics.

Ironically, postelection spirits were not appreciably higher in the government camp, for the distribution of spoils disappointed *chefes* and labor leaders alike. On Labor Day a large number of unions reiterated their support for Prestes but pointedly reminded him of his preelection pledge of a labor code.[13] (Washington Luís had forgotten his promises, it will be remembered.) Azevedo Lima complained that Irineu had not been appointed to the Senate finance commission: "It is incomprehensible that Rio, which for the first time in a very contested election . . . cast the majority of its votes for the government candidate, . . . did not receive any, not even *one,* seat on the important commissions of the Senate or Chamber, from which to defend Carioca interests."[14] Perhaps government leaders disliked Irineu's liberality with public funds. To make things worse, the Council seat vacated by Lacerda (elected to the Chamber) received little interest from the Frontin group. The mayor returned to his previous policy of vetoing patronage and special interest bills passed by the Council, to the detriment of the *chefes* and *cabos* who had to reward their followers. In exasperation, a suburban *chefe* and newspaper columnist requested that Prestes make good his pledge to electrify the Central's commuter lines, but the government claimed that no money was available.[15] Washington Luís, not due to step down until 15 November, seemed to have forgotten local politics; in fact, by mid–1930 national affairs demanded all his attention.

The Liberal Alliance showing had also been devastating for Rio Grande and Minas, where some younger politicians had contemplated armed revolt even before the election. After their defeat at the polls, they established ties with many disgruntled politicians in Rio and other states and even convinced exiled tenente revolutionaries of 1922 and 1924 to join them in a coup attempt. This plotting put Vargas in a delicate position between the young turks and the more cautious party hierarchs who were willing to abide by the election results.[16] The plotting against Washington Luís was openly discussed in Congress and in the press, and government officials became concerned with maintaining public order. The Senate could rarely muster a quorum, and the Council was wracked with patronage disputes and petty squabbles. The Chamber was usually dominated by the vocal opposition. The momentum of the plotting slackened in mid–1930 when party leaders still refused to permit a coup, but it was given new impetus by the August assassination of Vargas's running mate João Pessôa, governor of Paraíba. Gaúcho congressmen ominously reported that PRR boss Borges de Medeiros finally approved of the revolt, and police monitors decoded messages setting dates for an uprising, first in August and then in early September. There was now no doubt that a Gaúcho-Minas insurrection was a strong possibility.[17]

In Rio, the rumors of armed revolt, processed by the highly politicized press, turned public opinion further against Vargas. The militaristic threats appeared to be saber rattling, and the Cariocas pictured the Alliance politicians as poor losers. Moreover, the middle sectors probably believed that the Alliance coalition was no more reformist than the government. Were not the PRR and PRM old guard still firmly in control? A veteran observer for the *Jornal do Brasil* said,

> There may be some truth in [news of Borges's approval] but it is one of those truths no one believes. Not even if Mr. Color were to swear with his fingers crossed over his lips. That Borges is with the revolt nobody believes, even if the [PRR organ] *A Federação* were to proclaim it on Borges's orders and over his signature. There is not written nor spoken word, nor argument, nor evidence, nor proof, strong enough to convince one who lives here in these days . . . not even the Alliance politicians believe it. . . . There is only one way to be convinced: that is for Dr. Borges himself to come leading his troops, bringing the revolution . . . other than that, it is whistling in the wind.[18]

Such was the state of wishful thinking in Rio, for the plot was far advanced at that very moment.

In choosing a contact in Rio, Vargas's revolutionary coordinator, Oswaldo Aranha, passed over Bergamini, Lacerda, and other Alliance supporters, partly because of security. Anyone suspected of opposition was carefully watched by the police. Instead, the man who coordinated the revolution in Rio was the physician Pedro Ernesto Baptista, a man unknown in politics but well acquainted with the tenentes. Pedro Ernesto played a major role in politics from 1931 to 1937 as leader of the tenentes and more prominently as head of Brazil's first populist movement.[19] Although most of the revolutionary planning took place in the states of Minas Gerais and Rio Grande do Sul, he became the coordinator in the capital.

Born into a prosperous Recife family in 1884, Pedro Ernesto had enjoyed a good upbringing and education. He was early initiated into masonry, of which his father was a leader, and later he went to medical school in Salvador. A mediocre student, he showed strong leadership qualities among fellow Pernambucanos. After 1906 the family could no longer support him due to the failure of the bank where his father worked, but he stayed on for another year studying and doing odd jobs. In 1908 he traveled to Rio to complete his medical training in the leading charity hospital in the capital. He became self-reliant and disciplined during his years in school, yet he also gained a familiarity with economic hardship and learned to deal with poor patients in the last years of his training.

After practicing for several years in private clinics in Rio, Pedro Ernesto received financial backing from some Portuguese businessmen to build his own clinic, the Casa de Saúde Pedro Ernesto. Well equipped and spacious, it was one of the best surgical clinics in South America during the 1920s. With an aggressive business instinct and a natural skill for surgery, his personal finances prospered; he soon became a member of the new elite by purchasing a home in Copacabana and an automobile and by joining the right clubs.[20]

Pedro Ernesto's contact with the tenentes had begun in 1922 when a cousin who was an aide to Marshal Hermes da Fonseca was jailed along with the Marshal. Pedro Ernesto condemned the imprisonment as high-handed, and he sympathized with the subsequent revolt of the tenentes in Copacabana. Along with many other members of the new elite, he believed that the political system was profoundly corrupt and that a reconstitution of the nation was required. Inclined more to action than to reflection, Pedro Ernesto conspired in the 1924 mutiny of the dreadnought *São Paulo* and spent a brief time in jail as a result. In the following years he helped publish the revolutionary newspaper *5 de julho* and attended benefit activities for tenentes. His clinic, humorously called the "revolutionary blood bank" by insiders, was a refuge for the tenentes in the capital, where Pedro Ernesto was their personal physician. By the late 1920s, he was closely associated with the tenente movement.[21]

As the coordinator of the revolution in the capital, Pedro Ernesto handled information and money and sometimes carried soldiers and arms in clinic ambulances. He was credited with convincing ex-president Artur Bernardes to support the revolution, as well. In September he led a squad (including Bergamini, Pessôa, several tenentes, and a Gaúcho congressman) to Minas, but the revolt was called off. Shortly thereafter it was reset for 3 October, and he was given money and instructions for making preparations in Rio. Federal agents intercepted a letter from a Minas revolutionary stating that the fighting would begin in early October and on 29 September apprehended two tenentes with arms and ammunition in a clinic ambulance. They immediately circled the clinic, but Pedro Ernesto was able to escape and join the forces in Minas four days later. This time the revolt began on schedule.[22]

Rio was alive with rumors when the news of fighting in Minas and Rio Grande arrived late on 3 October. The early impression was that it would be easily contained by the government. Police put opposition politicians under twenty-four-hour surveillance, jailed many persons connected with the plotting or who spread rumors against the government, and imprisoned Bergamini, Lacerda, and Pessôa for short periods. Many unions and employee associations declared their solidarity with the government, and the police chief went so far as to suggest a workers' militia be formed should the revolutionaries draw near the capital.[23] Yet despite optimistic assessments by the government, support for Washington Luís clearly declined as October wore on. Bergamini and other reformers managed to distribute broadsides in workers' neighborhoods publicizing the extent of revolutionary advances, and rebel planes even dropped leaflets over the city. Meanwhile, reservists balked at mobilization orders, and the populace blamed Washington Luís for food shortages, lack of currency, and speculation.[24]

The decline of public order in Rio, plus the possibility of a full-scale civil war, led to the deposition of Washington Luís by the army high command in late October. They established a Peacekeeping Junta whose intentions were not clearly stated but which mediated between the old administration and the Vargas forces that had not yet made their way to Rio.[25] Army commanders had of course been approached during the planning stages of the revolt, but to no avail: most had adopted the attitude of Chief of Staff Augusto Tasso Fragoso, who would only support such an uprising as a last resort. By 20 October, however, Tasso and others had become convinced that Washington Luís's government was doomed and that they needed to act to prevent a total collapse of order. It was becoming increasingly difficult to prevent mobs in the city, some incited by communists, from sacking stores and other establishments. Moreover, middle-ranking officers appeared anxious to take matters into their own hands, to what end it was not clear. Therefore, the highest ranking officers in the army and navy forced Washington Luís to step down on 24 October.[26]

The Junta soon appointed a ministry and assumed command of Rio and São Paulo, requesting that the combatants lay down their arms. Bergamini, who had done all he could to bring about the fall of the government, was appointed mayor in Rio, and he quickly named many former Alliance colleagues to city offices. But by the end of its first day in power the Junta found that nine progovernment newspapers had been burned, stores had been sacked and weapons stolen, and armed men by the thousands milled in the streets. Gunfire was almost constant in the vicinity of the presidential palace. They failed, moreover, to secure recognition from the Vargas command, which believed that the Junta would attempt to bar them from power. From all indications, the Junta indeed intended to call new elections because they equivocated when Vargas pressed them for a declaration. Civilian mobs, meanwhile, wearing pieces of red cloth to identify themselves as Vargas supporters, became more aggressive. Some bands were led by communists; others seemed to have no leadership at all. Even the security forces in the capital contributed to the disorder. For example, on the twenty-fourth, fighting broke out between regular police, military police, and firemen, while

Revolutionaries meet with the Rio Peacekeeping Junta, 29 October 1930.
Pedro Ernesto is third from the left.

armed civilians joined in the melee. On the twenty-seventh, a gunfight erupted between the police, the army, civilian bands, and army cadets. It seemed that the revolt might trigger a thorough-going revolution. Given the deteriorating situation and Vargas's intransigence, the Junta announced that they would hand power over to the revolutionaries when they arrived.[27]

Although the details of the bargain struck between Vargas and the Junta have never been made public, it is possible to reconstruct its outlines from subsequent events. Vargas left Junta appointees in the Ministries of War, the Navy, the Treasury, and Foreign Relations, probably to assure that no radical changes would be introduced. Bergamini was allowed to continue as mayor, as a reward for his collaboration during the election and the revolt. Vargas (who claimed to have been duly elected in March) agreed to receive power as chief of the Provisional Government with no specified term in office. His authority, therefore, was considerably reduced by the restrictions imposed by the Junta. He was sworn in on 3 November.

Vargas had some administrative experience, especially as minister of finance and governor of Rio Grande do Sul (1928–30). In addition, as a leader of the PRR he had become disciplined in the regime created by Júlio de Castilhos and perpetuated by Borges de Medeiros. But unlike the other Gaúcho figures, famous for their courage and *caudilho* qualities, Vargas had perfected a style of conciliatory politics unusual in the south. He was friendly and personable but not very outgoing, and he was a methodical worker. Apart from a keen ability to judge and handle other politicians, Vargas's forte probably lay in finances. His wife Darcy had little to do with public life, dedicating her time to raising their three sons and two daughters. Such was the man who would dominate Brazilian politics for the generation after the 1930 revolution.[28]

Vargas's skills, although severely tested during the three and a half years of Provisional Government, turned out to be well suited to the demands put on him. The movement of 1930 had been no revolution in the classical sense; on the contrary, it triggered a period of intense political and institutional readjustment. First, the pronounced federalism of the Old Republic needed to be curbed to permit centralized planning and administration. Second, the laissez faire policies of previous governments, especially regarding labor relations, had to be overhauled in order to forestall middle-sector and working-class discontent. Finally, of course, the economy had to be nursed through the Depression and adjusted to the new international scene.

At no time in his first four years in government was Vargas ever entirely secure, which made him especially wary but also solicitous of support wherever he could find it. He rode herd over a diverse and shifting group of politicians in Rio and the major states, unable to give definitive shape to his government. He ruled by decree without legislative or judicial review, and his authority was often limited to the capital and a few states where he had loyal supporters. Statehouses were assigned to interventors, or federal agents, many of whom shared little in common with Vargas. His mandate was questioned at every turn. Among the major power contenders during the first half of the 1930s were Oswaldo Aranha, Gaúcho organizer of the revolution and first minister of justice; Colonel Pedro Aurélio Góes Monteiro, military commander of the revolt; General Leite de Castro, minister of war held over from the Junta; Borges de Medeiros and the interventor in Rio Grande, General Flores da Cunha; Governor Olegário Maciel of Minas, cosponsor of the revolution; and the tenentes, who had occupied key command posts during the revolt. The scores of power plays by these and other actors during the Provisional Government were too complex to relate here, although on occasion they affected Rio's trajectory toward populism.

Vargas made a genuine effort to win over the Cariocas, who did not like him, but he increasingly lost favor as the regime plunged toward dictatorship in 1931 and 1932. One of the ways he sought to appease them was by leaving Bergamini in office; as it turned out, Bergamini occupied the mayoralty of Rio for only eleven months. During his time in office, he attempted to gain autonomy from federal authorities and to broaden his electoral base. The first step came in mid-November, after the government abolished the City Council and made his acts as interventor subject to review by Aranha, the minister of justice. Bergamini declared to the press that this was a betrayal of the Liberal Alliance promise of autonomy for the Federal District. Bending to this criticism, Vargas acquiesced to make Rio administratively equal to other states. Bergamini also refused to accept suggestions from Vargas and Aranha for city appointees and instead cultivated support among civil servant representatives.[29] He revised the tax structure in order to shift a larger share of the burden onto business while reducing middle- and lower-income contributions; and he undertook to hold down the price of gasoline and coffee and to build low-cost housing in the city. These programs point unmistakably toward a multiclass sociopolitical strategy that might have led to populism and whose failure had as much to do with the revolution and the Depression as with Bergamini's own short-comings.

The interventor began his administration with a measure designed to replace business license fees with a progressive gross receipts tax. Associations of medium and small businesses, as well as the middle sectors, found the proposal attractive, but big business was opposed, since it would cost them heavier taxes. The AC-Rio, never friendly toward Bergamini, advised its member firms not to pay the tax, and by March 1931 a full-scale tax revolt was underway. Bergamini made several concessions and argued that the average business would not pay more, but eventually he was forced to issue municipal bonds for $7 million in order to cover his growing deficit. The tax revolt continued until the end of Bergamini's term, paradoxically hurting city employees (against whom a bond amortization tax had been levied) more than business.[30]

The gasoline tax case was tied to the gross receipts issue. The reform replaced automobile license fees with a tax on gasoline sales. Because the price of gas was fixed by the city, the new tax fell entirely on petroleum distributors, most of which were foreign. Owners of private automobiles and taxi drivers would benefit the most from the new system. The oil companies ignored the city price ceiling, however, and raised prices 40 percent to cover the new tax, whereupon the taxi drivers' union went on a week-long strike. Without federal backing Bergamini was forced to reach a compromise that raised prices substantially to the public.[31]

Bergamini's last and most popular campaign was for a penny cup of coffee, undertaken in the name of the common man. In early February, the city posted new price lists for basic commodities, which included the reduction of a demitasse of coffee to about one cent. Cafe owners staged lockouts, alleging that the price was ruinously low, and after several months of recriminations Bergamini agreed to a price of two cents if owners would post the price and pay a special tax to the city. Three days later he suggested that only cafes providing entertainment could charge two cents, which would encourage the employment of musicians. The dispute, of no small import to coffee-loving Cariocas, continued through August when owners eventually raised their prices.

Bergamini's reform efforts all failed, then, due to tepid support from the government as well as the desperate economic situation of the city. Bergamini had, nonetheless, followed his late 1920s strategy of building a coalition based on labor and reform-minded voters of the middle and upper strata. It was a valid approach but floundered on revolutionary politics. Bergamini and others assumed that Vargas was too weak to remain at the head of government long and that he would be replaced by a politician subservient to the party bosses in Rio Grande and Minas. Thus Bergamini had allied with Liberal Alliance people like Lindolfo Color and the chief of police, who demanded some independence in order to maintain their party commitments in Rio Grande. Bergamini was especially close to Color, who as first minister of labor played a brief but significant role in local politics.

A second way Vargas sought to win over the Cariocas was by creating new Ministries of Labor and Education. Labor and educational reform were attractive to the Carioca electorate and played a major role in the populist movement in the mid-1930s. The labor ministry had been proposed by Color and was created by Vargas in part to reward his former campaign manager. In addition, he appointed Francisco Campos, now a trusted aide of Governor Maciel in Minas, to the newly created Ministry of Education. Vargas's commitments to labor and educational reform were genuine, but in the turmoil of late 1930 it is likely that patronage reasons weighed as heavily as reformism. Vargas eventually gave more prominence to these agencies, even calling labor his "revolutionary ministry."

The core of the labor ministry was taken from agriculture, basically the old Department of Labor, Commerce, and Industry. In addition, an Indian protection agency and the National Labor Council were put under the new unit. Color was appointed minister two days after its creation in late November. Because all expenditures were meager in those days, Color set up offices in an unused municipal building ceded by Bergamini. The ministry operated entirely in and for the Federal District because well into the 1930s it had insufficient funds to support offices elsewhere. Until 1937, for example, it received less than 1 percent of the federal budget. Since São Paulo and Minas explicitly maintained jurisdiction over labor relations in their territories, the ministry dictated laws for the whole country but only enforced them in Rio.[32]

Color threw himself into the job of creating the ministry with the same energy he had displayed as campaign manager in 1929. He appointed Evaristo de Moraes as his chief counsel and Maurício de Lacerda to be a legal adviser. Together, for a little more than a year, they framed the legislation that would guide federal labor policy for nearly a decade. Color's political strategy was similar to Bergamini's: to remain somewhat independent of Vargas and to build support for himself in Rio. Likewise, he sought a multiclass coalition, hoping to draw upon unions, employers, and middle-sector citizens in general.[33] The first labor legislation illustrates this tack. Color's nationalistic Law of Two-Thirds required that at least 67 percent of the employees of any business be Brazilian nationals. It was directed especially at textile factories, merchant houses, hotels, and restaurants, which preferentially hired submissive immigrants. Nationalism was on the rise in the late 1920s anyway, due to economic hardships (blamed on Portuguese business) and to the reform spirit that asserted Brazil's need to strengthen its citizenry and institutions. As expected, the law was well received in Rio.[34] Another popular decree extended social security benefits to employees of public utilities companies. As indicated in chapter 3, retirement funds (CAPs) had been created for railroad and shipping companies in the 1920s. In addition to business contributions for retirement, the legislation also provided job stability after ten years, a particularly attractive feature for unspecialized employees. Vargas had promised to extend CAP coverage to the utilities companies during the 1930 campaign, and Color carried out the pledge early in his administration.[35]

A last program of the Ministry of Labor designed to elicit local support was the construction of low-cost housing in Rio. Such programs had long been contemplated, as noted in chapter 2, but with little effect. In December 1930 Color and Bergamini announced jointly their intention to complete a housing project in the Subúrbios, abandoned since World War I. At the same time a commission looked into plans for as many as two thousand units, with the subsidiary goal of employing the jobless. Yet these promises were not realized, and the only housing measures were authorization for CAPs to invest in members' housing and transferral of the Subúrbios project to the civil servants' retirement institute. An editorial cartoon in the *Jornal do Brasil* summed up the situation during Carnival 1931, depicting a parade float designed as a worker's home, pushed by Color, Bergamini, Evaristo de Moraes, and others. Low-cost housing, it implied, was just a fantasy.[36]

The last innovation of the early Vargas regime was the creation of the Ministry of Education. Francisco Campos was more a politician than an educator, his principal role being to maintain liaison with Governor Maciel of Minas. Nonetheless, he did compose federal legislation regulating university and secondary instruction in public schools, known as the Francisco Campos Reform. A controversial aspect was authorization for religious instruction in public schools. Because execution of the reform was of little interest to Campos, and because Bergamini's school director was not inclined to new undertakings, the Ministry of Education did not have an early impact in Rio. Only with the emergence of the populist government and the appointment of an energetic school chief would educational reform again inspire Cariocas. Campos quit the ministry in 1932 for political reasons and only returned to educational affairs tangentially in late 1935.[37]

The government's financial crisis was a major reason why Bergamini, Color, and Campos were unsuccessful in their first terms under Vargas; the government was not able to underwrite expensive new programs. By the end of 1930, hundreds more businesses had closed or cut back operations, leading to widespread unemployment and bankruptcies. Wages fell 10 to 15 percent and payrolls often went unmet. In the stock market (composed 80 percent of government bonds) prices and volume declined sharply in relation to the late 1920s. The cost of living dropped 13 percent relative to 1928–29 but not enough to stimulate consumption.

City revenues declined, municipal and federal governments cut spending, hard currency became scarce in the open market, and foreign trade fell sharply. The number of warehouse fires rose, as owners sought to cover bankruptcy with insurance settlements.[38] Unemployed workers milled about government offices expecting aid or jobs, and in December an assertive crowd paraded to the presidential palace for an audience with Vargas. The labor ministry registered eighteen thousand unemployed in Rio, upon whom forty-five thousand people depended for sustenance. There was even a temporary out-migration from the city as unemployed workers sought jobs in agriculture or stayed with relatives during the crisis. Passenger statistics suggest that as many as thirty-five thousand persons per month left Rio in late 1930, and in São Paulo seven thousand urban workers per month were given passage into the coffee zones. The Depression hit hardest in the cities.[39]

By mid–1931 the worst of the Depression was over, however, and early signs of recovery were perceptible. Industry and construction led the way in two divergent reactions to the crisis. Between 1930 and 1935 the growth of physical production in industry rose at a rate of 10 percent per annum and almost as rapidly for the remainder of the decade. Brazilian manufacturing had been protected by a lack of capacity to import and had begun to expand in 1931. Rio and São Paulo, Brazil's chief manufacturing centers, accounted for the bulk of new production. By 1934 an employer representative in Congress declared that industry had saved Brazil from the worst effects of the Depression and had helped balance the trade account by reducing imports. Though economists continue to debate the exact nature of the 1930s industrial recovery, they agree that it saved Brazil from worse economic consequences and fostered industrialization.[40]

A building boom occurred in the construction industry, spurred by increased investment in real estate by middle- and upper-class families attempting to protect savings from currency devaluation or revolutionary confiscation. Also, the city tax structure encouraged real estate investment by applying only minimal rates on unoccupied property. Rents were clearly not involved in the process because about eight thousand units were vacant in 1931 and rents had declined a quarter in relation to the late 1920s. Rather, anyone who was able took out a mortgage on a house or a lot. During 1931 over three thousand mortgages were executed, for a value of nearly $25 million, four times the value in 1925. The value of new mortgages declined after 1931 but remained above the 1920s average.[41]

While some new mortgages were simply rescheduled old ones, other evidence proves that most were used for real estate investments. As early as August 1930 some observers noted that the Depression had not hit the construction industry as badly as expected and that large projects were continuing. In early 1931 the *Jornal do Brasil* noted that six skyscrapers were being built in Cinelândia and that a number of others awaited licensing by the city. The boom was not limited to commercial property: middle sector and elite residential areas such as Copacabana, Tijuca, Gávea, and Andarai were among the fastest growing zones of the city. Late in 1931 the *New York Times* ran a feature on the construction boom in Rio, São Paulo, and other cities: "New subdivisions are being opened, improvements are being made in old subdivisions, and small farms bordering the cities are being purchased by city residents." The reason, they confirmed, was to safeguard savings from losses due to devaluation.[42]

The boom received further impetus from foreign investors. In mid–1931 a Copenhagen firm offered to finance and build 2,000 homes for low-income families in Rio, and the Chase Manhattan Bank advertised mortgage loans at 10 percent per annum. The *Correio da Manhã* ran daily ads for housing developments financed by foreign companies, typical of which was the following:

> CAPITALISTS: employ your money with security and intelligence. Consumer durables, merchandise, and short-term notes all fluctuate with frightening rapidity. Only real estate does not decline; it weathers the crisis and continues its solid growth. No one has yet regretted buying a lot or a house. The Land Investment Company [original in English] offers capitalists the best deal of the year, with the opening of Gavelândia, a new development of summer homes in Gávea, laid out with English landscaping. . . . Consider that twenty years ago land in Copacabana was only 100 reis per square meter. Today it is over 300,000 a square meter.[43]

In late 1933, U.S. engineers in Rio confirmed the feasibility of thirty-story buildings in downtown; and a New York real estate expert found Rio's land and property values highly inflated, noting that most foreign companies owned their buildings as investments.[44]

Rio's construction boom during the Depression had both positive and negative effects. It certainly contributed to rapid recovery by creating demand for building materials: the production of cement, paint, tiles, ceramics, and glass all rose at rates of between 9 and 33 percent per annum. It also greatly alleviated unemployment. On the other hand, the building boom induced serious distortions in the urban economy. First, by drawing off capital that might have gone into industry, it allowed São Paulo to further its lead over Rio in manufacturing. Second, it exaggerated the demand for manual labor in the city. The temporary outmigration of 1930 was reversed by the recovery, and internal migration to Rio was three times that to São Paulo in relation to host population.[45] Finally, it directed housing investment into commercial and upper-income housing at a time when poor migrants swamped the lower-income housing market. Let us look more carefully at these last two problems.

There was no doubt that the early recovery in manufacturing and construction stimulated migration to the cities. Color's Law of Two-Thirds began with this preamble: "One of the most pressing problems of the society is the forced unemployment of many workers, who flock to this capital and to other cities in great numbers in search of jobs." Complementary evidence confirms that most of these migrants were unskilled and thus sought out jobs in factories and building construction. Surveys of public school children in 1930 and 1932 showed a large increase in children from poor families. Over the next eight years the number from the Subúrbios rose from thirty-seven thousand to seventy thousand, much faster than the overall growth of the population.[46]

The second problem was the impact of poor migrants on the housing market. The construction boom dried up capital for tenements and low-income subdivisions at precisely the moment they were most needed, forcing newcomers in the 1930s into favelas. Surveys conducted in 1933 and 1940 reveal that the number of shacks rose from thirteen thousand to fifty thousand and that by the latter date nearly one hundred seventy thousand persons lived in favelas. This form of poor housing, with its high visibility and mobility, continued to grow until the 1960s, when it made up about 10 percent of the housing stock. It would inevitably become the focus for social reform and populist recruitment during the 1930s.[47]

The Depression was in large measure responsible for the poor results achieved by Bergamini and Color in 1931, but their attempts to remain independent from Vargas likewise undermined them. Vargas could not support them, even if he had been inclined to, and their reform efforts suffered. Vargas, instead, retrenched along the budget front and trusted no one for a year. Indeed, from mid–1931 until late 1932 Vargas presided over a closed, authoritarian regime that called itself a dictatorship. During this time Vargas made an alliance with the tenentes that, although saving his rule, ushered in reforms far more radical than those of the 1930 Liberal Alliance. It also changed dramatically the direction of Rio politics.

In February 1931 the tenentes had banded together in the Club 3 de Outubro, named after the date the revolution had begun. The first president was Colonel Góes Monteiro, who after a few months transferred the post to Dr. Pedro Ernesto. The latter was well suited to lead the tenentes because of his many favors for them during the 1920s. His clinic was a secure meeting place, and his civilian contacts made up for the tenentes' long estrangement from national affairs. Pedro Ernesto was not a politician but had the qualities to become one: he was self-assured, handsome, affable, devoted to improving his country, and untainted by the politics of the old regime. For these reasons, Pedro Ernesto remained president of the tenente Club 3 de Outubro during its year in power, helping to shape the destiny of the revolution.[48]

In August 1931 the tenentes were given key posts in the regime in an effort to put off civilian politicians and protect Vargas. During this tenente sweep it was decided to make Pedro Ernesto interventor of Rio so that he could help maintain security in the capital. Bergamini had created trouble with his tax reform and was associated with politicians hostile toward Vargas. Therefore in August the Club 3 de Outubro launched an effort to discredit Bergamini and force his resignation. Oswaldo Aranha, whose own position was becoming tenuous, was obliged to manage the dismissal. The accusations of the tenentes were used to justify Bergamini's "temporary" removal, and once he was out Pedro Ernesto was maneuvered into the position.[49] For over a year the tenentes ruled the city, endeavoring to keep Vargas in power by whatever means necessary. They also formulated their program, which called for thorough-going social and economic reforms for the country. Although these formulations are more significant to national than to Rio politics, they hold particular relevance to this study because of Pedro Ernesto's accession to the mayoralty in 1931, his close association with reformist tenentes, and the intimate relationship he developed with Vargas during the latter's most trying period. All of these would be crucial for the formation of the populist movement in 1933.

Color's position in the government also eroded rapidly during 1931, though he was able to hold out longer than Bergamini. No matter what he did in the labor ministry, Color seemed to threaten Vargas. Therefore, after some tentative experiments with labor management, the ministry saw its functions revert to the police department, where they had traditionally been handled by the DOPS. Vargas's well-known cooptation of the labor movement would have to await more propitious times. The 1931–32 federal budget allocated more money to the police department than to the labor ministry. In a February 1932 cabinet crisis Color resigned and was replaced by a former DOPS officer.

The election, revolution, and Depression had clearly dominated events in 1930 and 1931, when the trend was toward centralized dictatorship and retrenchment. The multiple crises of those years nonetheless contributed to the emergence of populism by provoking the total collapse of the old regime and the rise of Pedro Ernesto and the tenentes of Rio. All old formulae of *chefe* and interest politics were suspended, leaving the tenentes free to take a new approach. The lower class and the middle sectors, never firmly committed to a particular style of representation, were available for recruitment by the tenentes. Their approach would stress social reform and integration of the masses. It was perfectly suited to the emerging groups dissatisfied with the old politics.

6 □ The Populist Apogee

The multiple crises of 1930–31 were prolonged through the end of 1932 by a civil war in São Paulo protesting the Vargas-tenente dictatorship, but upon its termination Vargas was anxious to establish a constitutional regime. Rio was to play an important role in his plans by providing votes and legitimacy for the government. The first step had been to attenuate the militaristic character of the Club 3 de Outubro and to turn the tenentes into a national electoral force. Pedro Ernesto took a half-dozen close associates with him into the city administration, and in late 1932 he began to expand Rio's electorate. Within six months elections would be held for a constitutional assembly, and when the latter's work was accomplished the country would elect congressmen and local legislators. Vargas gave full backing to the mayor, who reciprocated by using his growing prestige to assure Vargas's election to a regular presidential term in 1934. The close relationship between the two leaders lasted for nearly three years, during which time experimentation with urban politics was the rule. The outcome was Brazil's first populist movement. The drive for Carioca support was the main dynamic of the populist birth, but social reform—very much a part of late 1920s politics—played a major role as well. This chapter details the recruitment side of populism, leaving the innovative social programs of the mid–1930s for chapter 7.

Pedro Ernesto enjoyed great freedom as interventor of Rio. His loyalty to Vargas had been proved during several crises, and by 1932 he was on intimate terms with the president. He regularly participated in meetings of the *gabinete negro,* or kitchen cabinet, made up of tenente and revolutionary leaders. In addition, Pedro Ernesto became physician to the first family, in which capacity he saved the life of Vargas's son and the first lady's leg from amputation after an automobile accident.[1] Pedro Ernesto was a newcomer to politics, however, and he followed Vargas's guidance in most matters, serving as a link to the Club 3 de Outubro and a coordinator for Rio affairs. As Vargas managed the transition toward open politics in late 1932, which would allow him to hold elections for a constitutional assembly, he had Pedro Ernesto leave the Club 3 de Outubro behind and concentrate on city politics. Ultimately the mayor would create popularity for the regime among Cariocas.[2]

Pedro Ernesto's campaign in Rio began with the creation of the Autonomist Party of the Federal District (PADF), whose primary function was to help narrow the separation between tenente militancy and middle-sector reformism. He and three former members of the Club 3 de Outubro issued a platform in March 1933 that sought such a conciliation.[3] The War Ministry, the Central do Brasil Railroad, and the Police Department were represented in the formation of the PADF, which at first had a strong civil service orientation. The platform of the PADF was necessarily eclectic. Besides the broad education and health programs to be described in chapter 7, it called for a bicameral council with politico-legislative and professional-technical branches; government chartering of worker and employer associations, with compulsory strike arbitration; and public assistance for workers, artists, intellectuals, and scientists. This platform was then backed up by putting the entire city government at the disposal of the PADF to help recruit voters.

The most important plank in the PADF platform was administrative autonomy for the city government, which provided the term "autonomist" for the party name. Autonomy was a doubly attractive issue for Pedro Ernesto, offering an increase in self-government for the Cariocas as well as added patronage through the transfer of some federal services to local control. Autonomy had been included in Vargas's Liberal Alliance platform in 1930 and had been a contentious issue between Vargas and Bergamini. With the return of open politics in late 1932, the municipal administration was favored by the transfer of most federal health services to local control. The effects of this and other changes, plus the rise in revenues brought about by the economic recovery, produced a 70 percent increase in city expenditures between 1932 and 1934. From the point of view of middle-sector city employees, autonomy promised greater job security through local control of patronage distribution. Opponents criticized the fact that autonomy represented new jobs and voters for the PADF, but city spokesmen responded that new teachers and physicians were needed to staff the schools and hospitals being built. Such an argument was difficult to counter, since virtually everyone agreed that the social programs were beneficial.

Pedro Ernesto's early electoral strategy was to register civil servants while setting up a patronage system that would attract the *chefes políticos*. This strategy was determined by the fact that all previous voter rolls had been cleared and that new registration and voting procedures were in force. The election law of 1932 enfranchised women, lowered the voting age to eighteen, created a federal judiciary for the elections, authorized government chartered associations and public agencies to register ex officio their members and employees to vote, and provided for secret balloting in sealed envelopes. The law also created a "quotient system" to stimulate party loyalty and to assure minority representation, guaranteeing parties one seat for each decile of the total vote captured.[4]

In order to reconstruct the electorate quickly, Pedro Ernesto coordinated a campaign to get government agencies and large organizations to register their employees to vote. Table 10 shows registration by major organizations, in groups of ten or more voters, carried out in the four months preceding the May 1933 Constitutional Assembly (ANC) elections. The fifty-eight thousand voters who registered in their place of work or union represented over 84 percent of the total qualified voters that year. The largest numbers were registered by the Central do Brasil and by the city government, which together accounted for half the total electorate. The war and navy ministries and the National Department of Public Health (being transferred to city control) registered another 12 percent. Government-recognized labor unions, led by the utility and maritime sectors, registered a fifth of all voters. Thus it was no accident that Pedro Ernesto had the army's chief of staff, the police chief, and the director of the Central do Brasil join him in creating the PADF. Civil servants were told that they could only expect autonomy and security if

TABLE 10: Ex Officio Voter Registration, 1933 (in 000s)

Agency	Voters Registered
Central do Brasil Min. Transport	21
Rio city government and police	14
Ministries of War and Navy	6
Maritime and dockworkers unions	5
Seven other unions	5
Public utilities unions	4
National Department of Public Health	2
Total, these agencies	58
Total registered voters	70

Source: Tabulated from Brasil, Supremo Tribunal Eleitoral, *Boletim eleitoral,* 2 Jan.–3 May 1933, passim.

they voted in favor of the official ticket. Simultaneously he gathered into the PADF a majority of Rio's *chefes políticos*, many of whom had been cut off from jobs by Bergamini. By March 1933 the PADF had about a dozen *chefes*, of whom the most important was Cesário de Melo, who agreed to deliver the Triangle.[5]

The massive job of rebuilding Rio's electorate required the creation of a new role in city politics, that of the party manager. The manager was usually a newcomer, without campaign experience or an electoral following, who served as an intermediary between the mayor and the *chefes*. Managers tended to be colorful figures—the tenentes, for example—who gave an image of reform and change to the party. The managers performed functions that had not been crucial in pre–1930 politics: they were speech writers, purveyors of large favors, media coordinators, and legislative whips. The managers kept the *chefes* in line, just as the *chefes* controlled the *cabos*. The critical difference was that, whereas *chefes* could always return to their constituencies for renewed support and were hence somewhat independent of higher authority, the managers owed their political existence to the party. Their only outside appeal was to national leaders. As long as Pedro Ernesto provided coherent and equitable leadership, the PADF functioned well.

One of Pedro Ernesto's top party managers was Padre Olympio de Melo, the popular Subúrbios priest who had collaborated for several years with Cesário de Melo. Born in the *sertão* of Pernambuco in 1886, Padre Olympio went as a youth to the seminary in Olinda, where he was ordained in 1909. There he participated in a Catholic utopian community made up of a sugar mill and a textile factory, an experiment inspired by the *Rerum novarum*, the 1891 papal encyclical discussed in chapter 7. The community failed, but Padre Olympio became acquainted with some leading church reformers, including Sebastião Leme, future cardinal of Brazil. On a trip to Rio in 1918 Padre Olympio fell ill with tuberculosis and was hospitalized for several years. After being cured he served as clinic chaplain and sought out contacts in the city, among them Pereira Carneiro, who solicited from him a weekly religious column for the *Jornal do Brasil*. In 1929 Cardinal Leme appointed him parish priest in the Triangle.

Padre Olympio worked with Cesário de Melo in the 1930 election and in 1931 moved to nearby Bangu to help stem unionization among the textile workers in Guilherme da Silveira's factory. With Silveira's help, Padre Olympio obtained many public services, including water, electricity, a public telephone, and a community center. At his insistence Bangu was made an electoral precinct. In 1933 Silveira invited Pedro Ernesto's campaign director to Bangu. PADF leaders lunched with Padre Olympio, who shortly thereafter joined the party. His appointment as treasurer of the party probably demonstrates Pedro Ernesto's desire to use leadership images familiar to rural migrants in the city.[6]

Besides Padre Olympio, who would eventually become mayor of Rio, the managers included a number of other colorful figures. Jones Rocha, the thirty-four-year-old medic who followed Pedro Ernesto from the Casa de Saúde into the 1930 revolt and eventually became his top lieutenant in the city government, was dapper and quick-witted. Augusto do Amaral Peixoto, son of one of the Casa de Saúde doctors and a tenente mutineer in 1924, was an effective speaker who easily assumed a command position in the PADF. Many of the other tenentes who took city jobs also played manager roles. Another colorful PADF manager was Luís Aranha, who took up Rio politics after his brother Oswaldo departed for Washington. Luís had some of the style and verve which characterized his more famous brother.

Bertha Lutz, the feminist leader during the 1920s, spoke with Vargas about advancing women's rights under the new constitution. At his suggestion she joined the PADF and ran for the ANC, to become one of the first women to serve in the national legislature. Olegário Mariano, the well-known poet from Pernambuco, and musical composer Villa-Lobos, also supported the PADF, an indication of sympathy within artistic circles. Finally, the owner of the *Jornal do Brasil*, Ernesto Pereira Carneiro, joined the PADF, giving it added respectability and a forum for policy discussion.[7] These new PADF managers had neither politically tested images nor secure electoral followings. Nor was there a common bond between them other than the desire to hold office and the belief that Pedro Ernesto's leadership provided the best chance of winning.

The PADF's first test, in the May 1933 elections for the ANC, indicated the success of Pedro Ernesto's initial approach (see table 11). With a high turnout, the PADF elected six of the ten Rio delegates to the ANC and captured the top four alternate positions, important should seats fall

TABLE 11: Rio Voter Turnout, 1930–45

Year	Voters	Offices
1930	64,000	President, senator, deputies
1933	70,000	Constitutional delegates
1934	110,000	Congressmen (who chose president and senators) and councilmen (who chose mayor)
1945	482,000	President, constitutional delegates

Sources: Jornal do Brasil, 3 Mar. 1930, p. 5; 1 July 1933, p. 8; 3 Feb. 1935; Hélio Silva, *1945, por que despuseram Vargas* (Rio: Civilização Brasileira, 1976), p. 515.

vacant. All six PADF delegates were newcomers to Rio politics, also party managers, and four were former members of the Club 3 de Outubro. The tenente-reformist image of the party, combined with intense campaigning among city employees, seemed successful in drawing votes.

Yet the 1933 election also revealed a weakness in the early strategy. Only eleven thousand (27 percent) of the ballots cast for PADF candidates bore the party name; the rest were either blank or carried the names of the *chefes* who distributed them. This indicated that voter loyalty, to the extent it existed, remained with the *chefes* rather than the party. This development determined a new PADF strategy for the next eighteen months, one of using Pedro Ernesto as a populist symbol.

Following the 1933 election, Pedro Ernesto began to adopt the image of *médico bondoso*, or humanitarian doctor, one which he already had in downtown precincts near his clinic. This new public personality supplanted his earlier identification with the brash tenentes and made him more attractive to the populace as a whole. It became the basis for his charisma, that is, his authority to lead conferred by the people. The *médico bondoso* was a familiar figure in suburban and small town politics in Brazil. Table 12 (see below) shows that doctors were nearly as numerous as lawyers in Rio politics, able to assume leadership positions because of their education, status, and ability to provide charity. In rural towns, where licensed doctors were few, pharmacists often played a similar part. For example, in a small Minas town a pharmacist-medic, by playing a mediating role between two traditional families and by building his popularity among the townspeople, became an influential *coronel* during the 1920s. A study of bossism in Bahia discovered an urban form, which might be called *doutorismo*, developing in coastal cities. There, too, medics frequently became politicians.[8] Pedro Ernesto easily adopted the *médico bondoso* image as his political personality, for it was a traditional role in rural society, immediately recognizable by recent migrants to the city. As treasurer of the PADF, Padre Olympio performed a similar function, furnishing a familiar leadership image and helping to generate trust among the urban masses.

The physical dispersion of Rio's population made voter recruitment difficult without recourse to the mass media, so the PADF managers mounted a modern publicity campaign using radio, newspapers, and other media. Radio was by far the most important element of this campaign, all the more effective because of its novelty. Several radio stations had operated in Rio prior to 1930, though they had not been used for politics. Four more commercial stations were installed in 1933 and 1934, by which time politicians came to rely upon them as much as on newspapers.[9] In these years stations competed to reach and keep audiences.

shifting from classical to popular music, promoting amateur performers, and invoking audience participation in studios. Between 1934 and 1937, six more stations were licensed in Rio, and the city's imports of radio receivers almost tripled, reaching a value of $2.4 million per year. In well-to-do homes and in bars and lunch counters in working-class neighborhoods, radio conquered a mass audience during the 1930s. Its political impact was enhanced by the fact that radio could reach the semiliterate population eligible to vote but unaccustomed to reading papers.[10]

The most lasting experiment in political radio was the "Hora do Brasil," begun in 1934 and still on the air in the 1970s. Its creator was Francisco Antônio Sales Filho, a Carioca politician who since 1933 had directed the National Press. Sales Filho, also a PADF candidate for the ANC, proposed to Vargas that they compose a daily forty-five-minute government broadcast to be carried by all commercial stations. It would begin in Rio and then reach other urban centers via telephone hookups. Sales Filho proposed a program of news, sports, and cultural information that would be liberally interspersed with editorials favorable to the government. For the sake of foreign residents, the program would also be summarized in English, French, and Spanish. Vargas approved these plans, and two months later Sales Filho reported that all Rio stations were carrying the "Hora do Brasil" and that the connection for São Paulo was ready.[11]

Sales Filho's propagandistic approach to public broadcasting quickly elicited criticism from the opposition. One of his more controversial editorials refuted a recent anti-Vargas statement by Artur Bernardes. Sales justified himself to Vargas: "Since Dr. Bernardes gave an interview to an evening newspaper, it seemed convenient to counteract immediately his unfounded assertions, emanating as they did from one who has held the highest office of the land."[12] Sales was accused of gross political abuse of his post as director of the National Press. One deputy called the "Hora do Brasil" the *fala sozinho* (lonely discourse) and the "hour of silence," when patriots should turn off their receivers.[13]

The forum nature of Rio politics and Vargas's desire to win urban support assured that national and local affairs would be mixed in public broadcasts. Sales Filho used the "Hora do Brasil" to aid the PADF campaign in 1934, and upon his election to the Chamber he passed the direction on to a friend of PADF manager Luís Aranha.[14] Besides this national program, a number of local broadcasts also enticed the public with political messages. In early 1934, for example, Anísio Teixeira and Roquette Pinto formed the Escola Rádio, a cultural and instructional station operated by the Department of Education. While not openly political, the Escola Rádio reminded citizens of Pedro Ernesto's health and education programs and urged listeners to use city services. Pedro

Ernesto's speeches and civic ceremonies were carried by the station as well. Rádio Mayrinck Veiga, the most powerful in Brazil, gave the PADF an hour of free campaign time each day for the 1934 election. In 1935 Pereira Carneiro founded the Rádio Jornal do Brasil, which was occasionally used to promote the PADF. Perhaps the most direct measure of the power of radio to create Pedro Ernesto's charisma is the fact that virtually all persons interviewed in the course of this study, whether friends or enemies of the PADF during the 1930s, remember the mayor as a humanitarian and charitable doctor.[15] Vargas also utilized the radio for reaching semiliterate masses: one of the crowning moments of political radio in this era occurred on New Year's Day 1936 when Vargas inaugurated a national broadcast hookup with a speech defending the social and economic programs of his government.[16]

Newspapers continued to be an important medium for political discourse, although their influence during the 1930s was diminished by the combined effects of voter mobilization, radio, and censorship. The *Jornal do Brasil* supported Pedro Ernesto and promoted PADF policies in its editorial columns. Between August and October 1934 the party published *O Autonomista*, a broadside with a more attractive makeup, but it proved ephemeral. In mid–1934 the working-class paper *O Radical*, formed originally in 1931 as a tenente organ, began to support the PADF as well. Yet the press in general offered limited aid for a campaign of the sort Pedro Ernesto mounted in late 1933 because the voter tended to read papers that reinforced his opinions. Rarely could a newspaper stimulate a nonvoter to register or a voter to change his affiliation. Moreover, a number of dailies divided the relatively small readership so that no paper could guarantee a truly mass audience.

Finally, the PADF managers experimented with film publicity. Vargas himself had made promotional films in Rio Grande do Sul in the late 1920s, and Color had speeches and trips filmed while minister of labor. Sales Filho's proposal to Vargas cited above also included a plan to splice propaganda strips into moving pictures shown in Rio. But this medium was generally too expensive to reach the voter to whom Pedro Ernesto's appeal was directed.[17]

Publicity by itself was not enough to mobilize the electorate. Registering new voters and getting them to the polls required a lot of work at the precinct level to complement the publicity campaigns, as the politicians realized. The PADF managers worked hard in poor precincts near downtown, while *chefes* were made responsible for getting out the vote in the North Zone. This perspective demonstrates how Pedro Ernesto's program and publicity were intertwined with traditional political activities, without which he could not have succeeded.

In late 1933 Pedro Ernesto and his nephew Jones Rocha began new efforts to expand the PADF following. The ANC would soon finish its drafting, and the country would then elect congressmen, local legislators, governors, and perhaps a president. The strategy Pedro Ernesto chose was to enforce party discipline regarding distribution of PADF ballots, so that all of the campaigning would enhance his image and not simply his vote totals. Door-to-door voter registration was organized in the dense tenement, commercial, and favela areas near downtown, under the supervision of Pedro Ernesto's party managers. These votes would bear either the mayor's name or the party label at the top, in exchange for which the managers would be guaranteed elective offices. The same discipline was imposed on *chefes* and *cabos*, who essentially transferred their voters' loyalty to Pedro Ernesto.

The *chefes* accepted the PADF rules for two reasons. First, by 1934 the number of votes required to be elected even to the Council surpassed the abilities of most individual *chefes*. Radio and newspaper publicity and party organization had become essential for urban political careers. In this situation, the *chefe* looked to a popular leader to *arrastrar a chapa*, that is, give wider appeal than was possible operating only on a face-to-face basis with voters. Second, Pedro Ernesto ran the PADF equitably with regard to patronage, rewarding deserving politicians with city jobs, public works, or elective posts according to their contribution to the party. If a *chefe* chose not to accept the PADF rules, the unattractive alternative was to run independently or with the opposition, in which case even winning elective office might not defray the costs of campaigning. Most *chefes* therefore brought their *cabos* into the PADF and agreed to enforce discipline with regard to building up the party label and Pedro Ernesto's image.

Between October 1933 and January 1934, managers, *chefes*, and *cabos* opened PADF headquarters throughout the city, hoping to bargain jobs and sufficient patronage to remain active in politics. In a short time voter registration climbed 25 percent over the May 1933 level.[18] Rocha took charge of the territory from downtown to Andarai, comprising the major favelas of Santa Ana, Gamboa, and Rio Comprido, working class São Cristóvão, and well-to-do Tijuca, areas which had accounted for about 40 percent of the votes cast in the 1930 election. Rocha convinced Lourença Mega, for many years councilman from Santa Ana, to join the PADF, and together they organized local *cabos* into the United Front of Santa Ana.[19] Rocha and his *cabos* registered ten thousand voters before the rolls closed. Luís Aranha was assigned several downtown precincts and eventually registered eight thousand voters. Augusto do Amaral Peixoto, organizer in the South Zone, registered two thousand voters, largely through the help of *cabos* from poor neighborhoods. Pereira Carneiro was given Flamengo-Botafogo, which added a few new voters to the PADF forces.[20] The politicians were completely in charge of the registration process, providing birth certificates, photographs, completed forms, transportation to and from the registrar, and sometimes even "literacy" classes for those who could not sign their names. Here is where the PADF served its most important function, mobilizing new voters and creating a loyalty for Ernesto which transcended the party itself. The PADF was especially active in the favelas, where the image of Pedro Ernesto as the *médico bondoso* who provided schools and clinics for the poor proved highly popular.[21]

Pedro Ernesto had numerous contacts with the favelas during 1932 and 1933, helping mediate eviction and land disputes, providing the first subsidies for samba groups during Carnival, and ordering installation of public services when possible. Growing rapidly during the 1930s, favelas concerned public officials and in part inspired Pedro Ernesto's social programs. The *Journal do Brasil* voiced this concern during 1934 and finally (somewhat rhetorically) called for the city to "take favelados more into account" in public planning. That was precisely what Pedro Ernesto was doing, offering favors to the favelados in exchange for their votes.[22] Party managers actively recruited votes and promoted the image of their beneficent leader among the poor and favela population. The culmination of their efforts came in June, when Pedro Ernesto and the PADF held a rally in Mangueira to announce the construction of a public school there, the first ever built in a favela. There were fireworks and military and samba parades for a crowd estimated at fifteen thousand, and songwriter "Zé com fome" dedicated several Carnival verses to the mayor. By the time of his death in 1942, Pedro Ernesto would have over one hundred godchildren in Rio's favelas, and the favelados turned out en masse for his funeral.[23]

Favelados did not constitute a large enough population to have a decisive effect on elections during the 1930s. Low literacy rates and lack of personal identity documents diminished their political participation, and voter registration books make no mention of favela residence. Interviewees who noted favela recruitment emphasized its novelty, not its extent. In large part, the favelados' importance derived from being the "people" who recognized the true leader. The favelas were a perfect synthesis of the Brazilian working class, with samba music, all manner of racial mixes, and a sampling of folklore from the interior regions. Their preference for Pedro Ernesto was an invaluable endorsement, a kind of people's opinion poll. His recognition of the favelados created a bond between leader and follower and helped legitimate his administration in the eyes of other social sectors. The discovery of the "people" in the urban working class was one of the most powerful innovations of 1930s populism.

A number of politicians shared in Pedro Ernesto's popularity, but Vargas was the long-term beneficiary of the mass urban support that the PADF won. After all, Vargas had encouraged the mayor and given him administrative autonomy, and like Pedro Ernesto, Vargas stressed protection for workers and offered traditional leadership. He gave Pedro Ernesto the freedom to undertake the voter mobilization, and the latter in turn pledged absolute loyalty to the president. The collaborative relationship could not continue indefinitely, though: the two were philosophically at odds, and Pedro Ernesto's increased prestige in politics made him a power contender potentially threatening to Vargas. Chapter 8 will show how the two men eventually clashed. But the underlying differences may even now be noticed in the political command structures. Vargas strove steadily for personal control over the political situation, while Pedro Ernesto could afford to relax his command and expand patronage, integrating more and more sectors of the population into his movement.

Populism as defined in the introduction became the overall approach of Pedro Ernesto and his party. They drew upon the communal urban tradition, promising to extend the vote and hence sovereignty to the people. The poor would be incorporated into urban society by means of social programs (described in the next chapter). Persons from all walks of life were drawn to the campaign to restore holistic society. And they responded: Pedro Ernesto received the support of the new elite, the middle class, and the masses.[24] It was the beginning of a new era in Brazilian history, during which big-city votes would multiply and eventually dominate national elections. Populism had come of age in Brazil.

The success of the PADF is especially evident when the party is compared to three other politically experimental groups formed in Rio during the 1930s, two class-based parties and a Catholic pressure group. Political opposition to Vargas, to the extent that it was allowed, focused on the PD, which was resuscitated by Bergamini, and the Republican Center, headed by Dodsworth following the death of Paulo de Frontin in early 1933. Neither party had much success in the 1933 elections, after which new approaches were designed to counter Pedro Ernesto's populism.

The first important experimental party of the 1930s was the Economist party (PE), organized by Rio businessmen. Leaders of the Commercial Association and the Industrial Federation formed the PE in November 1932 to represent their interests and to counter interventionist policies urged by the tenentes. None of the Economist leaders had participated in politics prior to 1930, yet they hoped to capture elite and middle-sector votes with a program based on private capitalism and the social responsibility of the business community. Classically liberal in its view of government-business relations, the PE nonetheless addressed the social question with an urban poverty plank proposing educational and welfare reforms of a self-help nature.[25] Political writer Gilberto Amado drafted the statutes and platform, and Mozart Lago assumed the executive direction of the party. Lago, a lawyer and journalist from an old Rio state family, was an astute politician who had studiously avoided party labels in order to play the role of *chefe*, expediter, and arranger. With several thousand votes from poor precincts downtown, Lago had won a seat in the 1930 Chamber, only to lose it because of the revolution. He also had gained support and financing by representing associations of chauffeurs, hotel owners, truck drivers, and market vendors. The Economist party paid Lago a handsome salary ($250 per month) to handle voter registration, campaign rallies, and news releases, and to publish a broadside with the unlikely name *A Trincheira (The Trench)*.[26]

Since much of the infrastructure of the PE was generously financed by the business community, many anti-Vargas politicians affiliated with it for the 1933 ANC election. Yet the party ran second to the PADF and only seated Dodsworth and Miguel Couto, both of whom had their own constituencies. Bergamini, running on both Economist and PD tickets, placed fifteenth, and the businessmen-candidates did even worse.[27] Part of the reason for the PE failure was that well-known candidates were reluctant to become too closely associated with the untested Economist image, thus undermining the party. Dodsworth and Couto distributed several thousand ballots with their own names rather than the party's, enough to have completed one minority quotient for the PE. Another reason for the PE failure was that the ex officio (union or workplace) registration differentially aided the PADF and labor parties, while the PE was forced to do most of its registration under the more laborious notarial rules.[28]

The PE made a more concerted effort to elect businessmen to the Chamber and to the City Council in the elections of October 1934. The CRC disappeared altogether, and Dodsworth became a leader of the PE. In April the PE formed a united front with the PD, and both mounted a large voter registration campaign in downtown areas. Anti-Vargas papers, such a *O Globo, Jornal do Comércio, A Noite,* and *Diário Carioca,* provided free space for PE releases. Even ex-tenente and Communist party member Agildo Barata, owner of an elegant shoe store in downtown Rio, joined the PE, considering it an honest experiment in class politics with some chance of defeating Pedro Ernesto.[29] Yet despite these renewed efforts, the PE failed to widen its congressional representation in the 1934 election, and it was virtually excluded from the Council as well.

Another political experiment of the early 1930s was the Carioca Pro-

Opposition broadside from elections of October 1934, showing prominent candidates.

letarian Convention (CPC), a working-class coalition attempting to overcome fragmentation in the union movement and to gain support from nonunion workers as well. The CPC was founded in late March 1933 by the Labor Federation, a union coalition with loose ties to the Ministry of Labor, and by the Maritime Federation, a powerful seamen's association.[30] Thirty-five of Rio's major unions participated in the formation of the CPC, representing a large electoral potential. The platform was nonideological, calling for labor unity, freedom of association, better wages and working conditions, and release of jailed labor leaders. The CPC organized a slate of ten candidates from major unions and distributed printed ballots in thirteen CPC rallies just prior to the election.[31]

The CPC was forced to compete against another worker coalition sponsored by remnants of the tenente movement, the Brazilian Socialist Party–Proletarian Political Union (PSB–UPP). This group was formed in late 1932 by a tenente congress presided over by Juarez Távora and Pedro Ernesto. It was attended by tenentes, northern politicians, labor leaders, and by some Old Republican politicians anxious to use the tenente movement for their reentry into politics. This party never developed a coherent program, as the name and origins suggest, and it did not receive consistent support from its founders.[32] Neither of these parties fared well in the May 1933 elections, for the labor vote was more effectively tapped by other politicians. The CPC polled fourth among the parties with 880 votes. This was more than twice the number received by the PSB–UPP, which at least indicated a mild repudiation of the labor-tenente-politician ticket. The PSB–UPP disappeared after the election; CPC leaders attempted to sound optimistic, but their experiment in politics was a failure.[33]

During 1934 attempts to form a working-class party renewed. Ex-tenentes Roberto Sisson and Hercolino Cascardo joined minority leftist leaders in April to form the Socialist Party of Brazil (PSB), but the group did not prosper. As the October election drew near, labor leaders formed the Proletarian United Front to replace the CPC and to draw together elements of the PSP, the Workers and Peasants Union (UOC), the International Communist League, the Labor party of Brazil, and the PSB. This effort failed as well, and by polling time the labor vote was hopelessly divided among a dozen minor parties. The UOC, a descendant of the 1920s BOC, received almost four thousand votes and was the third largest party, but it did not have sufficient ballots to complete one quotient. The rest of the labor parties received less than one thousand votes each.[34]

The last important new approach to politics in Rio was the Catholic Electoral League (LEC), a nonpartisan pressure group designed to give

Catholics a greater voice in political affairs.[35] LEC was created in 1932 to enhance Cardinal Leme's influence with Vargas, but in a few states (notably Ceará, Pernambuco, and Rio Grande do Sul) it won widespread support from the electorate. In Rio, LEC operated largely as an interest group to lobby for policies favorable to the church and to create adverse publicity for anticlerical politicians. The lay director of LEC was Alceu Amoroso Lima, leader in the Centro Dom Vital in the late 1920s and an influential Brazilian intellectual. Amoroso Lima drew up a Catholic program composed of measures which the church wished to see included in the new constitution, especially religious instruction in public schools, no divorce, and multiple labor unionism that would allow Catholic worker organizations. LEC also attempted to focus adverse attention upon potential enemies of the church. Amoroso Lima challenged politicians to accept or reject the LEC platform; predictably, most accepted it. In the 1933 election the LEC openly branded as anti-Catholic only the PSB–UPP, the UOC, and the CPC parties, which had little chance of success from the outset. Thus it is difficult to determine how effective LEC's veto threat was. The lobbying in the ANC, however, was quite successful, and Amoroso Lima claimed that virtually all of the platform was adopted.[36]

The competition generated by Pedro Ernesto's PADF and the other political groups of the 1930s drew new men to seek public office. Tables 12 and 13 demonstrate that new professional groups gained access to political posts. Law and medicine continued to furnish about half of the politicians, but military officers and employers replaced many profession-

TABLE 12: Professions of Candidates, 1926–30 (total cases = 58)

		Highest Office Held		Party Affiliation		
Profession	Total Frequency	Councilman	Senator, Deputy	PD	CRC	Other
Lawyer	20	8	7	7	10	3
Doctor	15	3	5	9	6	—
Teacher	10	1	1	7	4	—
Journalist	9	2	1	7	1	1
Engineer	8	—	2	2	6	—
Businessman	5	2	2	1	3	—
Notary	3	2	1	1	2	—
Labor leader	2	1	1	—	—	1
Intellectual	2	1	1	—	1	1
Military officer	1	—	—	—	—	1

Sources: Roster compiled from newspapers, campaign literature, and interviews. Dual occupations counted twice. Only persons for whom two or more data were available were tabulated.

TABLE 13: Professions of Candidates, 1933–35 (total cases = 102)

		Highest Office Held		Party Affiliation	
Profession	Total Frequency	Councilman	Senator, Deputy	PADF	PE–PD
Lawyer	24	2	3	6	14
Doctor	24	2	8	11	14
Teacher	9	1	3	2	6
Journalist	5	1	1	1	4
Engineer	5	1	2	1	4
Businessman	11	2	3	5	6
Notary	3	1	1	2	1
Labor leader	3	1	—	—	2
Intellectual	3	—	1	3	—
Military officer	13	4	3	13	1

Sources: Same as table 12. Labor parties not tabulated, nor persons who switched parties.

als, particularly in the Council. In all, the sample revealed thirteen officers and eleven employers, a marked increase over the pre–1930 figures. Pedro Ernesto's PADF showed the most divergence from the 1920s, for it brought tenentes and newcomers into local politics. The PE had a high frequency of employers, but so did the PADF, so the PE by no means spoke for the whole business community. The PADF also had a much higher frequency of doctors seeking political office, reflecting the political nature of staffing in city hospitals. Subsamples of newcomers in the PADF and the PE–PD suggest that the former were on an average ten years younger than the latter. A surprising fact is that the PADF, programmatically committed to the social question, had no labor leaders. This is probably because unions transferred their loyalty to the PADF without needing to create leaders in their own ranks.

The analysis of party affiliations before and after 1930 in table 14 provides evidence of considerable new recruitment of politicians by the

TABLE 14: Changes in Party Affiliation by Political Candidates (frequencies)

	Affiliation 1933–35			
Affiliation 1926–30	PE–PD	PADF	Other	Inactive
CRC	7	9	2	10
PD	5	3	—	7
Liberal Alliance	2	3	3	5
Inactive	14	35	—	—

Sources: Same as table 12. Inactive means other than for reasons of health.

innovative parties of the 1930s. Of fifty-six politicians active in 1930, for example, almost 40 percent dropped out of politics, either temporarily or permanently, a very high turnover in a period of five years. Of eighty-three politicians active in the mid–1930s, almost 60 percent were newcomers, particularly those of the PADF. Reading the columns of table 14 vertically shows that over two-thirds of the Autonomist candidates were newcomers to politics, compared to half of the Economists. Some party switching is also observable (from the CRC to the PADF, for example), but in general replacement of political ranks is the most common phenomenon. There is no doubt that in this sense the revolution of 1930 affected urban politics more than it did small town politics, where family and clan structures continued to be resistant to national affairs.[37]

The competition of innovative political forces and the recruitment of new politicians led to a marked expansion of Rio's electorate by 1934. Even with little time for voter registration, the 1933 election had 9 percent more votes than that of 1930, and the 1934 election received one hundred ten thousand valid votes, almost double that of 1930 (table 11). The new recruitment drives were conducted on a door-to-door basis and registered by the traditional notary process, rather than by unions. Politicians tended to concentrate in the dense commercial districts downtown, in favelas, and in the Subúrbios. A 1.3 percent casual sample of voter registration between June and September 1934 suggests that the majority of the new voters (51 percent) were unskilled workers from these areas. Tradesmen, professionals, and public employees made up the remainder, in almost equal proportions. The sample also suggests that migrants swelled the electorate, because 57 percent of the sample was born outside Rio, a significantly larger proportion than in the city's population as a whole. Only 9 percent of the sampled new voters were women.[38]

Thus the broader franchise, the new forms of registration, and the heated political campaigns of 1933 and 1934 contributed to a rapid growth of Rio's voting public. While the electorate (or potential voters) grew from two hundred twenty thousand to seven hundred fifty thousand between 1920 and 1940, the number of votes actually cast between 1922 and 1934 rose even more rapidly, at a rate five times that of the city's population. By early 1936, moreover, political planners would speak of five hundred thousand voters, a feasible goal given the experience of the mid–1930s recruitment. And it was clear to all that the populist politics developed by Pedro Ernesto were the most capable of reaping the votes of the newly enfranchised.

The election of 14 October 1934 left little doubt about the efficacy of the populist campaign conducted by the PADF. At stake were ten seats in the Chamber, twenty-two seats in the Council, and indirectly two senatorial seats and the mayoralty (the latter to be chosen by the Council in 1935). The PADF won eight of the ten Chamber and twenty of the twenty-two Council seats, assuring it control over the indirect elections as well. PADF managers and *chefes* were enthusiastic about the future, unanimously attributing success to their leader's popularity. Almost forty-five thousand ballots with "Pedro Ernesto-PADF" at the top were cast in the Council race, representing 42 percent of all valid votes.[39] Party loyalty, albeit identified with the mayor, was two and a half times greater than in the 1933 election, measured by the percentage of PADF votes in relation to the total. Pedro Ernesto held keys to political solidarity that the other experimental parties lacked.

Pedro Ernesto's campaign, the first city-based mobilization of mass electoral support in Brazilian politics, was not understood by all, and many questioned its propriety. Most critical were those tenentes who favored professional over electoral representation and who were hence sympathetic to the Economists and the labor coalitions. The president of the Club 3 de Outubro, which was now out of favor with Vargas, denounced PADF bargains with *chefes* like Cesário de Melo as no better than the corrupt politics of the Old Republic.[40] After the election, Abelardo Marinho, a tenente advocate of class representation, lamented the defeat of the Economist and labor parties. The Economists did everything correctly, he said: they hired experts, registered voters, and financed elaborate publicity campaigns, but they failed because they had no support from the bosses. The Economists might have won more seats if they had simply paid *cabos* to support their candidates. Similarly, the Carioca Proletarian Convention, a reconsolidation of socialist and labor splinter groups, did poorly despite the advantages of ex officio registration and the eventual support given it by twenty-seven important labor unions. Marinho, like many other tenentes, had lost faith in the renovative potential of the Vargas regime and was disturbed by the implications of Pedro Ernesto's populist campaign.[41]

Critics on the left generally understood more clearly that their own chances of building mass support were being eroded by the PADF. Tenente Agildo Barata (later a leader in the communist uprisings of November 1935) had joined the Economists to help defeat Pedro Ernesto, whom he perceived as the most serious threat to working class politics. Barata wanted the Economists to concentrate their efforts on gaining control of the Council, their only chance to defeat Pedro Ernesto. When the Economists failed to heed him, Barata angrily quit. The identification of Pedro Ernesto as a foil of class-based politics increasingly impressed leftists and was echoed a year and a half later by Luís Carlos Prestes, head of the Brazilian Communist party (PCB).[42] However, before analyzing the crystalization of ideological extremes that would undermine Pedro Ernesto's position in national politics (to be taken up in chapter 8), we must review the 1933 and 1934 campaigns to evaluate their impact on urban politics.

The masses of unskilled workers drawn to the city by economic recovery were not only available for recruitment but actually desirous of leadership to replace the loss of rural community solidarity. The populist movement reached out to the poor, whom it defined as the "people," and offered them a place in the city. In addition, unions and the middle sectors joined the movement. Unions that had been relatively leaderless in the 1920s backed Pedro Ernesto, and their members were attracted by his charisma. The middle sectors supported the party because it addressed reform concerns they believed in more than did the narrow class-based parties of the 1930s. The party made good its promise to incorporate politically the poor and working class into the burgeoning urban society, and the educated persons of the middle stratum did benefit from the thousands of new jobs spawned by the social programs (described in chapter 7). Finally, members of the new elite sympathized with the populist experiment, which they believed able to manage the masses and continue the pace of modernization they desired. Thus, the social support generated by populism worked politically.

The 1930 election had drawn sixty-four thousand persons to the polls, a record for the capital. The large turnout was caused by the superimposition of interest group politics over the still viable *chefe* and *cabo* system. But since the vote was split almost equally between the official and opposition candidates, Rio's votes counted little in the national scene. In the 1933 and 1934 elections, Pedro Ernesto (backed by Vargas) went beyond the push of 1930 to create a broad coalition which embraced the *chefes*, unions and employer associations, and even the poor and favela population. In a short time the number of voters had risen to 110,000 and promised to grow geometrically. His populist party resembled those of Latin American populists, such as Yrigoyen and Alessandri, although it was not national in scope. Although Rio's populist movement grew out of local politics, beset by the crises of 1930 and 1931, its importance derived from the fact that a whole new generation of urban-based politicians witnessed the possibilities of populist recruitment and learned the lesson well. Vargas himself would turn to populism during World War II.

7 □ Social Planning in the 1930s

With or without populism, new approaches to social problems were inevitable in the 1930s because of the reform sentiment built up during the previous decade and the visibility of the poor in metropolitan Rio. Both Pedro Ernesto and Getúlio Vargas owed much of their success in politics to new perceptions of social planning. Innovations in this previously private realm clearly distinguish pre– and post–1930 administrations. Neither the mayor nor the president had preconceived programs for social reform upon entering office, but instead drew upon the conviction that Brazilian institutions had become inadequate for modern urban society. The populist mayor's program in Rio focused on education, health, and charity, following reform directions of the 1920s. Vargas, it turned out, had an affinity for corporatism, the system in which private institutions are brought under the tutelage of the state. It must be kept in mind that social planning, singled out for attention in this chapter, was intimately tied to the political innovations of the 1930s, enhancing the appeal of Brazil's new leaders.

Pedro Ernesto's social reforms were largely designed to help integrate the poor into urban society, the promise of his populist coalition. If the poor, and especially the favelados, were the "people" who validated the new government, they merited programs that would make them good citizens and productive members of society. This approach appealed to the middle sectors, for it would eliminate the threat of social conflict and simultaneously create new jobs in the emerging professions. Thus Rio's reformism of the 1920s flowered in the 1930s, in a milieu of optimistic social planning.

Pedro Ernesto's personal commitment to social programs merits a word. Although he had been thought dictatorial during his tenure as president of the Club 3 de Outubro, Pedro Ernesto had actually helped formulate some of the most progressive elements of the tenente program. Among these proposals were the creation of a Ministry of Social Organization and Welfare; a labor code; a social security system; universal primary education; a public health service; and government chartering of voluntary associations. Because many of these proposals were included in the 1934 Constitution and were taken over by federal agencies, they were not attributed to the tenentes. Pedro Ernesto's dual role as tenente leader and populist in Rio, however, demonstrates that the tenente movement had a pronounced progressive strain.[1]

Pedro Ernesto's personal experience also contributed to his social reformism. His residency in the charity hospital of Rio was followed by continued aid to the poor in his own clinic. In fact, his reputation as *médico bondoso* first appeared among the residents of neighborhoods near his clinic. He felt a paternalism toward the poor and wished to offer them the means of self-improvement through education and good health. A last source of Pedro Ernesto's reform sentiment was Franklin Roosevelt's New Deal, which the mayor admired.[2]

One of the outstanding elements of the Pedro Ernesto administration was the educational reform directed by Anísio Teixeira. A leader in the Pioneer movement described in chapter 3, Teixeira immediately began to overhaul the city's school system to make it a model for the rest of the country. Although much had been accomplished by Fernando de Azevedo in the 1920s, Rio's schools were deficient by most standards. The primary schools lacked capacity and quality, causing most well-to-do families to send their children to private schools. Classroom additions had not kept pace with population growth, and the Subúrbios in particular needed hundreds of new classrooms. Teixeira, in a preliminary analysis of the situation and using criteria from the United States, reported that Rio's schools had space for only about 5 percent of the school-age children in the city. Moreover, a large number of the buildings were rented, a widespread and expensive arrangement inherited from the 1920s.[3]

Teixeira decided to build a score of new schools and ordered a comprehensive study to determine where they should be situated. First, realistic goals had to be established. The total school-age population was calculated, using censuses and housing surveys, at about one hundred ninety-six thousand for the year 1932. Of these, the public schools matriculated about ninety-three thousand, with actual attendance of only seventy-six thousand. The rest were by no means taken into private schools, whose global enrollments were only forty-six thousand. Thus, at best the public schools attended 47 percent of the children and private schools another 23 percent, and a third of the children went without formal schooling.[4] A comparison with the school system of Buenos Aires was sobering: there public schools took in 80 percent of the quarter of a million school age children, private schools had 14 percent, and only 6 percent went without formal education. Teixeira's program was formally proposed to Pedro Ernesto as a Plano Regulador, which recommended remodeling and new construction to assure facilities for one hundred fifty-six thousand students, covering virtually all children not enrolled in private schools. This would bring the city's proportion of the school age population to 77 percent, leaving private schools with 23 percent. No attempt was made to compete with private schools.[5]

The locational criteria of the Plano were designed to give means of social and economic improvement to the poor. The underprivileged, it said, "will increasingly require the help of the state to provide instruction and education that will stimulate them to change their present way of living." The model for such a philosophy was derived from Teixeira's studies abroad: "The United States has proved that education and instruction are the vehicles of progress." The Plano compared existing plant capability with needed space in each area, clearly revealing the deficiencies in the Subúrbios. The author noted, however, the existence of areas of poverty in the South Zone as well. Even elegant Copacabana had favelas and tenements whose children needed schools. The poor were not pariahs but necessary elements of the society who required the means for bettering themselves. A number of public schools were located near favelas and—for the first time in Rio's history—one was built in a favela, for the seventy-five hundred inhabitants of Mangueira.

Teixeira also sought to improve the quality of education, hoping to curb the high rate of attrition. Less than half of those entering the first grade stayed to complete the second, and only a tenth completed fifth grade. A particularly disturbing fact was that the poor had higher dropout rates than other children. Out of every one hundred students from poor families entering first grade, fewer than five completed fifth grade; by comparison, among the well-to-do 25 percent finished fifth grade. Rather than continue forcing poor children to attend classes that might be irrelevant to their life needs, Teixeira proposed to make the curriculum flexible and relevant to all social levels. The inspiration was John Dewey's: the child should be the center of the educational process, and his growth should determine what was necessary and important to learn.[6]

To apply progressive educational philosophy, which was termed the *escola nova,* was a difficult task in Rio's schools. A relative latecomer to the reform movement, Teixeira wrote and lectured extensively on the subject of the *escola nova* and became its principal proponent. The

Pedro Ernesto with schoolchildren.

traditional, academic approach had only given wisdom to a small elite endowed with both the leisure and the capacity to continue on to the university. Those not so endowed were likely to be left with a set of ideas of limited practical application. The traditional vocational school was also unsatisfactory, segregating underprivileged students for manual arts training and denying them the opportunity to experiment with science, literature, and the arts. Both the poor and the rich should be exposed to all sorts of learning to fulfill their natural inclinations and talents. The *escola nova* offered a relaxed environment dedicated to the present, in which the child could grow and develop his personality, his tastes, and his capacity for self-education.[7] It was heady stuff, but it offered such a clear and inspired break from the academicism of Old Republican education that it won over an entire generation of educators.

To introduce such radically new concepts in the 1930s among underpaid and poorly trained teachers long out of touch with educational theory would have been impossible. Instead, Teixeira concentrated on training new teachers and professors, for which purpose he transformed the old Normal School into the Educational Institute, utilizing a newly built center and a completely revised curriculum.[8] There would be experimental schools connected with the Institute, student teaching, a circulating library of books and films, and a new image for the elementary school teacher. Henceforth teachers would have tenure and access to city employee health benefits.[9]

To crown the system, Teixeira proposed the creation of the University of the Federal District (UDF), forerunner of today's University of the State of Rio de Janeiro. Created on 4 April 1935, the UDF was composed of the Educational Institute and all its experimental schools; the model Central Educational Library; laboratories of the city hospitals capable of training medical students; and four academic departments: science, economics and law, philosophy and letters, and art. The university assumed wide responsibilities for promoting cultural activities in the city, taking over management of the city's educational radio station, Escola Rádio. Moreover, composer Villa-Lobos and painters Portinari and Di Cavalcanti were engaged by the university to teach and to offer free programs for the public.[10]

The educational program achieved considerable success in its objectives. The city built twenty-eight schools capable of handling some one thousand students each, in the so-called platoon system of home rooms, rotating subject classes, and two shifts per day. The cost of these schools, architecturally simple, was much lower than those built during the 1920s, and additional savings were derived from reducing the number of buildings rented. Teixeira hired over eight hundred new teachers to serve in these schools. In two years enrollments climbed from ninety-three thousand to one hundred sixteen thousand (25 percent), a larger relative increase than had occurred during the entire 1920s. The number of children in the higher grades increased in relation to total enrollment, showing improvement in the attrition rate. At the same time, enrollments in the vocational schools doubled.[11] Finally, teachers gained an esprit de corps if not a complete understanding of the *escola nova*. Teixeira enjoyed remarkable success in these several years, the result of a decade of proselytism by educators and of a political willingness on the part of the mayor.[12]

Teixeira's progressive policies met with opposition from Catholic leaders and from Rio's political right, who with Vargas's consent mounted a campaign against the Department of Education. Vargas, as will be discussed more fully in chapter 8, began in 1935 systematically to eliminate political contenders on his left, with whom Teixeira was associated. The latter was forced to resign in December 1935, and in ensuing months widespread purges were carried out against his colleagues. The university was closed, professors were jailed, and the experimental schools returned to regular status. The cultural programs were shut down, often with immediate loss of the city's artistic patrimony. The intellectual leadership of the nation passed to São Paulo, where since the 1920s a vigorous cultural and university life had been developing.

Pedro Ernesto's health program was as ambitious as Teixeira's school reform, though not as philosophically innovative. Even before taking office Pedro Ernesto had called for increased spending on hospitals and related welfare services, suggesting that gambling be legalized to meet new costs. During the 1920s he had treated many indigent patients in the Casa de Saúde, and he believed that the state should assume wider responsibilities toward the poor. The city had run a modest first aid service since the Pereira Passos administration but had only one clinic at the time of Pedro Ernesto's appointment. The hospital was more than a decade old, and some seven hundred persons were daily turned away from its doors due to the lack of facilities.

During his five years as mayor Pedro Ernesto directed the construction of five new hospitals in the North Zone and one in Gávea; in addition, many health centers were built throughout the city. A number of rest homes, laboratories, and specialized services helped integrate the system. The cost was about three times that of the school construction, due to investments in clinical equipment. The delivery of medical services rose substantially during these years: house calls by public health nurses and doctors' consultations tripled, while hospitalizations doubled.[13] The philosophy was no different from that of the previous health program of the city; Pedro Ernesto simply expanded the facilities and staff to embrace a much wider population. The timeliness of the program, however, won the mayor great popularity, for rural migrants swelled the ranks of the urban poor during the 1930s, and reformers sought means of integrating them into city life. Pedro Ernesto emerged as a humanitarian doctor and a man of action during an often tense debate over the problems of urban poverty.

While most people agreed that a literate and healthy citizenry was a sound investment, much debate focused on the means of uplifting the poor. Shortly after the revolution, Evaristo de Moraes condemned the Napoleonic tradition that treated mendicancy as a crime: the state should instead deal with urban poverty through structural reforms and legal protection for the poor. Another writer, reflecting a growing uneasiness over the question of poverty in the city, called the favela an "invitation for social revolution." He proposed a large public housing program to eliminate this danger.[14] Some young artists chose the poor as subjects: for example, Portinari's 1930s canvas "Favela," which hangs in the New York Museum of Modern Art; Lúcio Cardoso's novel *Salgueiro* (1935); and a motion picture of the same period entitled "Sadness of the Favela." Even employer representatives in the constitutional convention recognized the need for public assistance programs, while warning against the depersonalizing effects of welfare.[15]

Pedro Ernesto's approach to charity was similar to that of progressive reformers in the United States during the 1900s. Aid to the poor should be a public responsibility in order to reduce the stigma of inferiority and dependency that often accompanied welfare. The *Jornal do Brasil*, reflecting the mayor's thinking, called for a new concept of public assistance which would uplift the poor and make them self-sufficient. The effort should be undertaken by the government, a neutral and disinterested agent. It concluded, "bands of poor and sick in desolate physical condition cast a pall over the panorama of the city, in contrast with its traditional image of comfort, prosperity, and cleanliness."[16]

Several months later, however, police chief Filinto Muller by-passed the city government in coming to an agreement with the Shopowners Syndicate. Muller proposed to take beggars into custody in order to make a file of legitimate mendicants and to exclude the able-bodied. Beggars would receive subsidies from the syndicate if they agreed not to beg in the stores. The *Jornal do Brasil* found Muller's approach lamentable, for it avoided a long-term commitment to the problem of poverty and it legitimized mendicancy.[17] Within days Pedro Ernesto took the initiative, forming the Social Assistance Institute (IAS). The mayor became the national president of the IAS, and the board of directors included Muller, the treasurer of the Bank of Brazil, the director of the National Department of Labor, representatives of the Shopowners Syndicate, and many prominent citizens. The approach was that of a united crusade, which would gather charitable donations from individuals and businesses to distribute among welfare agencies. It was probably not a coincidence that the same day the IAS was formed, the Shopowners Syndicate gave a public vow of support to Vargas and Pedro Ernesto for a decree prohibiting kickbacks for commercial rental agreements. Thus the populist integrative approach prevailed over the police solution.[18]

Two other welfare agencies formed during the same weeks revealed religious competition in charitable work. The Social Welfare Service (SOS) was composed largely of nurses from the federal and city health departments, making it appear a semipublic organization. The SOS had an American flavor, for many of its members had studied nursing or social work in the United States, and it received the endorsement of U.S. Ambassador Edwin Morgan. The Rotary and foreign companies provided the majority of the resources of the SOS, causing some to call it a "protestant" charity. Catholic leaders reacted quickly, forming the Archdiocesan Social Association (ASA). Since Pedro Ernesto was not a practicing Catholic, he was suspected of favoritism toward the former agency.[19] Nonetheless, the overall effect of the mayor's welfare stance was positive and enhanced his image as a humanitarian reformer.

The educational, health, and welfare programs enacted by Pedro Ernesto were modeled on reformist proposals of the 1920s. They did not threaten to modify the social structure or culture of Rio; rather, they were designed to alleviate poverty and to integrate the poor into urban society. Had more of the city's elite been receptive to reformism, such measures could have been enacted during the 1920s, but instead Old Republican planners concentrated on physical design. The Pedro Ernesto administration blamed the old regime for ignoring the social question. This attitude was best presented by the mayor's close aide and nephew, Jones Rocha, who charged that previous administrations had only addressed the material problems of the city, disregarding "the spiritual work of progressive improvement of popular education and social welfare. . . . The more the city improved materially the more obvious became the . . . disregard for popular culture and for the living conditions of the underprivileged."[20] Such an argument led Pedro Ernesto on several occasions to attempt to pass the costs of new social programs on to the wealthy.

The first proposal made by the mayor that would redistribute income toward the middle sectors was the 1933 *imposto único,* a land tax scheme first proposed by the nineteenth-century writer Henry George. Briefly, the *imposto único* was a single tax to apply progressively on the value of landholdings in and around the city. According to officials, the tax would have beneficial effects in the short, medium, and long ranges. It would immediately correct the inflated land market caused by the real estate boom because unimproved land or unoccupied buildings would have to begin paying taxes based on assessed rather than rental value. It would at the same time increase city revenues and reduce collection costs and evasion. By discouraging land speculation, the *imposto único* would free investment capital for more productive uses. The scheme would be redistributive by virtue of shifting a share of the tax burden from homeowners to investors in urban and suburban real estate.[21] The same organizations that had opposed Bergamini's business tax reform attacked Pedro Ernesto's, arguing that it would tax businesses excessively but not reach financiers, bankers, and holders of "idle capital." The mayor reacted by extending the city's property transfer tax to capital transactions such as loans, insurance policies, and sales of stocks and bonds. A vigorous debate of these measures took place over the following months, after which the mayor finally abandoned the *imposto único* proposal.[22]

The second major reference to redistribution came in early 1935, when Pedro Ernesto was sworn in as mayor of Rio. While he gave no ideological label to his program, he highlighted two concepts:

> The first is that perfection of the means of production has made possible, by increasing the social wealth, a more equitable distribution of goods, compatible with the needs of the modern workers. The second is that the state can no longer maintain an attitude of mere spectator or policeman of human progress, but rather must be a regulator of the life of the community during this phase of its historical evolution. . . . [We will press for] the progressive socialization of those [public] services which most affect the collective welfare of the people.[23]

Socialization of public services would be, through subsidized rates for consumers, to the decided advantage of the masses. By that point, however, the mayor's social program was deeply embroiled in union and leftist politics, which are discussed in the next chapter.

The Shift Toward Corporatism

While Pedro Ernesto's programs followed the reform direction of the 1920s, Vargas's approach to social planning gradually evolved toward corporatism. Vargas was not single-minded in his pursuit of any policy, and his corporatism emerged gradually and almost piecemeal. It first revealed itself in his dealings with the Ministry of Labor and by 1935 became firmly enough entrenched to create a philosophical breach between himself and Pedro Ernesto.

Corporatism was not a new idea. Medieval corporatism was the attribution of formal political powers to important societal groups: clergy, towns, military, and nobility in feudal systems, or guilds, hanses, and other economic associations in northern European cities.[24] By the late nineteenth century corporatism came into vogue again in Europe, especially in Catholic intellectual circles. Full-scale implantation of corporatism only appeared with the fascist regimes of Europe during the 1920s and 1930s, however, when war- and depression-battered societies needed extraordinary measures to survive. In Italy and later in Germany, Spain, and Portugal, pluralist groups were assembled into hierarchical "corporations," organized by sector: agriculture, industry, civil service, military, commerce, and so forth. The theoretical intent was to regiment social and economic institutions into corporatist structures which would reinforce rather than compete with the state. Private organizations would perform functions similar to the medieval estates. The defeat of the Axis powers in 1944 and 1945 brought an end to most fascist governments, and corporatism, because of its close association with them, was subsequently avoided by political theorists. Nonetheless, as recent analysts have pointed out, corporatism has continued to be a viable and attractive model for developing countries, particularly those in which Catholicism is the majority religion.[25]

For the most part, corporatism evolved in Brazil because Vargas required more authoritarian powers to rule the country under the twin effects of the Depression and the revolution. He rarely spoke of philosophical or ideological issues, concentrating instead upon the power struggles which surrounded his office. Taken individually his decisions reflect not so much a corporatist model of government as his need to maintain control over men and their ambitions. Nonetheless, there was a correlation between his authoritarian rule and the corporatism which was gradually implemented by the regime. Many of Vargas's ministers and councilors believed that corporatism was needed to reorganize and strengthen the Brazilian state, and their social policies in the areas of labor, family, social security, health, and education demonstrated this conviction. At one time or another, Aranha, Góes Monteiro, Campos, Cardinal Leme, Color, Juarez Távora, the Club 3 de Outubro, and other collaborators urged on Vargas measures which would contribute to a corporatist state. At the same time leading intellectuals also proposed corporatism as a nationalist model for Brazil.[26] To the extent that it was politically possible, Vargas favored these measures over those inspired by democratic liberalism. As the corporatist measures slowly accrued and the ideas meshed during the 1930s, Vargas assembled a corporatist state. He was neither overly purposive nor unbending in the process, as will be seen in the following case studies.

Lindolfo Color's Ministry of Labor pioneered much of the early Vargas social planning, and the president often called the new agency his "revolutionary ministry." The philosophical underpinnings of the labor unit were eclectic, drawing in large measure on the reform sentiments of the 1920s. Color, it will be remembered, had written most of the Liberal Alliance platform of 1929, including a detailed section on labor. His ideas on social legislation came partly from the International Labor Organization in Geneva and partly from labor programs in Uruguay and Argentina (the Colorados and the Radicals).[27] In addition, Color and others in the late 1920s had been impressed by the disciplining potential of Italian fascism, which seemed especially appropriate for the confused times following the revolution. Vargas and other PRR leaders in Rio Grande had experimented with the formation of producer cooperatives and federations similar to the Italian government for the regulation of trade and prices for the state's export products.[28] Color, as PRR deputy in Rio, frequently applauded this program in Congress and publicized it in his newspaper work. Beneath the eclecticism of Color's social ideas was the conviction, shared by many writers and politicians of the day, that the state had to intervene more actively in the society and economy to assure the nation's well-being.[29]

A major element of Color's program in the Ministry of Labor was the extension of retirement and disability fund coverage to employees of public utilities companies. Until 1930 only railroad and shipping companies were required to maintain such funds, called Caixas de Aposentadorias e Pensões (CAPs), but the ministry set out to create them for all skilled sectors of the urban workforce. Organized by individual companies, the CAPs regulated job security, accident indemnification, and retirement benefits. The legislation stipulated that employees with ten years of service could only be fired with just cause, to be determined by the National Labor Council.[30] Ministry officials also projected the unification of CAPs into industry-wide Institutos (IAPs) to absorb small, economically unviable CAPs. The first IAP, set up in 1933, covered seamen; soon thereafter stevedores, bank and commercial clerks, warehousemen, and factory workers were included in either CAPs or IAPs. The benefits of this social security system were substantial, and some labor groups fought hard for coverage. By the same token, employer associations and foreign companies vehemently opposed social security because of the costly contributions they were required to make.[31] During the early 1930s, much of Brazil's modern social security system was organized according to plans drafted by Color's staff.

The second major policy in Color's social program was syndicalization of worker and employer associations, that is, chartering by the Ministry of Labor in exchange for official recognition. In this way Color sought to incorporate unions and producers' organizations into the structure of the state; the government would then orient them with regard to economic planning and would mediate industrial relations in order to prevent conflict and strikes. It was time to stop thinking of labor as a commodity to be bought and sold, he said, and to recognize that economic progress was the cooperative goal of all classes; what was needed was "social cooperation of interdependent classes . . . in which the idea of progress is subordinated to the fundamental notion of order." Color envisioned a social system in which a technico-professional elite would direct the economic expansion of the country, yet in which control would remain in the hands of the syndicates. Strike arbitration, which he labeled the liberal prescription for labor conflict, simply exacerbated class tensions by admitting the existence of basic structural antagonism. "Syndicates, or class associations, will be the buffers of this antagonism."[32]

Syndicalization was received with little enthusiasm by unions and was repudiated outright by employers, mostly because both groups had opposed the Liberal Alliance in 1930 and distrusted Color's motives for wishing to give them semiofficial status. Moreover, the government now required submission of statutes and minutes of all meetings to the ministry, access to meetings and financial records by the government, and the power to impose direct administration (intervention) in certain cases. At first, weaker unions and civil servant groups were the only ones that desired to syndicalize, often in exchange for some Ministry favor. Major unions and employer associations in Rio avoided recognition in order to protect their autonomy. In 1931 and 1932, only fifty unions and three employer groups were syndicalized out of several hundred eligible associations.[33]

Resistance to syndicalization declined in 1933 when the government announced that official groups would be allowed to register their members to vote in general elections and to select representatives to the National Constitutional Assembly (ANC), which would soon draw up a new constitution. By late 1933 the ministry reported that legalized syndicates across the nation had one hundred ninety thousand members and annual receipts of $9.4 million. Even employer groups registered with the ministry, part of the Economist Party mobilization mentioned in chapter 6: by the end of 1933 they totaled twenty-seven, or a quarter of all of Rio's syndicates. Rio's syndicates, in turn, represented almost a quarter of all

Brazilian syndicates.[34] Again, the grass roots structure of unions and employer associations in Brazil today dates from the early plans of the Ministry of Labor.

Chapter 5 demonstrated that divergent political strategies had contributed to differences between Color and Vargas. Color attempted to build interest group support for himself through the labor ministry, while Vargas needed to establish control over a fluid coalition during the difficult years following the revolution. Color's alignment in 1931 with anti-Vargas factions separated the two men, and Vargas guietly shifted labor affairs from the ministry to the police department. Color might eventually have developed a more coherent program, but during his short period in office the Ministry of Labor responded to influences too eclectic for philosophical unity. In sum, Color concentrated on implementing the Liberal Alliance social measures he had drafted in 1929.

Vargas was less inclined to philosophical programs than Color, and shortly after the February 1932 cabinet crisis he implicitly rejected the Liberal Alliance program in a major speech: "The armed uprising of October 1930 did not have a program to impose upon the Brazilian people, nor was it necessary. Such movements are guided not so much by previously formulated clauses as by an instinct for the reality of the moment." The financial crisis, he continued, required a strong government imbued with special powers. Breaking from his prepared speech, Vargas enumerated instances when the French, English, and American governments had recently surpassed constitutional limits on executive powers. "Dictatorship," he said, "has emerged as the providential form of government today."[35] But if dictatorship suited his command requirements, corporatism offered an amenable organizational model, an antidote to the pluralism of the previous regime. Three major elements constituted Vargas's emergent corporatism—police surveillance of labor, class representation, and reestablishment of church-state collaboration.

Labor repression by the police counteracted Color's attempts to fortify unions through ministry chartering. Vargas's intentions with regard to labor were perhaps best revealed by his appointment of Salgado Filho, former head of the DOPS, as new labor minister in March 1932. Whereas Color had only opposed strikes against foreign companies, Salgado Filho prohibited all strikes and rounded up militant leaders regardless of their ideological positions. Salgado Filho's first task was to suppress a strike among electric power workers in May 1932. The police, now directed by tenente leader João Alberto, spared no efforts in the action. During the rest of the year strikes were not permitted. Gradually the government extended its control over the syndicates and social security organizations.[36]

Labor reacted to Vargas's attempts to control the unions and retirement funds with an increasing number of strikes in Rio, all opposed by the labor ministry and suppressed by the police. The press and congressional debates indicated the occurrence of twelve full-scale strikes during 1934. An employee of the Ministry of Labor at the time recalled that union militancy resembled that of the great strikes of World War I. Chapter 8 will trace this conflict between organized labor and police after 1934.[37]

Class representation was the second important element in Vargas's emergent corporatism in the 1930s. It was at heart a system for allocating seats in the constitutional convention and 1934 congress to delegates from labor, business, professional, and civil servant organizations. Representation by "class" (a term used by contemporaries to mean occupational sector) offered Vargas an opportunity to manipulate the votes of delegates friendly to the administration. But it also advanced corporatist organization, drawing on a long philosophical tradition. Perhaps the most ancient precedent for class representation was the division of medieval Portuguese society into estates. The impact of the Enlightenment discouraged such schemes in the name of egalitarianism, but the idea was resuscitated by Auguste Comte in the nineteenth century. Soon others embraced class representation: the papal encyclical *Rerum novarum* (1891) recommended it as a bulwark against anarcho-syndicalism; Emile Durkheim (a student of Comte and father of modern sociology) prescribed it against anomie, the psychological malaise caused by excessive division of labor in urban industrial society; Brazilian statesman Alberto Tôrres espoused it in his book *A organização nacional* (1914), as did his protégé Oliveira Vianna. The tenentes' Club 3 de Outubro included class representation in its plan of national reorganization, drawing upon the writings of Brazilian thinkers as well as Italian fascists. By 1933, when Brazil began to debate the form which its new constitution should take, class representation was a well-established principle.[38]

Opposition to the class representation scheme arose quickly, however. The pre-ANC drafting commission rejected the measure, and the *Jornal do Brasil* denounced it as an unfortunate imitation of fascism: "Far from being a stimulus for professional organization . . . Italian class representation is merely the conversion of those forces into instruments of the government—into tools of tyranny."[39] Private associations in Brazil were not strong enough to withstand the co-optive–repressive forces of the government. Indeed, Vargas saw class representation as a means for gaining a bloc of votes in the ANC larger than any of the state delegations. Besides police repression, he would hold out special favors and opportunities for those union leaders who collaborated with him. Some of the enticements Vargas used to co-opt labor were jobs in the ministry, the police department, and the retirement institutes; favoritism in labor-management bargaining; better treatment by police; and even seats in local and national legislatures.[40]

Largely at the insistence of Vargas and the tenentes, the class representation system was adopted for the ANC. In July and August representatives of syndicalized groups met in Rio to choose 40 of the 254 delegates to the ANC in the following proportions: labor, 18; employers, 17; liberal professions, 3; and civil servants, 2. Since the number of electors depended upon the number of syndicates chartered by the Ministry of Labor by mid–1933, the breakdown by regions and states provides an index of sanctioned associational strength.[41] About 60 percent of those from the northern and southern states came from worker organizations, and another 15 to 20 percent from the liberal professions. Employer groups were much better represented in the south, especially São Paulo; in contrast, a number of northern states sent no employer representatives at all. The center predictably had a heavy contingent of civil servants; in Rio they composed 39 percent of the delegation. A striking feature of the distribution of electors was their overwhelmingly urban origins. The *Jornal do Comércio* noted that legislative apportionment by state had not changed appreciably since 1875 and was still a touchy issue; yet class representation in effect gave more votes to urbanized states, where associations were active.[42]

The selection of the actual ANC delegates demonstrated Vargas's intention of using them for his own ends. Alleging that communists might infiltrate the proceedings, the labor minister personally selected an electoral board of subservient union leaders that excluded anti-Vargas militants. Seventeen of the eighteen delegates eventually chosen were from traditional unions in large cities, with a predetermined regional distribution of at least four from the north, four from the south, and three each from Rio and São Paulo. The Rio delegates were from the warehouse, bank, and store employees unions. The *bancada trabalhista*, as the labor delegation was known, was supplied with an advisory committee by the Ministry of Labor, and throughout the ten months of the ANC they voted in accord with the government's wishes. By 1935, however, many labor leaders had become disenchanted with class representation, and the government could not count on their votes in the legislature. Nonetheless, the system had the important effect of inducing private associations in Rio to charter themselves, giving the government legal access to their archives, financial records, and meetings.[43]

The third important corporatist policy followed by Vargas was rapprochement with the church. Sebastião Leme, made a cardinal in 1929, wished to reassert church authority in the public life of the country. By the time he helped convince Washington Luís to step down in 1930, Leme had already begun to take a more active part in public affairs. Vargas, though privately an agnostic, respected the influence of the church and decided to concede certain favors to Leme in exchange for his support during the early days of the regime. Vargas acquiesced to two of the three principal demands of the church, religious instruction in public schools and no legalization of divorce. This compromise, like police repression of unions and class representation, would have long-lasting social and political effects.[44]

Following the 1929 encyclical of Pius XI, Cardinal Leme attempted to expand Catholic influence in the educational system of Brazil. He was certainly aided by the accession of Francisco Campos to the Ministry of Education, who carried out a reform of secondary and university education as was seen in chapter 5. Among the decrees was one permitting religious instruction in public classrooms.[45] Campos justified this aspect to Vargas, emphasizing the political benefits: "In this moment of great difficulties, in which it is absolutely indispensable to muster all our material and moral forces, this decree . . . will mobilize the entire Catholic church to the side of the government."[46] Since he had already taken steps to allow such classes, the controversial measure was after the fact. A bitter, seven-year debate over the issue was thus begun, the consequences of which will be seen in chapter 8.

The second demand formulated by Cardinal Leme was to resist legalization of divorce. He convened an episcopal meeting in October 1931 to petition Vargas against such a move, and seven months later he wrote the president to warn of the socially dangerous consequences of draft legislation for divorce. Vargas privately assured church leaders that while he was in power there would be no divorce in Brazil. Aided by Francisco Campos, church officials altered the draft, and until 1977 divorce was prohibited in Brazilian law.[47]

Finally, Cardinal Leme promoted a Catholic labor movement, drawing on his early experiences with *círculos operários* (Catholic unions) in Rio and Recife. On this issue, however, Vargas would not compromise: he and the labor minister insisted on the "unitary syndicate," publicly chartered and without political, ethnic, or religious ties. After the 1934 Constitution again allowed multiple unions, the *círculos* made some headway, but only under the 1937 Constitution did they really prosper. Yet despite constant efforts since the 1930s, the church has not been noticeably successful in the labor movement due to the action of the Ministry of Labor. As other analysts have pointed out, the church-state rapprochement of the 1930s was erosive of church authority and integrity in the long run, particularly in the area of social policy.[48]

Vargas's corporatism in the 1930s, then, was not simply Machiavellian opportunism, enactment of the dictatorial system he had known in Rio Grande, nor imitation of European fascism. Rather, Vargas sought to control major groups in society through semipublic "corporations," or institutions. In labor policy, he was genuinely interested in providing social security and class representation as long as the institutions serving the working class could not be turned against his authority. Because large masses of urban poor sought security and authority during these years, Vargas eventually won their loyalty.[49] Vargas's actions toward the church may also be understood in these terms: he made significant concessions on some religious policies but took away the church's ability to act independent of the state in political affairs. His relations with the army also elucidate the corporate model at work. Vargas was not a militaristic person nor did he desire to rule solely with military backing; nonetheless, at the insistence of the high command he strengthened and unified the army during the 1930s, making it an essential pillar of his government.

Moreover, Vargas's treatment of the civil service demonstrates the influence of corporatism. Public employee associations, long an unstable force in Rio politics that championed reformist causes, were slowly depoliticized through syndicalization and were brought under his control. Vargas expanded the bureaucracy greatly during the 1930s and extended to it numbers of favors, yet at the same time he reduced civil servants' ability to bargain independently with politicians. He eventually even created a true corporation for them, the Departamento Administrativo de Serviço Público (DASP, 1938–), to rationalize the civil service and to channel its support into the structure of the state.[50] Throughout the 1930s Vargas created dozens of councils, institutes, federations, and commissions for the corporatist purpose of aligning private decision making with public policy. The government gradually suppressed the free play of pluralist, interest politics in Rio and segregated society into sectors that could be more readily controlled: labor, capital, civil service, professions, church, and bureaucracy were all to submit their demands and conflicts to state mediation. This corporatist system imposed in Rio was only possible during the period when strict social controls could be applied. Finally, it was conservative in the sense that it assumed that free interaction of men's wills would destroy society and that hierarchical rule was needed to orient men's behavior.[51]

The 1930s, then, saw the development of social planning in Brazil, in sharp contrast to the laissez faire governments that preceded the revolution. It was crucial for the emergence of Pedro Ernesto's populist movement, for it helped integrate the poor and provided jobs and a program for the middle sectors. Vargas's social policies, while corporatist in nature, served much the same function; the poor and recent migrants found in Vargas a leader whom they could trust. The federal government, meanwhile, grew rapidly with the addition of education, health, and labor programs hitherto nonexistent or run by the states. This attention to social planning was, together with economic interventionism, one of the most distinctive features of the 1930 revolution in Brazil. Rio was a testing ground for these reforms, most of which were later extended to the rest of the country. Populism has generally been associated with social legislation in Brazil, whereas authoritarianism, examined in the next chapter, has rarely included such programs; these biases were created during the mid–1930s.

8 Macabre Dance: Populism and Authoritarianism

Pedro Ernesto's success made him a national figure in 1935, by which time his party ruled the capital and his social reforms served as models for other cities. Two forces led the mayor to turn his party to the left in that year, a challenge from authoritarian-minded army and police officers and the advent of a labor-leftist coalition led by tenente hero Luís Carlos Prestes. Misreading Vargas's own growing sympathy for corporatist rule, Pedro Ernesto mistakenly veered toward a socialist position, which shattered his party and made him a target of rightist attacks. When it became clear that Vargas no longer supported him, the mayor steered back toward a conciliatory populist position, but it was too late: the president had him imprisoned on false charges and turned the city over to Padre Olympio de Melo. The clashes in Rio were symptoms of a growing confrontation between Vargas (now virtually dictator again) and his opponents who regarded populism within a democratic framework as viable. The 1937 election campaign for president saw these trends worked out in local politics, with a clumsy attempt by one candidate to replicate Pedro Ernesto's populism. Vargas tolerated the challenge long enough to create a crisis and then imposed authoritarian rule in his Estado Novo (1937–1945).

The roots of authoritarianism struck as deeply into the colonial urban bedrock as those of populism—they descended from the rights of kings to impose their will over the citizenry in times of emergency. The tradition held that in the long run there should be no conflict between patrimonial and local interests—yet sometimes the two might be in honest disagreement. This was roughly the situation that obtained in the late 1930s when the army and federal police sponsored Vargas as dictator and rolled back most of the populist advances of the preceding years. Vargas had considerable reason for desiring such a change in regime, for he had taken the country through some of its most difficult times in the early 1930s, and he believed that the people did not recognize the dangers inherent in a democratic system. Vargas had been apprenticed in the hard-bitten machine politics of Rio Grande and had learned to obey and be obeyed. Even though he had gained notable skills for conciliation and reform, he still preferred raw command; in his later years he concealed but never suppressed this preference. In the chaotic years which followed the 1930 revolution, Vargas had used a strategy of balancing those who were dictatorially inclined against those who insisted on constitutionalism. Balancing was always dangerous, however, and he strove in the mid–1930s to increase his executive powers by any means available. By 1935 he found that the army and police supported his efforts in this direction, and together they formed a covert alliance to impose an authoritarian regime. A biography of the late 1930s captured the situation nicely in its title *His Majesty the President*.

Authoritarianism was just as legitimate in Brazilian legal tradition as popular sovereignty, so it should be differentiated from dictatorship. The overall justification for authoritarianism is to preserve the collectivity from some immediate peril not perceived by the citizens. In the 1930s the threat was said to be impending civil war caused by agitators, as well as subversion by agents of both communism and nazism. Authoritarianism relies upon semipublic institutions to channel direction from the top down, as was seen in the discussion of corporatism in chapter 7. Extraordinary powers assumed by the executive are eventually codified into law, as happened with the Estado Novo constitution and several judicial codes promulgated afterward. Finally, authoritarianism exalts the state as the embodiment of the collectivity, which has the effect of enhancing executive prerogatives. Obviously such an increase of patrimonial authority decreases the authority of the people.

The Estado Novo was not a totalitarian state, then, nor was it even unrelieved authoritarianism because an undercurrent of populism (faint to be sure) survived. Populism had become engaged in a deadly dance with authoritarianism, in which each competed to rule. The dance was gruesome enough at times, for lives were lost and much suffering ensued. The situation may be likened to a counterpoint in which neither was permanently on top and each line moved in relation to the other. The "harmony" resulted from the common colonial traditions from which each sprang. It will be argued in the conclusion that the two modes of governance came to depend upon one another in a symbiotic relationship.[1]

As was noted in the introduction, some authors have treated populism and authoritarianism as similar regime types, arguing that only a veneer of liberality separated the former from the latter. The transition Getúlio Vargas made from dictator to populist is cited as an example, as are the Peruvian military government after 1968 and the Mexican "revolutionary" system. And the fact that both forms derive from a common colonial past might also be cited as evidence of their similarity. Nonetheless, as will be seen in this chapter, populism and authoritarianism need not be mutually supportive. Sharp differences separate them: patrimonial versus municipal traditions; charismatic versus anonymous leadership; electoral versus corporatist representation; open versus closed civil system; due process versus extraordinary judicial powers; social reform versus social control; and voter mobilization versus demobilization. Clearly there are other differences between populism and authoritarianism, but this list catalogues the major distinctions.

Looking at the examples cited above may help clarify this analysis. Vargas, it is true, moved from an authoritarian to a populist stance during the 1940s, a process discussed in the epilogue, but he accomplished this over a considerable length of time and with the aid of propaganda on an unprecedented level. Other Latin American politicians made similar transitions: Alessandri between the 1920s and 1930s; Ibáñez between the 1920s and 1950s; Perón between the early and late 1940s; and so forth. These men were undoubtedly in touch with the popular conceptions of legitimacy and drew upon both populist and authoritarian versions at different times. Such changes were not discordant with the colonial tradition that justified strong government in times of duress. Moreover, the Peruvian military government, which undertook reforms and distribution of land unusual for such regimes, may be regarded as the populist movement of General Velasco Alvarado because it fits most of the criteria elaborated in the introduction. Military leaders, in fact, often become populists. The Mexican regime, however, is not populist because it fits virtually none of those same criteria. (The exception is Lázaro Cárdenas.) To conclude, populism and authoritarianism are modes of governance that draw upon traditional notions of legitimacy; hence they can arise and fall quickly as the situation in a country varies. Because they are not institutions they do not have a lasting existence—when they disappear they blend into and reinforce the colonial heritage from which they originated.

Because of the special relationship that evolved between populism and authoritarianism in Brazil during the Estado Novo, some attention must be given to the peculiar forms the latter took. In particular, the police have played a special role in surveillance and repression during and after the era of populism. Therefore a brief history of the federal police after 1930 is necessary background for the rise of authoritarianism.

Growing Police Repression

Vargas's first police chief in Rio was João Baptista Luzardo, a disciplined lawyer-politician from Rio Grande who had commanded a contingent of troops during the 1930 revolution. In early 1931 Luzardo had announced a plan to reform the service, partly sloganeering to cover a purge of pre–1930 men from the force. Among those Luzardo chose to help carry out the reform was Evaristo de Moraes, the labor and criminal lawyer close to Bergamini and Color. The reform plan would have centralized and unified the department, incorporating independent night patrols and even the Military Police, which numbered five thousand men. The commander of the latter branch protested, and by late 1931 the reform was abandoned, partly due to Luzardo's ties with the opposition politicians in Rio Grande and São Paulo. He quit the job during the same cabinet crisis in which Color resigned.[2]

In mid–1932 Vargas appointed Joaquim Pedro Salgado Filho, former DOPS director, as minister of labor, and tenente leader João Alberto Lins de Barros as police chief. Labor control and presidential security were the prime goals of these appointments. João Alberto had served a tumultuous year and a half as interventor in São Paulo before resigning in frustration; his appointment in Rio bolstered the tenente Club 3 de Outubro and helped it secure control over the capital. With intended irony, João Alberto told reporters that *his* police reform would be a virtual charter for the city. Anticipating civil disturbances in São Paulo, the police set up round-the-clock radio contact with military garrisons and jailed opposition politicians implicated in the plotting. Following the São Paulo civil war (July–October 1932) João Alberto quit as police chief and returned to his native Pernambuco in order to run for Congress.[3]

The third Vargas designate for the Rio police answered neither political obligations nor security concerns; Filinto Muller, former DOPS director, was promoted to the job for the purpose of curbing labor and political opposition during the 1933–34 transition to constitutional rule. It was this role that most characterized the ten years he eventually served as Rio's police chief. A revolutionary from the 1920s. Muller had come to Rio following the revolution and joined the Club 3 de Outubro. After serving on the front in the São Paulo war, Muller was appointed DOPS director. Upon the resignation of João Alberto in February 1933 Muller was made acting chief, and in several months the appointment became permanent.[4] A quiet and assiduous worker, Muller harbored an intense dislike for labor organizers and leftist politicians. During the increased political by-play of 1934 and 1935 Muller became more convinced than ever of Brazil's need for an authoritarian state. His personal dedication to Vargas made him an especially valuable agent in Rio to keep watch during Pedro Ernesto's populist experiment.[5]

Muller gained fame as a tough police chief just as Pedro Ernesto reached the peak of his career. In August 1934 police broke up an antiwar rally with pistol fire and tear gas, and congressmen called for an explanation. The DOPS director replied that the rally lacked a parade permit and that, when confronted with the need for one, the leaders boasted of one hundred armed men who would guarantee their right to parade. One of the marchers allegedly fired on the police, who responded in kind.[6] The following month a labor delegate in the Chamber enumerated recent police attacks on unions: the offices of the bakeryworkers, chauffeurs, cabinetmakers, and railroad workers had been invaded by police and the latter's files confiscated. Police broke into a meeting of the hotel employees' union, resulting in one death and several injuries. The cabinetmakers' union was attacked again for helping textile workers organize a strike. The railworkers, meeting in the shoe-factory workers' union, were again attacked. Strike groups in textile factories were broken up by police gunfire. The congressman ended: "We are truly in a regime of governmental terrorism; shootings, deportations, imprisonments, attacks on unions and workers, jailings of the editors of the *Jornal do Povo*. . . . those imprisoned for labor conflicts are submitted to physical torture in the dungeons of this inquisitorial republic. Militant labor leaders disappear." Liberals also joined the protest of police violence. Dodsworth criticized Muller's use of tear gas on peaceful railworkers, and former senator Sampaio Correia called attention to a nonviolent strike of students which was broken up by tear gas and gunfire. Mozart Lago protested the arrest of a Portuguese leader in the chauffeurs' union. In short, Muller increasingly used unconstitutional police methods to intimidate opponents of Vargas during 1934 and early 1935.[7]

Muller also raised the level of censorship. During the period of tenente hegemony, the Department for Official Publicity had maintained a censor in each newspaper to prevent dissemination of "dangerous news." A *New York Times* correspondent was arrested for wiring a story damaging to Brazil's image abroad, and some antigovernment newspapers were closed from time to time.[8] During the period the ANC met, Vargas had Muller relax censorship, and he even donated $500,000 and a lot on the Castelo Esplanade to the Brazilian Press Association in an effort to win their friendship. By early 1934, however, these policies were seen to be ineffectual, and censorship was again instituted. ANC deputies read censored stories into the record, a 1920s usage designed to circumvent the police and to call attention to censorship. Vargas eventually revoked the Press Decree of 1923 but allowed Muller to continue monitoring news and closing unfriendly papers. Thus except for a brief period in 1933 and 1934, censorship continued through the 1930s and became institutionalized during the Estado Novo.[9]

Because Pedro Ernesto was making a strong bid for union support for the PADF during 1934, he became engaged in a power struggle with Muller. The two men had known one another during the tenente hegemony of 1932, but the mayor had soon disassociated himself from the authoritarian-minded members of the Club. By 1934 Pedro Ernesto was decidedly opposed to Muller and others, notably General Góes Monteiro, minister of war since early 1934.[10] Therefore, the mayor proposed creating a Municipal Guard to take over many police functions in the capital. The plan called for a public force of nineteen hundred men, including four hundred existing guards for public buildings and parks, to patrol the streets day and night. Former private night patrols (often created by *chefes*) were to be incorporated into the new unit. The cost would be met by a supplement to the property tax.[11]

The Municipal Guard proposal was politically attractive for the PADF. The need for a coordinated patrol service in the city was obvious, to supplement the investigative and traffic work of the civil and military police. Moreover, the new unit would give Pedro Ernesto more independence from Muller, allowing him to trade certain forms of protection—e.g., for union meetings—for political support. Finally, staffing out the new Guard would give the party fifteen hundred new jobs.

The Municipal Guard was created just prior to the 1934 election, and while it proved successful it also generated trouble. Góes Monteiro insisted that the Guard be issued only pistols and light machine guns and that its command be entrusted to Colonel Zenóbio da Costa, a career officer who disliked politicians and who would cooperate closely with Muller. In addition, the partisan staffing of the guard (positions were given to *chefes* for distribution) tarnished the reform image of the party. For example, the *Diário da Noite* called city government "Tammany Hall," and Pedro Ernesto undoubtedly lost some middle-sector support in the process. The creation of the Guard was a clear signal that the mayor expected to forge his own path into national politics. He would have to do so against stronger authoritarianism in 1935.[12]

Muller unleashed a second wave of repression against labor and liberal-left politicians in 1935. Citing the need for national security, the police began jailing union leaders and evoked criticism in the Chamber. Dodsworth protested the arrest of fifty bank clerks, to which Muller responded that only three were clerks and the rest were *fichados*, persons with police files of some sort. A labor deputy condemned the police closure of the Feminine Union of Brazil and the labor tabloid *Avante*, as well as attacks on the newspaper and publishers' employees and chauffeurs' unions. The DOPS director responded that police had merely taken in persons for interrogation regarding illegal, subversive cells. Finally, ex-propaganda chief Sales Filho, in a moment of unusual candor, proclaimed that "When Dr. Washington Luís was president, some said that the labor question was a matter for police. Just between us . . . labor problems are still police affairs."[13] Police repression, indeed, formed part of Vargas's larger strategy for bringing unions under federal control, as was outlined in chapter 7. Now that he was constitutional president, Vargas authorized more violent actions against labor leaders, many of whom were taking advantage of their new political rights to build a viable leftist coalition, making up for the years of repression.

In early 1935 Vargas requested Congress to legitimate antisubversive police actions by approving the National Security Act (LSN) drafted by government lawyers. The LSN was aimed at curbing the activities of an emerging popular front coalition in Rio that sought to bring together labor unions, the left wing of the tenente movement, and liberal opponents of Vargas. The movement was strongest in the capital and congealed into the Alliance for National Liberation (ANL), coordinated behind the scenes by the Communist party. In late March 1935 the group requested a city auditorium for their inaugural meeting, which was approved by Pedro Ernesto after clearing with Muller. During the meeting Luís Carlos Prestes (still wanted by the police) was proclaimed president of the ANL, directly challenging the government.[14]

Vargas responded by putting more pressure on Congress to pass the LSN, which it did within a week. Constitutionalists reacted vociferously against the measure. The Military Club condemned the law for authorizing excessive police power. Oswaldo Aranha, ambassador to the United States since mid–1934, wrote Góes Monteiro, "The Law you have composed makes me laugh, which is really crying when nothing can be done. . . . The police state cannot survive; it only leads to decadence, anarchy, and disorder." The police used their new powers to ban labor and leftist political groups from forming, and in July the government declared the ANL illegal.[15] In October a tenente deputy pronounced Brazil a full-blown dictatorship:

> Freedom of association? Public meetings are broken up by bullets, tear gas, and hand grenades. Recently the city witnessed a barbarous attack by police thugs on a meeting of university students. Right

> of association? Unions are raided daily. The National Unitary Confederation of Labor, legally founded by a labor congress in full view of the press (and certainly the police), saw its leaders imprisoned and its general assembly violently terminated during wage debates. Freedom of the press? Everywhere popular tabloids are confiscated and their editors jailed and persecuted. Freedom of organization? Political, beneficent, and cultural societies are stillborn, with the simple allegation by the police that they do not conform to some police model, which they will not identify. Individual rights? One has only to see the cases appearing daily in the courts, especially those of military officers.

The corollary of this repression on the left, he said, was police tolerance and even encouragement of ultra-rightist groups, themselves just as threatening to the state.[16]

Decline of the PADF

In the face of growing police attacks on labor unions, Pedro Ernesto decided to defend them and give his party a more socialist position. He also hoped, it is certain, to prevent Prestes and the communists from detaching labor from his populist coalition. The mayor interceded in two major strikes (postal clerks and merchant seamen) in early 1935, and his role proved successful and highly popular.[17] Pedro Ernesto was experimenting with various forms of leadership and coalition by this time, taking the calculated risk of alienating more conservative elements of his party. He did so with the support of Vargas, whose popularity rose with that of Pedro Ernesto. Yet Vargas played a double game, encouraging the leftward drift of the PADF while at the same time authorizing more police action, still waiting to decide his own path. By the time he chose to turn to the right, Pedro Ernesto was too committed to his own strategy to follow him.

Pedro Ernesto misunderstood the authoritarian trend of federal politics: An analysis in the PADF paper *O Radical* indicates that party leaders believed themselves to be in line with Vargas. *O Radical* divided the political field into right, center, and revolutionary left. Góes Monteiro clearly led the right, followed by Justice Minister Vicente Rao, the proto-fascist Brazilian Integralist Action (AIB), and the high bourgeoisie of industry and commerce. The centrists were state governors Lima Cavalcanti, Juraci Magalhães, Armando de Sales Oliveira, Flores da Cunha, and the urban petite bourgeoisie. The revolutionary left, *O Radical* editorialized, was led by Vargas, "but the overt leadership of this wing has been given to Dr. Pedro Ernesto." Then it cited a number of old tenentes as followers, some of whom had retired from politics. In 1932 a case could have been made for this analysis, but in 1935 it was completely—and dangerously—wrong. By 1945 it would be something else again.[18]

Pedro Ernesto apparently believed that Vargas concealed liberal-left sympathies in order to keep peace with his authoritarian cabinet. In this analysis, the mayor would hold together the liberal-left of politics while Vargas freed himself from his authoritarian captors in the army and federal police. Eventually Vargas would break from the right, reveal his true sympathies, and appropriately reward those who had kept the faith. Many politicians interviewed during the course of this study agreed that Vargas did encourage Ernesto in his leftward strategy, although none of the intimate dialogue between the two men was recorded.

The leftward shift also damaged the PADF, which had been haphazardly assembled in the previous two years. Party discipline, decisive in the 1934 election, had been enforceable because patronage was expanding, new legislative posts were to be filled, and *chefes* and *cabos* were confident of returns on their political investment in the party. The managers, however, were potentially unstable, for they had no constituencies of their own or at best represented institutions or pressure groups. For example, Amaral Peixoto defended navy affairs in the legislature and the executive; Padre Olympio represented the church; and Pereira Carneiro looked after interests of the business community. When in early 1935 political debts to the managers fell due, the resources of the party were too limited to satisfy everyone; indeed, there was even a slight decline in city expenditures. Since Pedro Ernesto had brought labor leaders and leftist intellectuals into the party to gain union backing, many of the managers believed that they had been betrayed by the mayor. These reactions were slow to be manifested, but a growing number of complaints were heard.

By April 1935, when Pedro Ernesto became the city's first elected mayor (indirectly by the Council), his new strategy was evident. During his acceptance speech in the Council chambers, he turned from the microphone and strode to a balcony overlooking the crowd that had gathered. Completing the address there, he called for strong local government, redistribution of income, protection of the working class, and socialization of basic public utilities.[19] The following month he repeated these themes in a speech inaugurating the Labor Center, an adult education facility designed for workers. The four instructors chosen by Anísio Teixeira had socialist leanings, and the program was termed communist by critics.[20]

The clearest break between Pedro Ernesto and those advocating authoritarian government came in July, following Muller's closure of the ANL. The mayor delivered a speech in the chauffeurs' union criticizing the action: "Never before has Brazil faced an hour as grave as this, for never before were the basic aspirations of the people as threatened as now, popular aspirations inherited from the Empire and upheld during the Republic. . . . The very right to a popular, democratic, and humane government is threatened with extinction." Pedro Ernesto went on to attack fascism and the AIB movement in Brazil as repressive and reactionary. The speech ran on the front page of the Communist daily, *A Manhã,* and was warmly received by liberal-left politicians. Hermes Lima, Maurício de Lacerda, and Costa Leite wired him congratulations, and João Neves applauded the speech in the Chamber. The chauffeurs' union speech underlined Pedro Ernesto's intention to adopt a leftist and prounion position in Rio politics, and it also gained him the enmity of the Integralist party, Muller, and many authoritarian military officers.[21]

Days later Pedro Ernesto took another stand that deepened his commitment to liberal-left leadership and cost him some elite support as well. Since 1931 the government had negotiated with foreign oil companies over foreign exchange quotas for petroleum imports. By 1934 the city's retail price ceiling on gasoline became an added variable, for with the mild inflation the companies had to raise wholesale prices. The issues were complex, and frequent changes in the ministries postponed a permanent solution. In July 1935, however, the companies decided to push for a final settlement, in what came to be known as the gasoline price case. Pedro Ernesto became the leading opponent of a price increase, posing as the defender of the working class against the impositions of foreign trusts.[22]

In July 1935 the Brazilian subsidiaries of Standard Oil, Caloric, Anglo-Mexican, Atlantic, and Texaco all agreed to raise the wholesale price of gasoline 9 percent. Retailers, held to a ceiling by the city, protested that their margins were erased by the increase. A number of garages that operated taxi fleets stopped selling gasoline, and the chauffeurs' union staged demonstrations calling for a return to the old prices. They portrayed the oil distributorships as foreign monopolies which made excessive profits. On the other hand, Rio required about half a million liters of gas per day in 1935, ten times the consumption of 1932, and the suppliers argued that the foreign exchange made available by the Ministry of Finance was insufficient to cover their imports. Thus they were obliged to buy currency on the open market, raising their costs. The case had been under consideration in several ministries, but in 1935 the companies appealed to the Federal Council on Foreign Commerce (CFCE), created to consult with industry and union representatives, technocrats, and government officials, for the purpose of recommending trade and development policies.[23]

The recently created CFCE was reluctant to take on the difficult politics of the gasoline price case, and its counsel only tentatively accepted jurisdiction, alleging that the price ceiling was a municipal rather than a federal issue. This was not altogether true, for any adjustment in Rio would spread to most of Brazil. In the meantime the chauffeurs received credentials from sister unions in nine major cities and states to fight the companies on their behalf, and a consultation of governors revealed them unanimously against the price increase. Class representatives in the Chamber attacked the foreign companies for acting in concert against Brazilian retailers and consumers.[24] When the conflict made front page news, Pedro Ernesto decided to step in and oppose the price increase. It was an attractive issue for his populist campaign because he could pose as a nationalist, a defender of the unions, and an activist mayor. The CFCE requested him to designate a representative to their meetings, which he did.

On 8 August the CFCE convened a group of interested parties, including two unions from São Paulo. The group failed to produce a compromise, and the following day Pedro Ernesto cabled his continued opposition to a price increase, repeating arguments used by the chauffeurs that the companies made sufficient profits without it. The companies responded that 80 percent of their employees were Brazilian and that the cost of their foreign exchange was now 50 percent over the official rate. They cut off supplies to various parts of the interior as a warning and offered Pedro Ernesto a blank check as a bribe, which he showed to his aides before rejecting the offer. The bribery attempt boosted the mayor's moral position, and he remained firm in his decision even after the CFCE recommended an 8 percent retail price rise.

In September the case was taken up by Valentin Bouças, IBM and Hollerith representative in Brazil, a personal friend of Vargas, and the new counsel of the CFCE. On the twenty-first he set up a meeting with Pedro Ernesto to discuss possible means of settling the case. The mayor expressed surprise that the issue was being reopened, but he heard several suggestions, including a scheme to mix surplus alcohol with gasoline in order to cut import costs. This alternative was rejected out of hand by the unions, which recommended importation of Russian gasoline. Nine days later Bouças wrote a final opinion on the case. He noted that the figures utilized by the unions (and hence by Pedro Ernesto) were unrealistic appraisals of company profits. The real figures were difficult to obtain, and Bouças said that to subpoena them "would be going too far, perhaps reaching socialism, for which . . . Brazil is not prepared." He pointed out Brazil's vulnerable trading position with the United States and England and advised against the Russian gasoline proposal, which might provoke retaliation from trading partners. Besides, he concluded, the retail price of gasoline was two-thirds impost, which threw the question back into government hands. The CFCE took a neutral position finally, saying that the price ceiling was a matter for the mayor of Rio to decide.[25]

The CFCE failure to take a stand on the gasoline price case appeared a victory for Pedro Ernesto, for it reinforced his authority in the city, won him the support of the unions without taking a radical position, and enhanced his image as a nationalist. Yet it also revealed the dangers of his new populist strategy. The tone of the CFCE opinions was sympathetic to the oil companies, reflecting the probusiness stance of most of its members. In private Vargas was probably told that the mayor's position was demagogic. Moreover, the militancy of the labor demonstrations and stoppages displeased the middle sectors. Finally, Pedro Ernesto's speech on the closing of the ANL, his association with the communist-led chauffeurs' union, and the hint of a deal to import Russian gasoline convinced many that he had moved too far to the left in courting the working class and had jeopardized his leadership.

Discontented PADF managers could not speak out against the nationalistic stance in the gasoline case, but some criticized Pedro Ernesto for other shortcomings. One was gambling corruption in city-supervised casinos. Early in his administration Pedro Ernesto had legalized gambling in order to promote tourism and generate revenues for social programs. The three casinos authorized in 1933 were in the South Zone and catered to upper-class patrons and tourists. By the end of the year the city received nearly $100,000 per month in taxes, and soon there were charges of corruption. The Club 3 de Outubro was the earliest critic, followed by the *Correio da Manhã*, whose owner informed Vargas of irregularities in the casinos. Pedro Ernesto investigated the charges and eventually fired the director of gambling inspection, but he refused to answer accusations that his aide Jones Rocha was channeling money into the PADF campaign chest. In mid–1935 Amaral Peixoto, jealous of Rocha's growing power in the party (he had been chosen for the Senate in April), broke ties with the mayor. He cited gambling corruption as a major reason, sensing that middle sector constituents would find it compelling. The PADF had begun to crumble.[26]

The issue of religious instruction in city schools was even more erosive of PADF unity. Since the Francisco Campos Reform in 1931, such instruction had been authorized but not mandatory, and Anísio Teixeira had steadfastly refused to provide more than token compliance. He did not allow priests to teach and only permitted attendance upon written request from parents. Church leaders attacked Teixeira on pedagogical grounds, charging that the Escola Nova only gave the student the means for learning, when it should also provide basic skills and moral values. Some PADF managers in the Council, coached by LEC leader Amoroso Lima, questioned Teixeira's professionalism, and the debate was quickly politicized in a way that destined Teixeira for defeat. Padre Olympio, president of the Council, and naval officer Atila Soares presented a bill to institute biweekly religion classes during school hours, taught by priests or by lay persons designated by the church. Parents would determine at the time of matriculation whether their children should receive such instruction and in which faith. In early May, to save the PADF from open conflict, the drafters gained unanimous agreement for its approval before sending it to commission. Then in exalted terms Soares lauded it as an important means of preserving the true social peace desired by God. His arguments were designed to tap middle-sector fears of social conflict, implying that working-class politics without the moral anchorage of religion would lead to communism.

Teixeira disliked the politicians who formed the backbone of the PADF and seldom dealt with them, but when the final vote on the religious instruction bill came in May, he conspired with Adalto Reis to generate opposition to the measure. The other councilmen refused to do so and indignantly accused Teixeira of meddling in their affairs. The debate degenerated into insults, and when Reis left the chambers for a phone call, Padre Olympio called the vote and the measure passed without opposition. The following day the recriminations continued, causing Padre Olympio to stop publication of the Council record. Pedro Ernesto failed to act on the bill, which Padre Olympio then signed into law on 4 June 1935.[27]

The image of the priest-politician signing a measure for religious instruction was rich in symbolism and signaled his ambition to challenge Pedro Ernesto's rule in Rio, but for the moment it badly shook the PADF coalition. Teixeira continued to resist implementation of the law, so Atila Soares sent him an insulting telegram: "Lament malign bolshevistic action Education Department. Tranquility Brazilian family cannot be left mercy individuals like you. Legitimate proletarian aspirations never rallied by epicurean materialists nor sinecure jobs." Pedro Ernesto, no longer able to remain neutral, wired his support of Teixeira's policies. Amaral Peixoto informed the mayor that he remained committed to Soares, and Pedro Ernesto responded that it was well to know one's enemies.[28]

The gambling and religious instruction scandals were party cleavages caused by Pedro Ernesto's leftist drift in 1935. As he reached out for union support, he inevitably lost some of the party managers, but he brought new men to replace them. One was the young physician from the Casa de Saúde, Júlio Novaes, to replace Amaral Peixoto as leader of the Carioca delegation in the Chamber. Party regulars vetoed this designation, however, and the position was finally given to a North Zone *chefe*. The manager level of the party gradually dissolved, and *chefes* and *cabos* unabashedly raked off patronage. Many PADF politicians no longer loyal to the mayor pronounced long and pointless speeches in the Chamber. What was true of the federal legislature was doubly true of the Council. Pedro Ernesto undoubtedly lost middle-sector support by allowing the party to degenerate.[29]

In August the mayor took steps to bring his party and administration back under control. He decreed the creation of five secretariats to make his office administratively parallel to those of state governors. The reorganization would bring new advisers into the government, and he liked to think of his new cabinet as a "brains trust" such as Franklin Roosevelt had formed in Washington. The secretariats, better paid and staffed than the earlier departments, were Interior and Security (including the Guard); Finance; Education and Culture; Health and Welfare; and Transport, Labor, and Public Works. The possibility of firing tepid collaborators to open positions for new supporters was not overlooked by PADF leaders. Atila Soares claimed that Pedro Ernesto was "sovietizing" the city. The measure passed despite these charges, and the mayor installed his new cabinet in September. The appointees hardly warranted Soares's epithet "bolshevist," for all but one were former department heads. The newcomer, appointed secretary of interior and security, was the outstanding lawyer Miguel Timponi, who would become Pedro Ernesto's defense attorney in coming years.[30]

During 1935 the PADF split into two major factions, those who supported Pedro Ernesto and those who followed Padre Olympio and Luís Aranha. Padre Olympio had challenged the mayor in the struggle for religious classes and privately wished to replace him. Luís (Lulu) Aranha's motives were more complex. He had acted as personal aide to his brother Oswaldo since the 1930 revolution, carrying messages and secret correspondence. While his brother was in Rio, Luís served as trouble-shooter and mediator during various political crises. Just as he was fiercely loyal to his brother, Luís became doggedly faithful to Vargas after Oswaldo left for Washington in 1934. Vargas appointed him to head the seamen's social security institute in that year, and he settled happily in Rio, where he could indulge his tastes for politics and horse racing.

Several factors appear to have motivated Luís's divergence from Pedro

Ernesto. As director of the IAP he might have come into conflict with union leaders loyal to the mayor. Moreover, the Aranha family was deeply Catholic, and the gambling and religious instruction issues probably pushed Luís toward opposition. Finally, as an intimate of the Vargas family Luís may have received private instructions from the president himself regarding his ties with Pedro Ernesto. By July 1935 Aranha was called an "honorary councilman" by the press because of the votes he controlled there.[31]

The antagonism within the PADF reached its greatest intensity in late August 1935, and as one politician remembered, Anísio Teixeira was a lightning rod. Pedro Ernesto announced a reorganization of the party to prepare for the coming cabinet changes. This would give the followers of the Padre Olympio–Luís Aranha faction a last opportunity to change their minds and join the mayor. In a party caucus held on August 29, Teixeira read a new PADF platform written by some socialist friends. Amaral Peixoto, Padre Olympio, Luís Aranha, and Atila Soares called the program communist and complained about the leftists, antifascists, and ANL members in the city administration. Teixeira, pedantic and disdainful toward the politicians, was the target of opponents' antagonism; Pedro Ernesto unwittingly became the ground cable two and a half months later.[32]

In his bid to win over more unions, Pedro Ernesto had relied upon Vargas to shelter him from attacks from the right. Vargas probably assured the mayor that he had such protection. The gambling and religious instruction scandals had been troublesome, but Vargas outwardly continued to support the mayor. After November, however, the situation shifted dangerously against Pedro Ernesto when communist revolts in several parts of the country brought army pressure to eliminate leftist and labor politics altogether. The revolts, amply described in the secondary literature, were weak, uncoordinated, and lacking in broad support.[33] Their main effect was to disorganize and demoralize the liberal left (largely uninvolved in the revolts) and to allow Vargas to implement authoritarian measures which had been unfeasible under the 1934 Constitution. Given the socialist overtones of the PADF reorganization of previous months, Pedro Ernesto and his administration became targets for rightist purges.

Immediately after the revolt in Rio, army generals demanded that Anísio Teixeira and many professionals in the Education and Welfare Departments be fired as subversives. Dozens of other city officials were fired, hundreds were taken into custody by the police, and for several days there were rumors that even Pedro Ernesto would resign.[34] The mayor resisted the pressures but was obliged to appoint Francisco

Campos secretary of education in December. Campos dismantled the UDF and did not object to the imprisonment of leftist faculty. He instituted regular religious instruction in public classrooms and abolished the experimental schools which had been set up in the Educational Institute. The Ministry of Education at the same time upgraded the Federal University in Rio, which had been eclipsed by the UDF, but faculty purges there too undermined morale. Congressional investigators called for the imprisonment of Teixeira, who was forced to take refuge on his family farm in Bahia. The obscurantism of these purges is conveyed by the fact that grade school murals by Di Cavalcanti and Georgina de Albuquerque, painters with leftist sympathies at the time, were covered over in 1936.

Attention focused on Pedro Ernesto who, as a leader of the liberal left in national politics, would reveal Vargas's long-range intentions. The mayor held tenaciously to his position and continued to monitor the communist underground. Correspondence captured later indicates that Pedro Ernesto continued to believe that Vargas was the unwilling ally of the authoritarian generals in December 1935.[35] This evidence parallels the analysis of *O Radical*, suggesting that the mayor persisted in the mistaken belief that Vargas would soon veer toward the left. In early 1936 however he realized that the president had made his choice, and he placed the PADF in opposition to the federal government. This was signaled by an invitation to Flores da Cunha (Vargas's arch-rival in Rio Grande) to visit him in the capital, followed by paid advertisements in daily papers advocating a plebiscite to choose Vargas's successor. Events moved quickly toward a climax.[36]

Pedro Ernesto announced a second reorganization of the PADF in March 1936, launching it with a promise of better leadership and a liberal program to appeal to the middle sectors. His secretary of interior proposed raising the electorate to four hundred fifty thousand, a reasonable projection given the techniques developed in 1933 and 1934. The new platform eliminated the obvious appeals to organized labor and stressed social conciliation again: freedom of speech, worship, and the press; honest, liberal-democratic government; personal and public security for the populace; socialization of basic public utilities; defense of the moral and economic welfare of the people; basic human rights; and development of a national consciousness. The mayor appointed seven prominent citizens to an advisory council in March and in turn was made honorary member of the AC-Rio. Definite signals emerged that the elite and middle sectors, faced with a choice between Pedro Ernesto's now moderate program and Vargas's dictatorial trend, preferred the former.[37]

Pressure rose however to remove Pedro Ernesto, especially after his name was found mentioned in papers captured in a communist safe house. The evidence was circumstantial, as later confessions demonstrated, but for political reasons Vargas decided to have Pedro Ernesto jailed. Disregarding pleas from governors and civic leaders throughout the country, he authorized Muller to arrest the mayor, which was done on the morning of 3 April. Olympio de Melo, who as president of the Council succeeded Pedro Ernesto, was instructed to ready himself for the oath of office, administered by the police chief. A series of police actions that day prevented demonstrations against the government. The populist experiment was nearly at an end.[38]

It is unnecessary to review the evidence presented during the months of trials held in 1936 and 1937 because the principal motive for Pedro Ernesto's imprisonment was political. Vargas had decided to create an authoritarian state, and anyone opposed to that choice had to be removed. Pedro Ernesto was the first prominent victim of that policy. Many more would follow before the Estado Novo became sufficiently stable in 1938. The popular mayor's arrest also pleased the army generals who preferred curtailment of leftist and labor politics, men who then began quiet preparations for a rightist coup.[39]

City politics, which had pitched perilously close to chaos in late 1935, degenerated rapidly after Pedro Ernesto's arrest. Padre Olympio lacked the skills for a smooth succession and conciliation within the PADF. He announced that one hundred more subversives in the city government would be fired immediately, mostly in the Welfare Department. He then appointed friends as welfare, interior, and finance secretaries, leaving public works and education (Campos) unchanged. Luís Aranha orchestrated much of the purge, trying to take over the PADF. The rapidity of these and other actions unsettled the Cariocas, most of whom knew Pedro Ernesto to be innocent.[40]

Within a month Padre Olympio's administration showed signs of disaster. Cesário de Melo quit the party and tried to take over the Council. The Guard was relieved of four hundred training rifles, several machine guns, two armored flatbeds, and four motorcycles. *O Radical*, which remained loyal to the imprisoned mayor, criticized Padre Olympio vehemently, risking closure by the police. Padre Olympio finally destroyed the PADF by filing charges of misappropriation against Pedro Ernesto. His chance of rebuilding the party was gone.

In August, Amaral Peixoto pronounced the party dead. One had only to observe the chaotic proceedings of the Council to see that the twenty PADF councilmen nucleated into "small groups formed around *chefes*," just as in the late 1920s. Novaes and Jones Rocha remained in touch with Pedro Ernesto, keeping alive a faction pledged to the acquittal and return of the former mayor. Most of the *chefes*, who had prospered under Pedro

Ernesto, joined in petitioning federal authorities to end the prosecution and release him. Vargas had no intention of doing so, however, until it suited his plans.[41]

Padre Olympio initiated few new projects in his administration, which was characterized by a growing rivalry between him and Luís Aranha. The outcome of his year in office was the inauguration of two hospitals, a new road to the statue of Christ on Corcovado Mountain, and an automobile race track (all begun under the previous mayor); a marching band for the Guard; and restoration of several historic churches. In view of this lackluster administration, Luís Aranha made his bid to take over the city by making deals with the *chefes.* Padre Olympio took up the fight, coached by Francisco Campos, and in December 1936 he fired some eight thousand persons on contract and began hiring new personnel loyal to his faction. By early 1937 he was hopelessly mired in dissent and requested Vargas to impose federal rule in the city, which was done in March. Padre Olympio was made interventor and the Council was closed.[42]

In mid–1937 Vargas managed a change of guard in Rio, partly to calm the city for the presidential campaign underway. Aranha claimed that Padre Olympio would deliver the city to the opposition, whoever it might be, adding ominously that Flores da Cunha was backing the Pedro Ernesto faction. Padre Olympio agreed to resign and was appointed judge on a newly created Accounts Tribunal, where he served until his mandatory retirement in 1956. In his place Vargas appointed Henrique Dodsworth, Frontin's nephew and erstwhile opponent of the government. Vargas's intent was to isolate the local government from presidential politics and put some order into municipal affairs.[43] Because Dodsworth remained studiously neutral in politics, his administration will be left for chapter 9, concerned with the Estado Novo. Our analysis of the populist-authoritarian counterpoint now requires an examination of the presidential campaign of 1937 and the subsequent coup creating the Estado Novo.

The Presidential Campaign of 1937

Vargas was constitutionally unable to succeed himself, and the strongest candidate for the presidential election scheduled for 3 January 1938 was Armando de Sales Oliveira, governor of São Paulo until late 1936. His candidacy was the culmination of six years of nearly uninterrupted efforts on the part of São Paulo to unseat Vargas. Sales was backed by Flores da Cunha, governor of Rio Grande, probably in exchange for a promise of support for the latter in 1942. Their two states had accounted for a third of all votes cast in 1934, and they would receive substantial anti-Vargas votes in other states. Moreover, Flores commanded a state militia that was strong enough to challenge federal garrisons and start a civil war should electoral fraud be attempted. Their campaign organization, called the Brazilian Democratic Union (UDB), began work in earnest in mid–1937.[44]

Vargas himself was covertly in the running, for which the constitution would have to be amended (an attempt failed) or abrogated, as it actually was. Since late 1935 Vargas had contemplated such a path at the urging of authoritarian generals. From mid–1936 on, several high-ranking members of government secretly coordinated efforts to have Vargas's term extended, preferably with a new constitution. They were Benedito Valadares, governor of Minas; Francisco Campos, Rio's secretary of education; Góes Monteiro, inspector of the central and northern military regions; and Agamemnon Magalhães, minister of labor since 1934 and interim minister of justice during the first half of 1937. These men cautiously sought allies for their plan, each in his own field of action.

A third alternative for the succession was the Paraíban José Américo de Almeida, the former novelist who had campaigned with João Pessoa and later with the tenentes and who had served as minister of transport between 1930–34. José Américo's nomination was pushed by the governors of Bahia and Pernambuco, who hoped to stop Vargas and put a fellow northeasterner in office. His backers counted on Vargas's inability to state publicly his intentions: the president was obliged under the constitution to run a fair, competitive election, and if Sales and José Américo worked hard enough Vargas would have no choice but to to so. They hoped to win Valadares to their side, perhaps with an offer of a future presidential nomination. Of the three candidates José Américo had the least chance of success, but his campaign merits closer attention because of its attempt to replicate the populism Pedro Ernesto had pioneered.[45]

José Américo hoped to capture the PADF working-class vote by imitating the former mayor's leftist stance of 1935, at first glance a reasonable strategy. José Américo knew from the outset that he did not have Vargas's genuine backing, so he could criticize the government obliquely for not fulfilling the promises of 1930. Moreover, the electorate existed but the party was in disarray, waiting for a leader of sufficient stature. His guess was right, for in a short time most of the PADF politicians backed him, desperate for some semblance of leadership. Many believed that Vargas leaned toward José Américo, despite promises of neutrality, because Vargas's real contenders were Sales and Flores. Local politicians therefore resuscitated the moribund PADF and threw themselves into the campaign.

José Américo gave his first major speech in Rio on 31 July, choosing to hold it outdoors in Castelo Esplanade. The locale was symbolic, he said, the site of Vargas's 1930 Liberal Alliance speech. He claimed to be heir to the 1930 movement and a defender of tenente idealism. Implicitly he also criticized the authoritarianism of Vargas since 1935 and his abandonment of the goals of 1930. José Américo listed his accomplishments as minister of transport and then detailed programs for major regions. He left his proposal for Rio until last, in order to heighten its impact on the crowd. If elected, he said, he would build low-cost housing: "We owe housing to the poor. Not doghouses. Whether they be small or model homes, they should be for people . . . not just proletarian housing, but homes for civil servants, bank clerks, seamen, for all those who face starvation in order to pay their rent. . . . And the money? That's always the easy retort, the depressing question that hangs in the air. Well it's easy, it's very simple. *I know where the money is. Instead of skyscrapers we will build 200 houses.*"[46] This last section proved immensely popular with the Cariocas, and José Américo decided he had hit upon a winning theme for urban audiences. National leaders, however, saw it as demogogic and disloyal to Vargas, at whose sufferance the Paraíban was running. José Américo later claimed that he was only referring to disposition of social security funds, but the common interpretation at the time was that he wanted to tax the rich to build low-cost housing for the poor.[47]

Rather than retreat from the theme or tone down his rhetoric, and probably urged on by leftist collaborators, José Américo made an even more shocking speech three weeks later.

> Am I the champion of the favelas? From the Esplanade . . . I saw Rio's hills and intoned an elegy to them. And I was deluged with reproach. I was called the champion of the favelas by those who thought I would be angry, when in fact they gave me a most moving title of human compassion. My answer was to mingle among the folk of the hills, sensing their souls, hearing their songs, shaking their hands, receiving their embraces. I wanted to understand them so that when in power I would continue to climb those heights where misery looks down on opulence, one of those contrasts in which Nature takes vengeance on human inequities, until the joy of the samba schools—a miracle of that popular soul—in order to hide hunger . . . is transformed into the bliss of body and soul.

A week later he repeated these themes in Salvador, a city in which perhaps half the population lived in *alagados*, squalid shantytowns built over tidelands.[48]

Simultaneously, José Américo's campaign workers made contact with many of the unions, noncommissioned officers' associations, favela organizations, and student groups which had backed Pedro Ernesto. This mobilization made the police and business community uneasy, just as it had in 1935. Typical of the criticism was that of José Soares Maciel Filho, an industrialist, owner of *O Imparcial,* and a crony of both Vargas and Góes Monteiro. Maciel wrote that José Américo was an "ambitious criminal" for trying to gain the support of labor unions, military associations, and the leftist remnants of the ANL. The candidate "wants to raze skyscrapers to make houses in the favela, forgetting that with only the value of his own home he could build 20 workers houses." Anonymous leaflets circulated accusing José Américo of courting the left: his campaign paper, *O Popular,* was edited by Domingos Velasco, the congressman who had denounced Muller's police in 1935 and who was jailed as a suspect in the ANL revolt. Other *O Popular* writers were leftists, and the paper openly criticized the church and fascism. The police monitored such complaints and kept Vargas informed.[49]

José Américo's persistence in the face of mounting elite and middle-sector criticism is best explained in terms of his misreading of Pedro Ernesto's strategy in 1935. Apparently José Américo and his aides believed that their demogogic speeches to the poor would bring them the popularity Pedro Ernesto had enjoyed. They failed to perceive that the PADF had been a multiclass, integrative party that offered something for all groups and alienated as few sectors as possible. The former mayor had articulated interest group politics, campaigned with a charismatic image, and drawn in the *chefes* with well-regulated patronage. His provision of schools and clinics for the poor responded to broadly felt needs of the 1920s, not foreign doctrines chosen opportunistically. Even when Pedro Ernesto had spoken of redistribution in 1935, he phrased it as "more equitable distribution," singled out foreign companies for higher social costs, or was prepared to retreat, as in the *imposto único* case. He never sided with one class *against* another, so that when he shifted to union politics in 1935 he could still count on a great deal of active or latent support from the middle and upper strata. José Américo, on the contrary, took the side of the poor from the outset and posed as their defender against the other classes, generating immediate opposition.

José Américo should have retreated when people reacted adversely to his "I know where the money is" speech, but instead he worsened his position by entrenching himself in the role of champion of the favelas. This error was perhaps due to his and other Rio politicians' expectation that Pedro Ernesto would join their party upon his release from prison. By this time, however, Vargas controlled the situation and had changed tack. He abandoned political means of continuing in power and decided to rely upon the army to carry out an authoritarian coup. This required not conciliation and even-handed administration but rather an ambience of crisis that would convince the army to act on his behalf. That was the main dynamic of politics between July and November 1937.

The Estado Novo

Pedro Ernesto's lawyers had appealed his conviction of May 1937 to the Supreme Military Tribunal (STM), which had final jurisdiction in national security cases. By July his chances for acquittal were good: both José Américo and Armando Sales pulled strings on his behalf, and public expectations (aroused by the press) created a propitious climate.[50] It may also be that Vargas favored the former mayor's release in order to heighten the tension in Rio politics, which it certainly did. It was a classic phrase in the populist-authoritarian counterpoint.

Pedro Ernesto's two loyal supporters throughout the trials had been Jones Rocha and Júlio Novaes, who had early thrown in with Armando Sales. While in jail, however, Pedro Ernesto remained neutral in the presidential contest in order not to jeopardize his case. When he was finally acquitted and released on 13 September, he was besieged with demands for a choice.[51] Supporters of both major candidates organized rallies the following day to celebrate his release and induce him to join their side. He spent the night drafting a vigorous speech condemning his enemies and dramatizing the suffering to which he had been subjected. At the last minute, however, aides convinced him to give a moderate speech consonant with his role as conciliator. Because the demonstrations had swelled to mass proportions, the city declared a holiday so that employees could attend. Tension mounted, for politics seemed to hinge on what Pedro Ernesto would say.

Crowds of well-wishers had massed at three principal sites: outside the mayor's hospital in Tijuca; in Plaza Onze, the traditional gathering point for samba groups; and in Castelo Esplanade, where the main speeches were to be made. When Pedro Ernesto left the hospital his car was pushed toward downtown by supporters. The crowds at Plaza Onze were too dense for the car to enter, so speeches were given without him. The caravan attracted more and more people as it moved down the Avenue, and a member of the Property Owners' Association remarked, "It's the revolution!" The main rally began when Pedro Ernesto arrived at the Esplanade. The samba leader Paulo da Portela led the national anthem, and then several deputies and councilmen welcomed their leader. Shouts of "José Américo and Pedro Ernesto" rang out. The former mayor was visibly weak when he took the microphone. He thanked the Tribunal for a just decision and the many newspapers for favorable coverage. He went on to stress that he could never have participated in the revolts of 1935 because, "I am not, was never, and will never be a communist." He ended his short speech by denouncing the current city administration as an "infamous intervention" and promising to take up the banner of autonomy again. "We do not possess arms nor do we desire them . . . because we have the great weapon of the vote to rid the city of its enemies." Exhausted, Pedro Ernesto was driven home.[52]

The rally and speech had an unsettling effect because Pedro Ernesto had failed to reveal his choice for the presidential election. For a week he rested and weighed the options. One would be to drop out of politics and allow his health and personal finances to recuperate. Later he could reenter, for his popularity had been manifest in the great rallies of the fourteenth. Another was to support José Américo, with whom most PADF politicians were already aligned. The last choice was to join Armando Sales's campaign, which had been gaining force in recent weeks. Pedro Ernesto chose the latter course, largely because Sales was the only person capable of defeating Vargas. There was no doubt that the president was maneuvering toward a coup, and the forces of São Paulo and Rio Grande were the only deterrents to its execution. Jóse Américo was pitifully weak, and his backers in Bahia and Pernambuco were on the defensive. Thus Pedro Ernesto joined the UDB in the final weeks of drift toward the authoritarian resolution.

Pedro Ernesto made public his decision to back Armando Sales in a dramatic rally in João Caetano Auditorium on 29 September. He recalled in his speech the social programs of the PADF, all of which had been consonant with the constitution. The cities of São Paulo and Rio had both undergone progressive health and education reforms in recent years, contributing to the welfare of the urban poor. He also mentioned his courageous campaign against the foreign oil companies on behalf of the populace. At the end of the speech he announced that if the UDB won in January he would return to the mayoralty of Rio. Thus Pedro Ernesto became a target of the coup proponents and inadvertently precipitated their plans.[53]

Whether or not Vargas intended it, Pedro Ernesto's release triggered the Estado Novo coup by creating a sense of political crisis in Rio. Maciel Filho, commenting on the rallies of 14 September, wrote: "The Avenue is full of people deliriously applauding Pedro Ernesto. Tens of thousands, without the least exaggeration. Absolved unanimously by the STM, he returns to be the boss of the city. . . . Conquistadores always joined combat to conquer lands, castles, and treasure. In Brazil candidates join battle to conquer the favelas. . . . The fight will be furious, the favela is at stake."[54] Military leaders took Pedro Ernesto's acquittal as an affront and held a counter-demonstration on 22 September to honor loyalist soldiers killed in the 1935 revolt. Pressure for tighter police controls also grew. A Minas political leader wrote later: "The release of Pedro Ernesto, received by boisterous popular demonstrations, was answered with the civic-military ceremony for those killed on 27 November 1935. That in turn gave rise to the call for a new state of siege, for federal control in Rio Grande, and . . . the stone rolled down the mountain." Populism created unrest that justified authoritarianism.[55]

Minister of War Eurico Dutra was a critical figure in the coup plans, and in the days following Pedro Ernesto's acquittal Vargas agents pressed Dutra to agree to call off the election. Finally, when asked directly by Vargas, he endorsed the plan, which included closing Congress and abrogating the 1934 Constitution. Dutra's decision was followed by a meeting of the general staff, in which he argued: "The communist documents are plentiful and explicit; the antagonistic attitudes of certain persons released from jail are public and self-evident; the street demonstrations are familiar to you all; the position taken by the press does not leave the slightest doubt about the danger." The references to Pedro Ernesto's acquittal and the subsequent rallies show that Dutra believed authoritarianism to be the antidote for a populist threat.[56]

Once Dutra agreed to the coup, the plans moved quickly. Releasing copies of a bogus communist conspiracy, the "Cohen Plan," the government obtained from Congress a new state of siege, the first act under which was an order for Pedro Ernesto's arrest. The former mayor and his son fled to São Paulo to escape the country but were apprehended and placed in a prison camp for four months. Filinto Muller became executor of the state of siege in Rio, joined by former police chief João Alberto and by Vargas's brother Benjamin. Many more persons who endangered their plans were sent to improvised prison camps. There was little anyone could do. A week before the coup was scheduled, José Américo and Armando Sales obtained incontrovertible evidence of a conspiracy. A manifesto against the plot was read in Congress and distributed in army barracks, forcing Vargas to move up his plans five days. On 10 November army units closed Congress, and Vargas presented a new constitution to his cabinet for ratification. That night Vargas went on the "Hora do Brasil" to justify the coup and outline the policies that would guide the Estado Novo. The authoritarian solution was nearly complete.[57]

The coming of the Estado Novo went back almost three years and was intertwined with the decline of the populist movement in Rio. To regard it as merely power politics ignores the important symbiotic relationship that developed between these two dominant modes of governance in modern Brazil. Other factors to be sure contributed to Vargas's rightward trend (e.g., the challenge in Rio Grande and São Paulo and the possibility of an army conspiracy), but the political by-play and rhetoric became a populist-authoritarian counterpoint. This dialectical relationship began in early 1935 when Pedro Ernesto turned his successful populist movement toward the left to counter growing police repression and the labor-leftist front led by Luís Carlos Prestes. The mayor achieved his aim, certainly with the backing and advice of Vargas. The latter, nonetheless, was charting an opposite course for his regime, toward an authoritarian state that would complement the corporatism embodied in most social and bureaucratic reforms of the 1930s. His long-range goals were to curb regional power bases such as those in the south and to bring state institutions fully under his control. The 1935 populist-socialist episode in Rio was clearly a tactical diversion, looking at Vargas's strategy in hindsight.

Nevertheless, the little-known story of Pedro Ernesto's popularity and defense throughout 1936 and 1937 indicates that populism had become firmly based by that time. It not only existed but resisted, and Pedro Ernesto remained one of the most popular men in Brazil during his prosecution. That was precisely why José Américo chose to attempt a populist campaign in 1937. The populist-authoritarian relationship is also important because most accounts of the Estado Novo attribute it to Machiavellian intrigues, imitation of European fascism, or the communist threat. This chapter argues instead that authoritarianism (especially of those other than Vargas) emerged as much to counter populist recruitment as any other cause. In the eyes of authoritarians, populists dangerously mobilized the masses and pitted them against the established order. We have seen that that was not true, and Vargas himself would turn to populism within several years.

9 Epilogue: Populism During the Estado Novo

Despite the predominantly authoritarian character of the Estado Novo, an undercurrent of populism persisted and grew. This little studied part of the story is important because it reveals Getúlio Vargas's adoption of the populist style for which he later became famous. Also during this period populism moved from city to national politics, where by 1945 it would constitute a major new source of votes. Thus, during the Estado Novo the populist-authoritarian counterpoint became firmly established in Brazilian political culture. Vargas was the central figure of this new phase, gradually building (with the aid of his labor ministry) a charismatic authority among the working class. Paradoxically, as national politics drifted toward Vargas's own populist experiment, local affairs were kept tightly leashed by the new mayor.

Henrique Dodsworth had been sworn in as interventor-mayor of Rio in July, a position he held for eight years. He was chosen by Vargas largely to stabilize and if possible depoliticize local administration while the Estado Novo conspiracy ran its course. Dodsworth was nearly the opposite of Pedro Ernesto, and appropriately his job was to demobilize political groups. Vargas trusted Dodsworth's administrative abilities, demonstrated in the finance commission of the Chamber for many years. Moreover, Dodsworth was exceptionally weak by 1937 and would probably not be re-elected to Congress. Vargas's choice resembled other instances when he selected able but politically weak men whom he could control, such as Benedito Valadares for Minas in 1933. Beholden to few others, Dodsworth faithfully served the president throughout the Estado Novo.[1]

Dodsworth's long administration was characterized by fiscal austerity and reduced commitments to social programs. As his biographer said, "given the great undertakings of Pedro Ernesto, unexpectedly brought to an end by political and financial crises, it was not strange that the city should revert to lean times." Spending was cut back and the city collected budget surpluses for the next eight years. In addition, the hospital and welfare programs were decentralized to prevent their misuse for political ends. The public works expenditures were shifted from the development of parks and gardens to the building of roads, most of which benefited residents of the South Zone. It was definitely a reversion to a pre–1930 type of municipal administration, in which Dodsworth emulated his uncle Paulo de Frontin.[2]

The centerpiece of Dodsworth's term was President Vargas Avenue, a grand boulevard built perpendicular to Rio Branco Avenue, decongesting downtown and serving as a traffic artery to the North Zone and Subúrbios. The project, first recommended by Agache, necessitated razing 525 buildings between 1941 and 1944, including 4 churches, 6 banks, and a marketplace. The project proved controversial, especially the sacrifice of historic buildings and means of indemnification, but in the end it met its proposed objectives. The imitation of Frontin, who directed the Avenida Central work, was obvious, as was the effort to aggrandize Vargas's reputation. By the early 1940s, in fact, a conscious effort was made to generate popularity for the president.[3]

Dodsworth had few political functions throughout the Estado Novo since elections were not held and no legislature existed. To be sure he found jobs for most of the *chefes* and *cabos*, who gravitated to Dodsworth the way they had toward Frontin, but there was little need for patronage politics. Instead the mayor worked long hours at his desk, much as Vargas did, even foregoing the customary summers in Petropolis. So lackluster was the city government that one of Vargas's cronies complained that it was *detracting* from the president's popularity. But the focus of politics was on the national level: Vargas even got credit for the long awaited electrification of the Central do Brasil lines, completed between 1937 and 1945. Dodsworth, fifty years old at the end of his term, was unable to continue his career any longer, and he went to Portugal as ambassador. The populist way of politics in Rio had completely bypassed him.[4]

Yet populism was alive and well, as signaled by the huge crowds that assembled for Pedro Ernesto's funeral. He died in August 1942, a victim of cancer at the age of fifty-eight. He had suffered much during the Estado Novo. For three years he had defended himself against charges of graft in a trial that drained his personal wealth; he lost his share of the Casa de Saúde and was obliged to practice in another clinic. In 1939 he and six

EDIÇÃO DAS 5 HORAS DA TARDE

DIRECTORES: CANDIDO CAMPOS JOAQUIM DE SALLES

A NOTICIA

FUNDADOR: OLIVEIRA ROCHA

SÉDE: AV. RIO BRANCO, 134

ANNO XLV — RIO DE JANEIRO, SEXTA-FEIRA, 19 DE JULHO DE 1940 — NUMERO 545

NA GUERRA A HESPANHA

Presume-se que Franco pretende sahir das difficuldades internas com que se acha em lucta, auxiliando a Allemanha a conquistar Gibraltar

Esperados dentro de vinte e quatro horas acontecimentos de transcendental importancia

WASHINGTON, 19 (United Press) – Informações diplomaticas chegadas a esta capital dizem que podem ser esperados, dentro das proximas vinte e quatro horas, acontecimentos de transcendental importancia na politica externa da Hespanha.

Ao que se soube, esses acontecimentos estariam relacionados com a posição da Hespanha diante da guerra européa, presumindo-se que o general Franco, premido pelos elementos favoraveis á Allemanha e Italia, chefiados pelo sr. Serrano Suner, talvez declare a Hespanha em guerra com a Inglaterra, para contornar certas difficuldades internas decorrentes de uma negativa de passagem ás tropas allemãs para o ataque a Gibraltar.

General Franco

REUNE-SE HOJE O REICHSTAG

O governo fará uma declaração

BERLIM, 19 — (United Press) — A D. N. B. deu a conhecer o seguinte communicado do marechal Goering, presidente do Reichstag allemão: "Hoje, ás 19 horas, reunir-se-á o Reichstag. Na Ordem do Dia figura uma declaração do governo germanico. A sessão será transmittida por todas as emissoras allemãs.

ESCOLAS E HOSPITAES!

Enaltecida pelo Club de Engenharia a administração do dr. Pedro Ernesto

Em sessão solemne, ser-lhe-á entregue o premio que conquistou, por votação unanime, em reconhecimento pelos serviços prestados á cidade

O ex-prefeito dr. Pedro Ernesto

REJEITADA A PAZ DE HITLER

LONDRES, 19 (United Press) – Durante as duas ultimas semanas, o governo britannico rejeitou categoricamente tres propostas de paz da Allemanha.

Os circulos britannicos assignalam que o facto de insistir o sr. Hitler em seus esforços para persuadir a Inglaterra a negociar a paz reforça a crença de que o Reich se debilita á medida que os dias passam, e que o sr. Hitler comprehende que não poderá sahir victorioso em uma guerra prolongada.

Batalha naval no Mediterraneo

LONDRES, 19 — (United Press) — O almirantado annuncia que em uma batalha naval travada no Mediterraneo o cruzador australiano "Sydney" afundou o cruzador italiano "Bartolomeo Colleone".

Headline in *A Noticia* recalls schools and hospitals built during the Pedro Ernesto administration.

others finally were acquitted in a decision that most people regarded as fair.[5] After all, Pedro Ernesto's transgressions had been political, not criminal. In the last two years of his life Pedro Ernesto did all he could to get Brazil into World War II on the side of the Allies. Upon his return from a medical examination in New York he gave his last speech, in which he praised the U.S. role in the conflict and called for unity in the Americas against the Axis. He died just two weeks before Brazil declared war.

The enormous crowds that turned out for his funeral were the largest since the demonstrations of 1937. One newspaper called it the longest procession the city had ever seen. Poor people from the samba groups and favelas walked among the limousines of the cortege, carrying messages of homage to the former mayor. *Time* magazine called him the best loved man in Brazil, pointing to the masses of poor who joined the funeral. A carnival verse was composed:

> Your Honor understood, the poor were without cheer,
> They needed Carnival at least three days a year.
> For that I raise three shouts, to echo evermore,
> "Viva Pedro Ernesto! Viva the Interventor!
> Viva our revolution, he's our beloved defender."

Newspapers from all over the country carried the story of his death and funeral, and religious masses in his honor continued through October.[6]

Vargas, who along with some of his top officials avoided the funeral, was devising a populist strategy for the elections that would be held following the war. Put simply, Vargas elicited the allegiance of the working class through social legislation and publicity without using party recruitment or elections. Just as Pedro Ernesto had done, Vargas developed a charismatic image as father of the poor *(pai dos pobres)*, causing the masses to trust him. They came to believe in his dedication to their well-being, which strengthened the legitimacy of the president. In order to analyze this major change in Vargas's leadership and authority, we will examine social legislation and government relations with the working class for the origins of Vargas's populism. We will also look at the publicity methods he used to draw the people closer to him.

The growing importance of labor and social legislation in Vargas's administration was evident in the responsibilities given to the labor ministers. The first was Agamemnon Magalhães, a tough and effective politician from Ceará who held the post from 1934 until 1937. He laid the groundwork for implementing one of the ministry's long-range goals, turning satisfied social security members into pro-Vargas voters. One of his major accomplishments was a census of industrial workers for subsequent organization in 1938 into the single largest social security institute, the IAPI, that in turn became a model for other institutes. By 1939 the IAPI membership reached eight hundred thousand, about half of all persons covered by social security.[7] Magalhães, in the latter years of his term, covered justice in addition to labor and coordinated the Estado Novo conspiracy.

The next minister of labor, Waldemar Falcão (1937–41), consolidated earlier programs without undertaking many new ones himself. A lawyer who in 1932 had participated with Pedro Ernesto in the formulation of the tenente program, Falcão canceled all syndicate registrations and carried out new ones designed not only to enhance the government's influence in the sector but to eliminate unviable groups. Falcão also oversaw the formation of three institutes, including the IAPI, and introduced better management of social security assets. Finally, he created a minimum wage system and set up a judiciary for hearing labor grievances, entirely separate from the regular courts. It is noteworthy that Falcão appeared little in public ceremonies, allowing Vargas to reap the popularity for social legislation.[8]

By 1941 Vargas was ready to give greater prominence to his labor program, and this was carried out by the new minister, Alexandre Marcondes Filho, a Paulista lawyer and politician. Marcondes instructed his staff to codify all labor and social security legislation, as had been promised in 1930. The result was the 1943 Consolidation of Labor Laws (CLT). Marcondes also became political coordinator for Vargas. There had been no minister of justice since the resignation of Francisco Campos in mid–1941, and Marcondes was made acting minister of justice in a July 1942 cabinet shakeup, a post he occupied until March 1945.[9] Unlike his predecessor, he assumed an active role in public life, filling in for Vargas at labor rallies and broadcasting the benefits of the regime to the working class. He probably drafted Vargas's labor addresses, and he gave scores of speeches on the "Hora do Brasil" praising the president's government and publicizing the social advances. In several cabinet changes and confrontations between 1942 and 1945 Marcondes nearly always won. During the postwar transition of March 1945, the justice ministry was given to Agamemnon Magalhães, a former minister of labor; the fusion of political and labor affairs was nearly complete.[10]

Brazil had gotten a bad reputation internationally from the mid–1930s repression of labor and the left, followed by the fascistic Estado Novo Constitution, so after 1940 Vargas began to pay more attention to foreign opinion. It was natural that he should choose to emphasize labor and social advances which helped assuage the dictatorial image abroad. He sent the eminent constitutional lawyer Pontes de Miranda to the International Labor Conference, held in New York in late 1941, with instructions to give a favorable picture of his social programs and to avoid criticism of Brazil in the sessions. At the same time, the ministry began submitting articles and news about Brazilian labor law to the ILO for publication in the *International Labor Review* (London). The material published was legalistic and designed to heighten Vargas's reputation. Vargas was steadily creating a charismatic authority based on benevolence toward the working class.[11]

In labor ministry broadcasts, speeches, press releases, and in its *Boletim* (circulation 100,000), Vargas received credit for every detail of work accomplished on labor's behalf. Vargas was always referred to as a great benefactor, a man of supreme insight into the national conscience, whose spirit was present in all articles of social legislation. He granted benefits to the workers and personally signed every decree in their favor. He was also portrayed as a political genius, implying that the people could follow him without regard to representative institutions or elections. As Vargas said, the people "don't satisfy hunger with the right to vote nor educate their children with the freedom of assembly."[12]

Social legislation composed most of the domestic output of the government in the early 1940s, and the Ministry of Labor was its executor. It was accompanied by systematic efforts to create and mold public opinion favorable to the regime and to Vargas in particular. During the authoritarian period from 1935 to 1939, police had concentrated on censoring adverse news and had used official channels for public announcements of an informative nature. Censorship was detested by the press, and a strong aversion to the regime developed among intellectuals. In late 1939 Vargas changed tack and began to offer positive inducements for cooperation from writers and journalists. In response to a major protest against censorship in December, he moved the old publicity and censorship agency from the police to the presidency and changed its name to Department of Press and Publicity (DIP). The first director of the DIP was thirty-nine-year-old Lourival Fontes.[13]

A lawyer and writer from the state of Sergipe, Fontes had migrated to Rio in the 1920s, helped by the prominent Amado family. Like so many other provincials he took a job with the city, becoming chief of the tourism department. Not inclined to make trouble, he rode out the difficult years of the revolution and participated in Sales Filho's experiments with radio and publicity. Fontes also wrote for newspapers on the side, which had occasioned his signing the censorship protest in 1939. Fontes's principal attributes for director of the DIP were writing ability, no political ambitions, and flexible political standards. As heir to the Sales

Filho operation of the mid–1930s, Fontes took over the "Hora do Brasil" broadcasts, tourist promotion, foreign press relations, censorship, and government publications.[14]

The DIP proved more acceptable to the press under Fontes's leadership because he was imbued with both positive and negative sanctions with which to exert influence. Crude harrassment of the press became rarer after 1940, and the government began subsidizing the cost of newsprint (and hence publishers' profits). Many intellectuals agreed to write anonymous articles praising Vargas and his regime in exchange for substantial commissions. Official releases by DIP, meanwhile, emphasized wartime problems or political crises. DIP also published books lauding the social and labor programs of the government. In short, it became a fairly sophisticated propaganda agency, comparable to its Italian counterpart in the 1920s. Fontes was wrongly identified with a pro-Axis position in 1942 and was obliged to resign during the cabinet reorganization of July. His next post, as delegate to the ILO headquarters in Montreal, undoubtedly revealed the growing association of labor and publicity in Vargas's mind.[15]

Vargas almost never spoke openly or in private about his political strategies or preferences, leaving contemporaries (and historians) only external evidence from which to reconstruct his thoughts. Presidential addresses are one of the best indications of the growing indentification of labor, politics, and publicity during the Estado Novo. Vargas was a skillful speaker according to a contemporary publicity specialist who has compared his radio talks to the Roosevelt fireside chats.[16] I have scanned some thirty speeches Vargas made to labor between 1930 and 1945 for three specific elements: for identification of the "people" in the populist sense that we have used the term; for references to self; and for slogans that indicate a relationship between people and self.

Over the fifteen years of Vargas's first administration, he continually spoke to the working classes about his social and labor programs. The references to labor benefits and social harmony were consistent from the 1930 speech on the Castelo Esplanade until his resignation communique in 1945, but the manner in which he identified the beneficiaries of his programs changed noticeably. Through 1938 he addressed his labor speeches to the *provo brasileiro,* or "Brazilian people." Only once did he refer to class and that was in 1932 when he addressed the *classes trabalhadoras*, or "laboring classes." It seems clear that he wished to avoid references that might indicate a divergence of interests between classes, a concept that he always explicitly refuted.

In 1938 he began addressing them as *trabalhadores do Brasil,* or "workers of Brazil"; the first time he gave the term prominence was during an impromptu speech to workers in São Paulo, whom he called *trabalhadores de São Paulo.*[17] By 1940 "workers of Brazil" became his exclusive way of addressing labor, and soon it was rendered an incantation to the masses. It must be recalled that many middle-sector employees—clerks, civil servants, teachers, and so forth—could identify themselves with the masses because they had received substantial benefits from the social legislation in force. Therefore Vargas created his "people" in the late 1930s from the working class and the lower levels of the middle sectors, from whom he elicited charismatic authority.

Vargas's verbalization of self was also indicative of an emerging populist relationship with the masses. In the early 1930s he chose such impersonal terms as "my government," "my acts as head of state," "the acts of the government," "our organization," "our will." The most frequent was "my government." However, in the impromptu speech in São Paulo in 1938 he used "I" several times. Thereafter the singular personal pronoun became more frequent, although the plural never disappeared. In addition, the approximation with the masses was explicit in his press conference statement of early 1944: he wished to eliminate intermediaries between the people and the government and to run an "open door" administration. The culmination of the increasing grammatical proximity between Vargas and the "people" came in his 1 May 1945 speech when he began, "Workers of Brazil! *Here I am at your side* to join in the commemoration of Labor Day."[18] Although Vargas never recorded his ideas about such matters, it is clear in retrospect that he was creating a new personal self available to the masses as the "father of the poor" to be the recipient of charismatic authority.

The slogans in his various speeches also show Vargas's emerging populism. Nationalism was, of course, always present in his labor addresses. A principal message through 1940, and especially during the authoritarian period, was for the patriotic worker to beware of seduction by insincere politicians and leftist ideologues. Rather, he stressed, the dignity of the citizen came from work. Two slogans of 1940 may be regarded as representative: "Order and work" and "Union and work." By 1944 a new message, that of economic nationalism, had emerged that would infuse his speeches for the next ten years. Typical were the search for "economic emancipation of the country" and the desire to "combat economic colonialism."[19] By extension, Vargas told the working class that by following him it would be assured employment with dignity and just wages and benefits. The threat was no longer foreign ideologies but international monopolies. Vargas was the man who could be trusted to defend the interests of the masses.

What, then, can be concluded of Vargas's early 1940s strategy of employing labor policy and publicity for political ends? First, he was unquestionably preparing for a populist movement similar to Pedro Ernesto's a decade earlier. The proof of the pudding would be the December 1945 elections, but the approach was unmistakable. The multiclass nature of his growing support was observed by many. A German political scientist visiting from the United States noted: "Perhaps the most striking feature of present day Brazil—and one that is universally admitted—is that Vargas personally and the regime in general are extremely popular among the laboring masses. Vargas has won the soul of the common man."[20] An article by a leftist writer came to much the same conclusion. The middle class had been divided about the Estado Novo, he wrote, but soon they began to accept the regime because their interests were satisfied. Moreover, "since a year ago the president has the support of the masses as no other did before him."[21] It was clear that the middle sectors backed Vargas for reasons of self-interest while the masses responded to the charisma fostered by the Ministry of Labor and the DIP. Finally, Vargas enjoyed the support of a coterie of industrialists and merchants who prospered from the wartime economy. As cynics quipped, he was "father of the poor and mother of the rich," but by being the president of all the classes Vargas was becoming a populist.

A second conclusion to be drawn from Vargas's labor and publicity activities was that he intended to remain in office after the war by creating a labor party. To be sure, little mention of what came to be the Brazilian Labor Party (PTB, 1945–65) was made before the close of the war, but the direction of Vargas's policies was unmistakable.[22] As was seen in chapter 6, Vargas recognized the growing role that urban voters would play in politics and had backed Pedro Ernesto's populist experiment in order to win support for himself. By the early 1940s cities with more than twenty thousand inhabitants held over a sixth of the population and were growing much faster than the national average. An urban populist strategy, then, was all the more attractive to Vargas in order to complement his network of traditional politicians. It is unthinkable that Vargas would dedicate such time and resources to labor without a political motive, that is, the creation of mass popularity for eventual electoral use. The question was one of timing, and by 1943 a schedule was emerging.

Marcondes Filho and Vargas hinted at an administration timetable in late 1943. Throughout most of the year a strong push had been underway to register workers with the government-recognized syndicates in anticipation of using work cards for voter qualification. In November they announced that at the end of the war new voting rules would be promulgated for holding a plebiscite and general elections. To sweeten the news Vargas decreed increases in the minimum wage and in civil servant salaries, along with other labor benefits. The following April he promised a return to democracy after the achievement of peace. As the war came to a close in Europe, political spies from across the country sent Vargas reports, and collaborators began giving advice, solicited and unsolicited, regarding the transition to constitutional government. Most perceptive, from the populist point of view, was the advice of Francisco Campos: Vargas's best strategy would be to lead the opposition *against* the government.[23] Given his attempt to curry multiclass backing for eventual elections, Vargas could best succeed by expanding his promises from social programs to democratic freedoms, much as Pedro Ernesto had done in 1935. But Vargas persisted in maintaining dictatorial controls through the police and DIP, providing easy targets for the opposition. In other words, the populist-authoritarian counterpoint was becoming stronger, but Vargas's ear did not pick it up.

Demands for Vargas's resignation arose in all quarters, including the army, and the president was caught in a trap of his own making, similar to that of 1937: by instinct he wished to stay in power, but he was unable to declare his candidacy. It was an unenviable situation, for this time the army wanted him removed.[24] Marcondes proposed that Vargas be nominated by the workers, or "the people," who would be mobilized by the Ministry of Labor. His draft manifestoes to that effect, dated late December 1944, called for Vargas to serve a new presidential term after 1945. One went on to laud Vargas in familiar ministry language: "President Vargas gave the country [social] legislation which puts us in the vanguard of civilized peoples and on defense against demands which in other countries have provoked crises." A second version, apparently addressed to the middle sectors, stated that "The entire nation . . . is deeply and totally convinced that Getúlio Vargas . . . in virtue of his past record and his political wisdom, is the individual most capable of leading the country through times as difficult as those in today's and tomorrow's world."[25] These manifestoes, if distributed by the ministry, would have been signed by millions of persons. The differing language of the documents indicates that Marcondes and probably Vargas intentionally sought support from the lower and middle strata, a populist strategy. In December 1944, however, Vargas shied away from this approach and the manifestoes were not used.

During the ten months Vargas held office in 1945 he demonstrated a continuing lack of nerve and grasp of populist strategy, despite excellent intelligence and advice from insiders. For example, his daughter Alzira and crony Maciel Filho told him of intrigues in his cabinet and false friends, and there is no doubt that by early 1945 the number of his genuine supporters was becoming small. In this situation, Vargas would have enjoyed far more advantage outside the presidency or at least, as Compos counseled, if he had pressed for political liberties while attacking authoritarian elements in the government. Indeed, Vargas several times considered resigning so that he could join the "people," but he never did.[26] The antitrust law of June 1945 also revealed Vargas's ambivalence. Drafted by the new minister of justice, Agamemnon Magalhães, it required all corporate entities to be approved by the government, which was empowered to break up monopolies and companies that enjoyed unfair competitive advantage. The law especially scrutinized corporations with foreign ties, suggesting that Vargas was about to implement his promised economic nationalism. Yet he did little to defend the law against detractors, and even after entering into force it was not used.[27] Vargas had cut off potential backing from the business community without compensating with new labor and leftist support. The antitrust law echoed Pedro Ernesto's 1935 call for nationalizing basic utilities and regulating foreign conglomerates, but Vargas was unwilling to stand by it. After his ouster it would be a different story.

Vargas's relationship to Luís Carlos Prestes was yet another failure of nerve. Urged to release political prisoners by the U.S. State Department, Vargas pardoned a number of persons in April and May, including Prestes. The latter soon came out in support of Vargas and collaborated with the labor party being formed, indicating that the two saw their interests as parallel for the time being. Yet Vargas did not make any shift to the left that might win over those who admired the tenente hero of the 1920s. Prestes worked with the system for six months until he was elected to the Senate on the Communist party ticket, which was the major beneficiary of the leftist resurgence after 1945. It is evident that Vargas, like Pedro Ernesto in 1935, wished to co-opt the left, but his unwillingness to follow through undermined these efforts. The *queremista* ("We want Getúlio") demonstrations staged by the labor ministry and the PCB in late 1945 were transparent maneuvers that did not enhance Vargas's charisma. Prestes, on the other hand, became the best-known communist leader in the hemisphere.[28]

The final way in which Vargas failed to utilize populism advantageously was his continued reliance on police repression despite mounting pressure for a return to political freedom. From July 1944 until March 1945 Coriolano de Góes (police chief under Washington Luís) was in command of the Rio police, after earning a bloody reputation as head of the São Paulo security forces. Students dubbed the police "Góestapo" due to his strong-arm measures. When a relaxation became inevitable in 1945, Vargas appointed João Alberto, another veteran of the post. The DIP too kept tight controls over publishing until February 1945, causing a number of newsmen to become "martyrs for freedom" by forcing them to write on restricted topics before the inevitable lifting of censorship. Indeed, the final act that triggered the coup of October 1945 against Vargas was the appointment of his brother Benjamin as police chief and João Alberto as mayor of Rio.[29] Apart from the conspiratorial aspects of these appointments, they continued the unacceptably authoritarian controls in effect since the mid–1930s. In fact, Vargas erred by trying to intone both lines of the populist-authoritarian counterpoint.

The election returns of 1945 revealed Vargas's successes and failures in trying to create a populist movement. Since he was not a candidate, we must analyze the results by party and state.[30] The PTB, like its sponsor the Ministry of Labor, barely existed outside the states of Rio and São Paulo, where it received over 60 percent of its votes. This showed Vargas's wisdom in appointing a Paulista minister of labor in 1941, who would revitalize the agency's operations in the country's leading industrial center. The PTB took the largest share in any single state by winning 27 percent in Rio; nationwide its portion was ten percent. It was aided by a pledge from official candidate Eurico Dutra to consult the party on the appointment of the labor minister and to honor all social legislation on the books.[31] The PTB's chief rival was the Communist party because they both vied for the working-class vote. The PCB ran best in Rio (20 percent) and São Paulo (14 percent), and it came out only one point below the PTB in the overall returns. Therefore, the ambivalent association of Vargas with Prestes failed and the labor vote was rather equally divided between the two charismatic figures.

The next major election, that of January 1947 for state assemblies, demonstrated that Vargas out of power was more effective than in power because the PTB (with which the public now identified him) picked up one hundred thirty thousand votes, the only important party to grow. The PCB remained stable between the two elections, while the others declined in absolute and relative terms. The PTB was definitely a mobilization party similar to the Autonomist party of the 1930s because in the postwar period it tripled its electorate while the other parties stagnated or declined.

Rio continued to be the proving ground for populist politics after 1945. With Vargas gone and a government in power that was unsympathetic to labor, the PCB as an opposition party gained a substantial lead over the PTB in the capital. In the state assembly elections of 1947 the communists received 25 percent of the vote compared to the PTB's 20 percent, and they held a plurality of seats. For a time Vargas and Prestes played a cagy game with one another, vying for leadership of the working class, but in 1947 the PCB was outlawed and the following year communists were removed from elective office, effectively ending their challenge of Vargas's popularity among the masses. The PTB was the principal beneficiary of the closure of the PCB.[32]

Vargas also crossed swords with another charismatic figure, Adhemar de Barros, the lawyer-politician who had served as interventor in São Paulo State between 1937 and 1941. As the Estado Novo drew to a close in 1944, Adhemar recognized that authoritarianism was on the wane, and he built a reputation as a man of the people who favored leftist causes. Without risking trouble with the police, he said that the people wanted "another kind of democracy." He was the most popular man in the Paulista capital by the time the war ended, especially among workers. In 1947 he ran for governor on his own party ticket and defeated the Vargas-PTB candidate handily. Vargas had wished to ensure the hegemony of his party in São Paulo, the only other city with over a million inhabitants and an important base for his political future. Adhemar dueled with Vargas for the next several years, but finally in 1950 he traded his party's votes for the vice presidency and the two senatorial seats from Rio.[33] The details of the maneuvering (which included a fascinating role for the PCB) do not require analysis here; suffice it to say that Vargas, although undoubtedly the most popular man in Brazil, had much to learn about new forms of populism evolving in Rio and São Paulo.

Through the early 1950s urban politics continued to follow the pattern of the 1930s, awarding large numbers of votes to the man who could build a multiclass coalition of the middle and working sectors. Integrative populism of the sort Pedro Ernesto pioneered still worked because no single stratum had sufficient votes to win elections, at least not nationally. By 1955, however, the urban working-class vote had become large and predictable enough to be courted on its own, creating a shift from mass- to class-based urban politics. Candidates and parties increasingly addressed narrower interests and evoked class antagonism. This new form of populism, termed syndicalist by Francisco Weffort and Peronist by Di Tella, was far more complicated and even dangerous than the multiclass integrative variety.[34] It opened a new phase of urban politics that ended with the military takeover of 1964.

The populist-authoritarian counterpoint in this new phase was far more strident: by the time of Vargas's death the military had become the guardian against leftist and class-based politics and intervened in every presidential succession. It is uncertain whether the old style populism was still viable. Jânio Quadros employed it in 1960, but he soon resigned, vainly trying to circumvent opposition in Brasília. Goulart encountered such obstacles in 1963, which contributed to his shift to the left and the 1964 coup. Casual analysis suggests that the old form of populism was no longer workable; but such speculation takes us beyond the scope of this chapter, the intent of which has been to identify the origins of Vargas's populism during the Estado Novo.

Vargas's conscious effort to create a charismatic authority among working class voters in the early 1940s was unmistakably based on the experience of Pedro Ernesto as mayor of Rio from 1931 to 1936. Vargas chose labor rather than health and education as his social program (a division between municipal and federal responsibilities existent in the 1930s), but its use for political ends was nearly identical. Thus it was the labor ministry that provided the recruitment work that had been earlier performed by Pedro Ernesto's Autonomist party. The sectors of the population targeted and the means of recruitment were virtually the same. Both men, likewise, made much use of newly available mass media. Vargas became the protector of the poor, the defender against foreign exploitation, the trustworthy and beneficent leader, the man of the people—all images that had been utilized by Pedro Ernesto in the 1930s.[35] The borrowing was naturally unacknowledged: Pedro Ernesto's removal from the public eye in the late 1930s and his death in 1942 allowed Vargas to make the transition from dictator to populist without much awkwardness.

Yet others also perceived the possibilities of populist recruitment and style, which became the dominant mode of urban politics between 1945 and 1964. The legacy of social planning from the 1930s and the universal projection of Vargas's paternalistic image gave him a decided advantage among the 1950s populists. Nonetheless, Vargas himself fumbled at times, misunderstanding the dynamics of populism or not overcoming his autocratic preferences. Despite his grand skills in politics he was fallible, and others were anxious to attack him. His last failure led to suicide in 1954. From then on populism evolved into more sophisticated forms but usually played out themes first raised in the 1920s and 1930s with the rise of urban politics.

10 Conclusion: City and State in Modern Brazil

The genesis of urban politics in the 1920s and the subsequent rise of populism as a dominant form of leadership have been the central themes of this book. The city educated and socialized migrants, who then began participating in voluntary associations and elections. Reform became a major goal of the urban voter, who sought to make the government responsive to emerging social groups and their problems. Vargas's first administration drew heavily on urban reformism when it overhauled the state following the 1930 revolution. Yet the 1930s and early 1940s were among the most trying times in modern history, and the creation of a new state capable of governing Rio and other huge cities was neither peaceful nor entirely successful. On the one hand, the rapid mobilization of a populist electorate representing all strata of society did not create a true citizenry; rather, it gave the vote to multitudes who might be swayed by ambitious politicians. On the other hand, conservative forces arose to take firm control of the government and to reform the state from the top down. The interaction of these two trends gave rise to a populist-authoritarian rivalry that is perhaps the most important legacy of the era.

The rise of urban politics was not an automatic response to industrial and demographic growth—instead, it was created by flesh-and-blood men and their ideas and the interplay between them. The way urbanites saw themselves as grouped into classes with differential shares of income, power, and prestige also affected the emerging politics. As the working class grew, it could no longer be taken for granted. Popular leaders of all sorts harangued and convinced the poor to join unions and mutual aid societies in order to improve their standard of living. In the 1920s it was difficult to sustain labor militancy, but certainly the spread of voluntary associations throughout the working class presaged greater mass participation in public life. Some members of the elite recognized the need for reform, as did the middle sectors who would be the administrators of programs for the poor. If any single cause for the rise of urban politics existed, it was the desire of citizens to correct the ills caused by the republican generation and to restore the autonomous, socially holistic, and representative tradition of former times.

The rejuvenation of traditional urban politics preceded and contributed indirectly to the revolution of 1930, an event which is gradually being demoted in historiographical importance. The role of cities in the revolution was neither direct nor simple, however. The rapid increase in voters in Rio that had occurred between 1926 and 1930 was due to interest-group electoral activities superimposed over the traditional clientelism of the *chefes* and the *cabos*. By definition the new politics addressed broader issues, most of which spoke to labor, civil service, business, and city planning concerns. Both candidates for the presidency in 1930 promised to enact reforms favored by urban voters, despite the fact that the latter still counted little in numerical terms. The new urban politics most influenced the rhetoric of national politics, providing more complex issues than before.

Getúlio Vargas was billed as a reform candidate in 1930, but paradoxically he lost in Rio's election. His popularity among the middle sectors and the poor was offset by the organized labor vote, which expected greater benefits from the official nominee. When Vargas came to power eight months later at the head of an armed revolt, he faced such formidable problems nationally that urban politics were relegated to a minor position. He did, however, have a genuine commitment to labor and social reform, which was manifested during the early 1930s in the new labor and education ministries and in his alliance with the tenente movement. That they were used to fortify Vargas's position need not detract from his interest in their programs. Experiments in recruitment of urban support for his regime led directly to populism.

Vargas's encouragement of the tenente party (led by Pedro Ernesto) and his sponsorship of official unions that could be manipulated by the labor ministry were essential mechanisms for the emergence of populism. They also, in an improvised way, contributed to reshaping the state, which hitherto had discouraged both labor and urban political movements. The state gradually became corporatist during the 1930s by organizing agencies and bureaucracies that would manage new urban interests from the top down. During the transition to autocratic rule corporatism and populism coexisted, both attempting to conciliate class relations. As a number of authors have argued recently, no necessary antagonism exists between the two phenomena, one of which is a structure of government, the other a means of electoral recruitment.[1] The proper emphasis is on the urban nature of both.

Social programs undertaken in the 1930s broadened the purview of the state markedly: whereas the pre–1930 regimes were characterized by a view that the "social question is a police matter," later politicians chose the social question for innovations that would appeal to the masses. In the case of Vargas, the goal was to make private decision makers, especially employers and workers, subject to government supervision in exchange for federal protection and favors. The latter included social security coverage for most urban laborers and employees; official tutelage of unions and employer associations; police repression of militant and leftist leaders; class representation in Congress; and collaboration with the church's social goals. The first two programs, begun by Minister of Labor Lindolfo Color, followed the 1930 Liberal Alliance platform and were direct responses to reform sentiments of the 1920s. After Color resigned, the top-down corporatist approach prevailed. Although the model was not implemented as fully as in Europe (much of the 1937 Constitution was ignored, for example), corporatism does explain the broader outlines and intent of Vargas's social programs.

Pedro Ernesto's career in Rio politics, as interventor and mayor (1931–36), provided the first glimpse of a style of politics that became widespread after the war. His administration built schools and hospitals in the lower-class districts and Subúrbios concomitant with electoral recruitment in those zones. The school program was directed by Anísio Teixeira, a reformer deeply influenced by the social critics of the 1920s and by the U.S. progressive education movement. Teixeira overhauled Rio's school system and created a university and a cultural service. Despite these praiseworthy undertakings, Teixeira fell victim to a rightist upsurge in 1935; his ideas, however, influenced a generation of Brazilian educators and intellectuals. The hospital program was managed by Pedro Ernesto, who drew on experience operating his own downtown clinic. The facilities he built even today form the core of Rio's public health system. In addition, the mayor supervised a united charity agency. Populism needed no preconceived design of the state, and Pedro Ernesto's programs were eclectic and cumulative, much as were Franklin Roosevelt's in the 1930s.[2]

Urban class structure yielded to Vargas's corporatist and Pedro Ernesto's populist politics. The elite grudgingly accepted Vargas's leadership in credit, trade, and labor policy and took part in the various business-government commissions formed in the period. Vargas had never hesitated to protect Brazilian producers from the ravages of the Depression and international competition, but the beneficiaries of federal protection usually disliked the required state intervention in the economy. To members of old wealthy families Vargas was a product of small town, borderlands society who could never be more than a political opportunist. Nonetheless, they worked with him during the 1930s because no other form of leadership was available. This was in part because their vision of the state, as manifested in the Economist platform of 1933 and 1934, was laissez faire and antiquated. By 1937 most businessmen and wealthy persons realized that their fortunes would be best served by working with Vargas. A comparison of the 1920 and 1940 censuses suggests that Rio's elite made the right choice: Brazilian nationals had accounted for only 17 percent of the city's industrial capital in 1920, but by 1940 they controlled 44 percent and shared ownership in another 8 percent. Brazilians also gained control over commercial establishments in about the same proportion, with a tendency to form large Brazilian-foreign firms. Thus the elite acceptance of Vargas, after a long period of estrangement, initiated a mutually beneficial relationship.[3]

Rio's middle sectors grew dramatically during the 1930s, as was seen in table 4, yet by the early 1940s they no longer unequivocally championed reform causes. Certainly such programs had given them new jobs and protection, since the most rapidly expanding areas were social and educational services. In addition, middle sector employees gained universal social security coverage in the 1930s, with privileged benefits subsidized by the treasury.[4] Pedro Ernesto was a pioneer in this regard, by providing pensions for city employees disabled by common diseases, civil servant status to teachers and day laborers, and job stability after two years of service. Yet the middle sectors feared the escalation of populist-authoritarian conflict in 1936–37. Among other things, it threatened civil servant purges such as those by Padre Olympio and the Ministry of Education. And of course their civil liberties were curtailed during periods of repression. As suggested in the preceding chapter, the middle sectors were wary of the Estado Novo but soon accepted it to be in their best interest. Thus began a lasting middle-sector willingness to give up political liberties in exchange for stability. Indeed, the middle sectors opposed most populists after 1955, considering them as threats to their well-being and harbingers of the end of multiclass integrative urban politics.[5]

The most dramatic result of the new politics and state of the 1930s and 1940s was the successful incorporation of several hundred thousand rural migrants into urban life. Here had been the real challenge of the social question of the 1920s: to educate and make citizens of poor, racially mixed, unskilled, illiterate pariahs. The task seemed fraught with danger, yet populism and corporatism proved it otherwise. The migrants saw the city as a great opportunity, and they happily took industrial or service jobs regarded as menial by urbanites. Even the favelas, termed an invitation to revolution by a 1930s social critic, grew rapidly by offering substantial advantages over downtown slums. In Rio, as in most other Latin American cities, the masses proved adaptable to urban life. Accommodation rather than revolution occurred.

The rural masses in the city contributed to many of the positive accomplishments of the first Vargas administration. They provided the manpower for economic expansion. Industrialization in particular depended on the growth of the work force: one hundred thousand more laborers were employed in Rio's factories between 1920 and 1940. Pedro Ernesto helped the process of mass accommodation by providing familiar leadership images and by creating a sense of participation and hence belonging in the city. The new masses became the consumers of popular culture, including samba music and the propaganda of the Estado Novo. In the postwar era they would also become objects of political recruitment on a scale far more ambitious than Pedro Ernesto ever imagined.

Recruitment of the poor, as opposed to their incorporation, was the issue that finally drove Vargas and Pedro Ernesto apart. The level of voting had been very low in national elections, and even in the big drive of 1930 only 5 percent of the population voted.[6] After 1932, however, urban politics lost their episodic quality and became continuous. Participatory politics in Rio overcame the limits of patronage and even interest group politics and reached out to the masses. Voter contact was maintained through visits by recruiters and pervasive media exposure to popular figures like Pedro Ernesto and Padre Olympio, creating loyalty that could be activated at election time. For a time, then, many working-class persons enjoyed a voice in politics, a powerful and seemingly irreversible process. It was one Vargas was not prepared to sustain for long in the mid–1930s. The 1935 prounion drive by Pedro Ernesto, while encouraged by the president to pre-empt the left and keep Luís Carlos Prestes from forming a labor-tenente coalition, alienated the military and other proponents of dictatorship. The 1936 imprisonment of Pedro Ernesto marked the beginning of a long struggle between populism and authoritarianism.

Vargas, always shifting strategies and seeking new alliances, saw a need for dictatorial powers in the mid–1930s. Elections cost money and diverted attention from administration, and managing the new state was complicated in the extreme. From his point of view it was time to demobilize parties and alliances and to concentrate power in his hands. Thus, while he incorporated the masses through corporate agencies, he eliminated electoral politics from the scene.[7] The army and the police, with their broad powers of investigation, incarceration, and censorship, imposed a calm on the cities, in contrast to the effervescent quality of urban politics in preceding years. The interventor in Rio, Henrique Dodsworth, would be remembered for a constructive administration, but he could not have won an election for mayor. So from 1936 until about 1940 the authoritarian theme was dominant over the populist or participatory one.

In the early 1940s Vargas effected his most noteworthy transition, this time from dictator to populist. Using as a model Pedro Ernesto's electoral movement of the mid–1930s, Vargas put the labor ministry and propaganda agencies to work fostering a charismatic image of himself among the masses. Vargas was widely credited with the social legislation of the 1930s and was the best known person in Brazil, so the task was not difficult. The challenge was to forge a movement without actually holding elections. This was done through the media and cooperative labor leaders known as *pelegos.* This popularity campaign on behalf of Vargas, boldly called *trabalhismo* (laborism), created the cadres who in 1945 would organize the Brazilian Labor party, Vargas's own movement. A new phase of urban politics was at hand.

In 1945 Vargas mishandled the populist strategy, uncertain of what to do with the authoritarian controls still at his command, but he was inadvertently saved by a military coup against him and the subsequent election of General Eurico Dutra as president. Although Vargas probably did not fully understand the dynamics of the populist-authoritarian counterpoint, he was in fact aided enormously by the developments of late 1945. Freed of the need to maintain discipline, Vargas could pose as the father of the poor, protector of the working class, defender of national sovereignty, and so on, images that were familiar in Brazilian politics and that had proved effective in urban elections during the 1930s. It is this last role of Vargas that has become famous, giving him a reputation as one of Latin America's foremost populists.

The new Vargas will remain an enigma until researchers study his private papers from the postwar period, but some insights may be gained by comparing his later career with that of Pedro Ernesto, the pioneer of Brazilian populism. Both practiced what theorists call multiclass integrative populism, that is, the formation of expansive electoral movements by charismatic leaders. The bond between the leader and the masses, the basis for his charisma, is a perceived quality that makes the populist into the benefactor of his "people." Usually the populist is a reformer, although the commitment and effectiveness of his efforts may vary. Certainly Vargas and Pedro Ernesto appeared as reformers, even though neither envisioned radical changes in the distribution of wealth, prestige, or power in society. In each case reform was a means—certainly not dishonest—for gaining middle- and lower-class support. These parallels between the 1930s and the 1950s leave little doubt about the origins of Brazilian populism.

Another striking parallel between the two decades is the authoritarian role assumed by the military. The army high command, with few exceptions, has stood as a bulwark against populism and class politics that might disturb the orderly conduct of government. This position dates from the mid–1930s, forged by Góes Monteiro, Eurico Dutra, and others in the wake of the communist uprising. The military has increasingly found support among the middle sectors, large portions of which view populism (especially that based on class appeals) as dangerous to their own and to national interests. The antipopulist stance of the military since Vargas's second presidency has placed it directly athwart the main trend of urban politics, which was expanded participation by the masses. Until 1964 the army had an indirect influence, pressuring civilian leaders from behind the scenes, but after the takeover by General Castelo Branco the influence became direct and often oppressive. The main justification for continued military rule was to combat the communists, but the real target was populism. The populist-authoritarian counterpoint continued.

Urban politics have followed the same trajectory they first took in the 1920s toward greater participation and reform beneficial to the masses. The support is now predominantly working-class, but the direction is the same. Repression has only accentuated the tendency for urban voters to defy the forces of authoritarianism. Cities now contain a majority of the population, and the opposition parties today are entirely urban in makeup. The bigger the city, the greater the opposition vote. To stem this tendency, censors keep close watch over the mass media rather than newspapers, perhaps remembering the lesson of the 1930s that only an elite, literate audience responds to written propaganda. Throughout the 1970s the opposition was barred from radio and television campaigning. The roots of the dilemma are in the 1930s, which suggests that the solution cannot be a simple denial of urban politics.

This is not to say that the urban electorate has become radical. Although the controlled nature of post–1964 politics makes ideological analysis difficult, it would appear that the working class vote is center left. Even when the Communist party grew rapidly in the postwar years, Luís Carlos Prestes led it with a conciliatory, even populist, stance. Certainly the Brazilian Democratic Movement, which captured most urban votes in the 1970s, was not a leftist party, though sectors within it might have taken different stances if permitted. Indeed, the repressive nature of the regime, as at various times in the 1930s and 1940s, provokes radical opposition from otherwise moderate quarters. That is one of the classic elements of the populist-authoritarian rivalry.

Therefore, the Brazilian state created in the 1930s—one committed to address the issues of urban life—faces a major structural obstacle: how to accommodate the political wishes of the working class without attacking the rights of the middle sectors and their military protectors. Because the state is nominally democratic, it must find a solution. Some regime theorists would change the state to eliminate its representative aspects, allowing technocrats to concentrate wholly on economic growth and international projection, but in recent years that has not been a dominant sentiment in the high command. Were it to become so it would pit them against the democratic and social reformist trend of urban politics since the 1920s. At the moment city and state are in potential conflict.

In sum, Rio's society and politics from the 1920s until the 1940s clearly show that the city had become a critical influence in the evolution of the modern Brazilian state. Late 1920s reformism gave rise to a new brand of politics that attracted the middle sectors. The new politics supplemented and gradually replaced the traditional patronage distribution of neighborhood bosses. This led to expansive coalition-building and the appearance of the first genuine populist party in the 1930s. A combination of personal leadership qualities and propitious timing vaulted Pedro Ernesto, mayor of Rio, into the center of an experimental movement that cut across social boundaries and extended participatory politics to the masses. The interaction between Pedro Ernesto and Getúlio Vargas, however, revealed inherent limits to democratic processes. Authoritarian forces grouped behind Vargas in 1935 and pitched the regime to the right, undercutting the populist movement. Yet the interplay between the president and the mayor was complex, for Vargas was learning the techniques of mass politics. In a sense Pedro Ernesto was Vargas's alter ego, developing a populist style that could not endure in the 1930s but that Vargas himself would perpetuate in the 1940s and 1950s. Thus populism not only was central to Rio's history but also played a leading role in the evolution of urban politics in Brazil.

NOTES

BIBLIOGRAPHY

INDEX

Notes

Chapter 1: Introduction

1. Richard M. Morse, "Brazil's Urban Development: Colony and Empire," *Journal of Urban History* 1 (1974):43–44.

2. The best-known studies of colonial cities are Nestor Goulart Reis Filho, *Evolução urbana do Brasil, 1500–1720* (São Paulo: Livraria Pioneira/Universidade de São Paulo, 1968); Pedro Pinchas Geiger, *Evolução da rede urbana brasileira* (Rio: Instituto de Estudos Pedagôgicos, 1963); Nelson Omegna, *A cidade colonial,* 2d ed. (Brasília: EBRASA, 1971); and Edmundo Zenha, *O município no Brasil, 1532–1700* (São Paulo: Instituto Progresso, 1948).

3. Charles R. Boxer, *Portuguese Society in the Tropics* (Madison: University of Wisconsin Press, 1965), esp. the introduction and ch. 3; Stuart B. Schwartz, "Cities of Empire: Mexico and Bahia in the Sixteenth Century," *Journal of Interamerican Studies* 11 (1969): 616–37; Rodolfo Garcia, *Ensaio sobre a história política e administrativa do Brasil, 1500–1810* (Rio: José Olympio, 1956), pp. 91–106 (hereafter cited as *História política*).

4. Morse, "Brazil's Urban Development," pp. 45–46.

5. The most penetrating view of this process is Rae Jean Dell Flory, "Bahian Society in the Mid-Colonial Period: The Sugar Planters, Tobacco Growers, Merchants, and Artisans of Salvador and the Recôncavo, 1680–1725" (Ph.D. diss., University of Texas, 1978).

6. A. J. R. Russell-Wood, *Fidalgos and Philanthropists: The Santa Casa da Misericórdia of Bahia, 1550–1755* (Berkeley and Los Angeles: University of California Press, 1968). On the concept of organic society in Latin America, see Richard M. Morse, "The Lima of Joaquín Capelo: A Latin American Archtype," *Journal of Contemporary History* 4 (1969):95–110.

7. Garcia, *História política*, p. 92; Morse, "Brazil's Urban Development," p. 43.

8. Cf. Charles R. Boxer, *The Dutch in Brazil, 1624–1654* (Oxford: The Clarendon Press, 1957), p. 19. It can be argued that the municipio should be regarded as a county and the *câmara* a county commission, with jurisdiction over rural as well as urban affairs. In Brazil, however, the *câmara* did not generally deal with rural problems, which were left to the powerful sugar planters. Thus in effect the *câmara* was a city council, and most studies treat it as such.

9. Richard M. Morse, "The Claims of Tradition in Urban Latin America," in *Contemporary Cultures and Societies of Latin America*, 2d ed., rev., ed. Dwight B. Heath (New York: Random House, 1974), pp. 480–94.

10. The urban changes which accompanied the rise of export agriculture in the late nineteenth century may be sampled in E. Bradford Burns, "Manaus 1910: Portrait of a Boom Town," *Journal of Interamerican Studies* 7 (1965):400–21; and Gerald M. Greenfield, "The Challenge of Growth: The Growth of Urban Public Services in São Paulo, 1885–1913" (Ph.D. diss., Indiana University, 1975).

11. On the impact of these doctrines, see Robert G. Nachman, "Positivism, Modernization, and the Middle Class in Brazil," pp. 1–23; and Richard Graham, *Britain and the Onset of Modernization in Brazil, 1850–1914* (New York: Cambridge University Press, 1968), ch. 9.

12. Michael L. Conniff, "Voluntary Associations in Rio de Janeiro, 1870–1945," pp. 64–81.

13. The classic statement is Antônio Carneiro Leão et al., *A margem da história da República: ideais, crenças, e afirmações* (Rio: Annuário do Brasil, 1924).

14. Steven Topik, "The Evolution of the Economic Role of the Brazilian State, 1889–1930," *Journal of Latin American Studies* 2 (1979):325–42, and "State Interventionism in a Liberal Regime: Brazil, 1889–1930," ms. article, Aug. 1979. An outspoken proponent of tried and true ways of governance was Alberto Tôrres, the early twentieth-century writer and politician. See *A organização nacional* (Rio: Imprensa Nacional, 1914).

15. This conception owes a great deal to Richard M. Morse's work on culture and urban history. See for example his discussion of the Catholic-patrimonial heritage and the search for a new organic solidarity in, "Cities and Society in 19th Century Latin America: The Illustrative Case of Brazil," in *The Urbanization Process in America from Its Origins to the Present Day*, ed. Jorge E. Hardoy and Richard P. Schaedel (Buenos Aires: Instituto Torcuato di Tella, 1969), pp. 303–22.

16. For a definition and collection of studies which follow this line of analysis, see Michael L. Conniff, ed., *Latin American Populism in Comparative Perspective* (Albuquerque University of New Mexico Press, 1981).

17. The concept of "multiclass, integrative populism" is developed in the article by Torcuato S. Di Tella, "Populismo y reforma en América Latina," *Desarrollo económico* 4 (1965):391–425.

18. Cf. Gino Germani, "The Concept of Social Integration," in *The Urban Explosion in Latin America*, ed. Glenn H. Beyer (Ithaca: Cornell University Press, 1967), pp. 175–89.

19. It was precisely in the 1930s that Claude Levi-Strauss, working in Brazil, began developing his famous theory of structuralism, starting with the idea that primitive social groups are microcosms that can reveal much about the makeup of complex societies. By the 1950s a considerable "national character" literature had accumulated in Latin America.

20. Max Weber, *On Charisma and Institution Building*, ed. S. N. Eisenstadt (Chicago: University of Chicago Press, 1968).

21. The best study of messianism in Brazil is that by Maria Isaura Pereira de Queiroz, *O messianismo no Brasil e no mundo* (São Paulo: Dominus/Universidade de São Paulo, 1965).

22. Alistair Hennessy, "Fascism and Populism in Latin America," in *Fascism: A Reader's Guide, Analyses, Interpretations, Bibliography*, ed. Walter Laqueur (London: Wildwood House, 1976), pp. 255–94. Although he does not analyze the relationship between populism and authoritarianism, he correctly notes that they are different types of regimes. See also the study by Aspásia Alcântara de Camargo, "Autoritarismo e populismo, bipolaridade no sistema político brasileiro," 22–45.

23. The best-known study on patrimonialism in Brazilian history is Raimundo Faoro, *Os donos do poder*. Ch. 1 discusses the medieval origins of the patrimonial state.

24. Tôrres's disciple Oliveira Vianna forcefully argues that the patrimonial-imperial mode predominated in colonial cities. See *Instituições políticas brasileiras*, vol. 1: *Fundamentos sociais do estado, direito público e cultura* (Rio: José Olympio, 1949), ch. 6.

25. The historiography of authoritarianism in the twentieth century is even scantier than that of populism. One of the most thoughtful recent approaches is that of Vamireh Chacon, *Estado e povo no Brasil: As experiências do Estado Novo e da democracia populista, 1937–1964* (Rio: José Olympio/Câmara dos Deputados, 1977).

26. *Cadernos do nosso tempo* (Jan.–June 1954):139–49.

27. Weffort's writings on populism have been conveniently reprinted in a new volume, *O populismo na política brasileira* (Rio: Paz e Terra, 1978), from which these and subsequent citations are taken: pp. 28, 34, 38.

28. Ibid., pp. 62, 71, 84–85.

29. Octávio Ianni, *O colapso do populismo no Brasil* (Rio: Civilização Brasileira, 1968); English trans. by Phyllis B. Eveleth, *Crisis in Brazil* (New York: Columbia University Press, 1970), p. 198.

30. (Rio: Civilização Brasileira, 1975), esp. pp. 9–48.

31. Trans. Marjory Mattingly Urquidi (Berkeley and Los Angeles: University of California Press, 1979), esp. ch. 5.

32. In *Ideology and Social Change in Latin America*, eds. June Nash, Juan E. Corradi, and Hobart A. Spalding, Jr. (New York: Gordon and Breach, 1977), pp. 200–36. A very fine, recent analysis of labor and populism in the 1950s is José Alvaro Moisés, *Greve de massa e crise política: estudo da greve dos 300 mil em São Paulo, 1953–54* (São Paulo: Livraria Editorial Polis, 1978), esp. pp. 108–11.

Chapter 2: *Cidade Maravilhosa*

1. The best physical survey of Rio (Brazil's federal district between 1834 and 1960) is Sylvio Froes Abreu, *O Distrito Federal e seus recursos naturais*.

2. A great deal of material on this period is contained in Adolfo Morales de los Rios Filho, "O Rio de Janeiro da Primeira República," and in Fernando Nascimento Silva, comp., *Rio de Janeiro em seus quatrocentos anos* (hereafter cited as *Rio quatrocentos anos*). No competent synthetic history exists, however. For a comparison with Argentina, see James R. Scobie, *Buenos Aires: From Plaza to Suburb, 1870–1910*.

3. Afonso Arinos de Melo Franco, *Rodrigues Alves, apogeu e declínio do presidencialismo*, 1:307–60; Norma Evenson, *Two Brazilian Capitals*, pp. 37–40.

4. Nancy Stepan, *Beginnings of Brazilian Science* (New York: Science History Publications, 1976), ch. 5; Franco, *Rodrigues Alves*, 1:361–436; Gilberto Freyre, *Order and Progress*, pp. 263–76.

5. *Jornal do Brasil*, 15 Mar. 1928, p. 6; 14 Apr. 1928, p. 7; U.S. National Archives, *Records of the Department of State Relating to Internal Affairs of Brazil, 1910–1929*, microfilm collection M519, file 832.00, political reports/1, Jan. 5, 1928 (hereafter cited as *Internal Affairs of Brazil*); Rios Filho, "O Rio," 274:54–57; 272:163–69.

6. Freyre, *Order and Progress*, pp. 277–78; *Jornal do Brasil*, 21 Apr. 1927, p. 9; 6 July 1927, passim; *Internal Affairs of Brazil*, file 832.796, passim; Rios Filho, "O Rio," 274: 74–81.

7. 4 May 1926, p. 12.

8. José Oliveira Reis, "As administrações municipais e o desenvolvimento urbano," in Silva, *Rio quatrocentos anos*, pp. 143–44.

9. Preston James, "Rio de Janeiro and São Paulo," 143–44; Everardo Backheuser, "A planta atormentada da cidade," 408–10.

10. Francisco Agenor de Noronha Santos, *Os meios de transporte no Rio de Janeiro;*

Nestor de Oliveira Neto, "Os meios de transporte," in Silva, *Rio quatrocentos anos*, pp. 338–56.

11. Much unsystematic information may be gleaned from Rios Filho, "O Rio," and Francisco Agenor de Noronha Santos, *As freguesias do Rio antigo*, ed. Paulo Berger (Rio: Edições O Cruzeiro, 1965). These older zones correspond to those described in Sam Bass Warner's classic, *Streetcar Suburbs*. For Latin American suburbanization, see Scobie, *Buenos Aires*, ch. 5; Charles S. Sargent, *The Spacial Evolution of Greater Buenos Aires, Argentina, 1870–1930*, pp. 66–83; María Dolores Morales, "La expansión de la ciudad de México en el siglo XIX," pp. 70–104; E. Jeffrey Stann, "Transportation and Urbanization in Caracas, 1891–1936," pp. 82–100.

12. See, for example, the Sunday supplements of the *Jornal do Brasil;* and Henrique Dias da Cruz, *Os subúrbios cariocas no regime do Estado Novo*.

13. 23 Apr. 1926, p. 4; 28 Apr. 1926, p. 5.

14. Eneida and Paulo Berger, *Copacabana; Jornal do Brasil*, 4 Jan. 1931, p. 14; 18 Dec. 1930, p. 6.

15. *Jornal do Brasil*, 5 May 1927, pp. 8, 12; *Correio da Manhã*, 3 July 1926, p. 6; Nelson Nunes da Costa, *História da cidade do Rio de Janeiro* (Rio: Prefeitura do D.F., 1934), p. 176.

16. Luiz Dodsworth Martins, *Presença de Paulo de Frontin*, pp. 40–41, 190–91 (hereafter cited as *Frontin*). The Derby merged with the Jockey Club in 1932.

17. The classic study of poor housing at the turn of the century is Everardo Backheuser, *Habitações populares*.

18. Lawrence Fulton Salmen, "The *Casas de Cômodos* of Rio de Janeiro," pp. 6–10. Azevedo's novel is available in English translation as *A Brazilian Tenement* (New York, 1926).

19. The surveys are contained in Brasil, *Recenseamento 1920*, vol. 3, pt. 3: *Estatística predial e domiciliária da cidade do Rio de Janeiro* (Rio: Imprensa Nacional, 1925), and Brasil, Ministério do Trabalho, *Estatística predial, Distrito Federal, 1933* (Rio: Imprensa Nacional, 1935).

20. Rios Filho, "O Rio," 273: 30–40; Armando Magalhães Correia, *O sertão carioca*.

21. A large literature has grown up regarding the favelas, some technical and much alarmist. For the early history, see José Alípio Goulart, *Favelas do Distrito Federal*, pp. 11–29; "A cidade livre da Favella," *A Noite*, 26 Nov. 1919; Andrew Pearse, "Some Characteristics of Urbanization in the City of Rio de Janeiro," pp. 191–92; Backheuser, *Habitações populares*, pp. 45–46; Alberto Passos Guimarães, "As favelas do Distrito Federal"; Luciano Parisse, *Favelas do Rio de Janeiro*.

22. Figures on favela shacks and population are based on the two housing surveys cited in n. 19 above. Only groups of five or more shacks within the planning department's "urbanized zones" were tabulated. Population estimates are based on 4.5 persons per domicile, the average in the 1940s. Among the low cost housing plans for the city in the 1920s, see Antônio Jannuzzi, *Escorço histórico do problema da construcção de casas populares;* J. A. Matos Pimenta, *Casas populares;* Gustavo Eugênio Leopoldo Estienne, *A cidade do Rio de Janeiro, o que falta fazer;* Armando Augusto de Godoy, *A urbs e os seus problemas*. Cf. Decree Number 14.813 of 20 May 1921 that created special tariff and tax subsidies for low cost housing. *Correio da Manhã*, 8 July 1926, p. 5.

23. 1 Apr. 1926, p. 4.

24. *Jornal do Brasil*, 6 Jan. 1927, p. 6; 5 Apr. 1927, p. 5; 10 July 1927, p. 6; 26 July 1927, p. 10.

25. Alfred Agache, *Cidade do Rio de Janeiro;* Evenson, *Two Capitals*, pp. 40–52.

26. Agache, *Cidade do Rio*, pp. 22–23; Godoy, *A urbs*, p. 79; *Jornal do Brasil*, 19 July 1927, p. 8.

27. *Jornal do Brasil*, 4 Nov. 1927, p. 9; 8 Jan. 1927, p. 6; 20 Mar. 1927, p. 20; 10 Feb. 1928, p. 6; 8 Apr. 1928, Sunday Supplement, pp. 22–23. The verse is from ibid., 21 Feb. 1928, p. 17.

Chapter 3: Social Structure and Reformism in the 1920s

1. John J. Johnson, *Political Change in Latin America*, Introduction. Cf. James R. Scobie, "Buenos Aires as a Commercial-Bureaucratic City, 1880–1910."

2. For a description of the data base, see Michael L. Conniff, "Voluntary Associations in Rio de Janeiro, 1870–1945." Theoretical and comparative discussions are available in John J. Bailey, "Pluralist and Corporatist Dimensions of Interest Representation in Colombia," in *Authoritarianism and Corporatism in Latin America*, ed. James M. Malloy (Pittsburgh: University of Pittsburgh Press, 1977), pp. 259–302; Richard D. Brown, "The Emergence of Urban Society in Rural Massachusetts, 1760–1820"; P. H. J. H. Gosden, *Self-Help Voluntary Associations in the 19th Century* (London: B. T. Batsford Ltd., 1973); Graham E. Johnson, "Voluntary Associations and Social Change"; Kenneth Little, *West African Urbanization: A Study of Voluntary Associations in Social Change* (Cambridge: Cambridge University Press, 1965); Eugene W. Riding, "Interest Groups and Development"; and Philippe C. Schmitter, *Interest Conflict and Political Change in Brazil.*

3. Freyre, *Order and Progress*, pp. 265–66; F. J. Oliveira Vianna, "As elites," *Correio da Manhã*, 3 Jan. 1926, p. 4; 14 Jan. 1926, p. 4; Rios Filho, "O Rio," 272: 65–97.

4. Rios Filho, "O Rio," 272:113–15.

5. *Annaes da Associação Comercial do Rio de Janeiro, Relatório . . . 1930*, 2: passim; Raul de Góes, *A Associação Comercial no Império e na República*, pp. 170–78. Typical daily activities of the AC-Rio may be sampled in *Jornal do Brasil*, 23 Dec. 1926, p. 6; 7 June 1928, p. 9; 16 Dec. 1926, p. 8; 10 Feb. 1928, p. 11; 3 Feb. 1928, p. 6; 19 Jan. 1928, p. 8; 27 Jan. 1928, p. 11; 10 Feb. 1928, p. 11; 11 Feb. 1927, p. 10; 20 July 1928, p. 8.

6. Câmara Portugueza de Comércio e Indústria, *Relatório do conselho director 1921–1922* (Rio: Jornal do Comércio, 1923), pp. 166–213.

7. See, for example, *Jornal do Brasil*, 21 June 1928, p. 7; 2 Dec. 1926, p. 8; 7 July 1927, p. 12; 27 Jan. 1927, p. 10; 20 Feb. 1927, p. 7.

8. Ibid., 7 Oct. 1926, p. 7.

9. Albert Fishlow, "Origins and Consequences of Import Substitution in Brazil," (hereafter cited as "Import Substitution"), p. 317; *Jornal do Brasil*, 3 Aug. 1927, p. 9; 7 Dec. 1926, p. 13; 3 Apr. 1927, p. 8; 2 May 1929, p. 10; 21 Mar. 1928, p. 11; 15 May 1927, p. 14; 1 Nov. 1926, p. 10. Cf. the recent book by Edgard Carone, *O Centro Industrial do Rio de Janeiro e sua importante participação na economia nacional, 1827–1977* (Rio: Centro Industrial do Rio de Janeiro, 1978).

10. Perhaps in defense the Chamber published a magazine for its members throughout the 1930s. See the Chamber's *Relatórios* between 1912–1936 in the National Library in Rio. Cf. Rios Filho, "O Rio," 272:108–13; *Recenseamento 1920*, vol. 5, pt. 1: *Indústria*, pp. lx–lxiv, on foreigners in business.

11. *Correio da Manhã*, 2 Jan. 1926, p. 5; *Jornal do Brasil*, 7 Oct. 1926, p. 20; 9 Mar. 1927, p. 8; 3 Nov. 1927, p. 11; 15 Dec. 1926, p. 10; 13 Jan. 1928, p. 6; 13 Mar. 1927, p. 7; 22 Aug. 1928, p. 20; 15 Oct. 1926, p. 8; 2 Feb. 1928, p. 10; 26 July 1927, p. 8; 1 Nov. 1927, p. 11; 22 Oct. 1926, p. 12.

12. Interview with Countess Pereira Carneiro (widow), 8 Dec. 1972, and mimeographed

biographical statement; *Jornal do Brasil,* 2 May 1928, p. 7; 22 Dec. 1927, pp. 7–8; 5 May 1927, p. 6; 20 Dec. 1927, p. 8; 5 Oct. 1926, p. 5; 14 Apr. 1927, p. 5.

13. Décio Saes, *Classe média e política na Primeira República brasileira, 1889–1930,* pp. 9–15; Johnson, *Political Change in Latin America,* ch. 8; Luís Aguiar Costa Pinto, "As classes sociais no Brasil"; J. S. Huilhon Albuquerque, comp., *Classes médias e política no Brasil;* Maria do Carmo Campello de Souza, "O processo político-partidário na primeira república," p. 221; Edgard Carone, *A República Velha,* 1:175–89.

14. Rios Filho, "O Rio," 272:32–39, 63–65. The clergy might be mentioned as a traditional profession, but as will be seen below they were uninfluential in the 1920s. Only a few intellectual and political leaders in the church stood out.

15. Martins, *Frontin,* pp. 161–65; *Revista do Club de Engenharia* 32 (1930).

16. Evaristo de Moraes Filho, interview, 30 Jan. 1973; and "Introduction," in Evaristo de Moraes, *Apontamentos de direito operário.*

17. The one profession that has been studied is "intellectual." See A. L. Machado Neto's *Estrutura social da república das letras (sociologia da vida intelectual brasileira, 1870–1930)* (São Paulo: Universidade de São Paulo, Grijalbo, 1973).

18. Conniff, "Voluntary Associations," pp. 69–70.

19. *O Jornal,* 20 Nov. 1928, p. 1; *Jornal do Brasil,* 1 June 1928, p. 8.

20. *Jornal do Brasil,* 20 Jan. 1927, p. 6, provides a history of the society. See also ibid., 22 Feb. 1927, p. 6; *O Globo,* 21 Jan. 1929, p. 5.

21. *O Globo,* 6 Mar. 1929, p. 7; *Jornal do Brasil,* 26 Oct. 26, p. 14; 2 Oct. 1926, p. 6; 7 Dec. 1926, p. 20; 24 Dec. 1927, p. 9; Decree 5622 of 28 Dec. 1928, reported in *Internal Affairs of Brazil,* 832.00/Gen'l Conds./15, 18 Jan. 1929.

22. *Jornal do Brasil,* 26 Oct. 1926, p. 8; Charles F. O'Neil, "The Search for Order and Progress: Brazilian Mass Education, 1915–1935" (hereafter cited as "Brazilian Mass Education"), pp. 211–22; Jorge Nagle, *Educação e sociedade na Primeira República,* pp. 123–24.

23. Rios Filho, "O Rio," 274: 19–29.

24. *Recenseamento 1920,* vol. 2, pt. 1: *População do Distrito Federal,* pp. 132–37.

25. In U.S. measure the recruits were 5′5″ and 128 lbs. "Anthropological Considerations of the Brazilian Male," *Internal Affairs of Brazil,* 832.22/-, 5 Dec. 1927; for a fuller analysis of this study, see Frank D. McCann, "The Nation in Arms: Obligatory Military Service During the Old Republic," in *Essays Concerning the Socioeconomic History of Brazil and Portuguese India,* eds. Dauril Alden and Warren Dean, pp. 235–38 (hereafter cited as *Socioeconomic History of Brazil*).

26. "The Wage Question," *Internal Affairs of Brazil,* 832.504/22, 25 Aug. 1927.

27. Maurício de Lacerda, *Evolução legislativa do direito social brasileiro,* pp. 32 ff.; José Albertino Rodrigues, *Sindicato e desenvolvimento no Brasil,* pp. 46–58; Azis Simão, *Sindicato e estado,* ch. 2.

28. *A Batalha,* 22 Aug. 1930, p. 1; *Revista dos Ferroviários,* May 1930, p. 3.

29. Everardo Dias, *História das lutas sociais no Brasil,* pp. 86–95 (hereafter cited as *Lutas sociais*); Boris Fausto, *Trabalho urbano e conflito social, 1890–1920;* Sheldon L. Maram, "The immigrant and the Brazilian Labor Movement, 1890–1920," Alden and Dean, *Socioeconomic History of Brazil,* pp. 178–210; and "Labor and the Left in Brazil, 1890–1921: A Movement Aborted," *Hispanic American Historical Review* 57 (1977): 254–72.

30. Caio Monteiro de Barros to ILO Conference, reported in *Jornal do Brasil,* 6 July 1928, p. 10. The press carried news daily about these powerful groups.

31. José Oiticica, respected labor reporter, in *A Pátria,* 19 Nov. 1928, p. 19; *Internal Affairs of Brazil,* 832.00/524, 25 July 1925.

32. E.g., *Jornal do Brasil,* 2 May 1928, p. 8; 29 July 1927, p. 7; 9 Nov. 1926, p. 10; 3 June 1927, p. 10; 21 Apr. 1927, p. 12; 4 June 1927, p. 8; *A Pátria,* 21 Sept. 1928, p. 4.

33. *Internal Affairs of Brazil,* 832.504/31, 17 Apr. 1928. Cf. Conniff, "Voluntary Associations," p. 71.

34. *Jornal do Brasil,* 25 Aug. 1926, p. 21.

35. *Correio da Manhã,* 22 Apr. 1926, p. 5; *Jornal do Brasil,* 7 May 1926, p. 13; 8 Aug. 1927, p. 19.

36. Thomas E. Skidmore, *Black Into White,* ch. 6; Rios Filho, "O Rio," 272:97–108.

37. Skidmore, *Black Into White,* pp. 190–92.

38. Cf. Edison Carneiro, *A sabedoria popular.*

39. João Camilo de Oliveira Torres, *Estratificação social no Brasil, suas origens e suas relações com a organização política do Pais,* ch. 7, argues that the Old Republic as a whole was a time of great social stability.

40. Paulo Neuhaus, *História monetária do Brasil, 1900–1945,* pp. 81–85; *Jornal do Brasil,* 4 May 1927, pp. 13–14; 6 May 1927, p. 5; 10 Feb. 1928, p. 5.

41. *Correio da Manhã,* 18–19 Mar. 1926, passim; *Jornal do Brasil,* 4 May 1926, p. 15; 20 June 1926, p. 17.

42. Debate by João Jorge de Costa Pimentel, in Congresso Operário, *Jornal do Brasil,* 28 Apr. 1927, p. 11.

43. *Correio da Manhã,* 20 Mar. 1926, p. 7; 19 Jan. 1926, p. 6; 16 Apr. 1926, p. 3; 2 July 1926, p. 4; *Jornal do Brasil,* 18 Mar. 1927, p. 10; Aug. 1926, passim; 26 Oct. 1926, p. 8; 20 Oct. 1926, p. 7; 10 Feb. 1927, p. 14; 5 Feb. 1927, p. 6; 8 Apr. 1927, p. 18; 12 Apr. 1927, p. 8; 27 Apr. 1927, p. 19; 9 Dec. 1927, p. 13.

44. *O Globo,* Feb. 1929, passim; 15 Apr. 1929, p. 7.

45. *Jornal do Brasil,* 2 May 1928, p. 5; cf. Paulo L. Burlamaqui, *As associações profissionaes,* pp. 7–150.

46. Gilberto Freyre, *The Mansions and the Shanties,* p. xxiv.

47. *Jornal do Brasil,* 23 Nov. 1926, p. 7.

48. Freyre, *Order and Progress,* pp. 386–405; Gaston V. Rimlinger, *Welfare Policy and Industrialization in Europe, America, and Russia,* ch. 1. James M. Malloy has analyzed the origins and impact of social security in *The Politics of Social Security in Brazil.*

49. *Correio da Manhã,* 20 Jan. 1926, p. 5.

50. Simon Hanson, *Utopia in Uruguay* (New York: Oxford University Press, 1938), pp. 150–71; Samuel L. Baily, *Labor Nationalism and Politics in Argentina* (New Brunswick, N.J.: Rutgers University Press, 1967), ch. 2; Frank R. Brandenburg, *The Making of Modern Mexico* (Englewood Cliffs, N.J.: Prentice-Hall, 1964), pp. 54–56; James O. Morris, *Elites, Intellectuals, and Consensus.*

51. Napoleão Lopes, *Todas as associações de classe são 'casos de polícia',* p. 8; *Jornal do Brasil,* 1 May 1927, p. 1; 4 May 1929, p. 12; *Correio da Manhã,* 5 Jan. 1926, p. 6; 2 Jan. 1926, p. 5; 8 Jan. 1926, p. 4; 8 July 1926, p. 4.

52. Speech by Lindolfo Color, future minister of labor, in the Chamber of Deputies, reprinted in *A Pátria,* 24 Oct. 1929, p. 10.

53. Vargas had presented the draft to the Chamber of Deputies Justice Commission, of which he was a member. *O Globo,* 12 July 1928, p. 12; 8 Jan. 1929, p. 2; *Jornal do Brasil,* 21 July 1928, p. 6.

54. See n. 22 above.

55. *O Jornal,* 4 Dec. 1928, p. 1 and passim; *O Globo,* 11 Jan. 1929, p. 1.

56. *Brazilian Culture: An Introduction to the Study of Culture in Brazil,* trans. William Rex Crawford (New York: Macmillan Co., 1950), pp. 446–88; O'Neil, "Brazilian Mass Education," pp. 253–61; Nagle, *Educação e sociedade,* pp. 134–260. Educational reforms of the late 1920s and 1930s will be dealt with more systematically in chapter 6.

57. Azevedo, *Brazilian Culture,* pp. 451–53; Sônia Botelho Junqueira, "A criação do

Ministério da Educação e Saúde Pública"; *O Globo*, 15 Apr. 1929, p. 1; John D. Wirth, *Minas Gerais in the Brazilian Federation, 1889–1937*, pp. 89–91.

58. *Jornal do Brasil*, 4 June 1926, p. 17; Freyre, *Order and Progress*, pp. 293–309.

59. Ralph Della Cava, "Catholicism and Society in Twentieth-Century Brazil," *Latin American Research Review* 11 (1976): 7–50; Thomas C. Bruneau, *The Political Transformation of the Brazilian Catholic Church*, pp. 30–37; Laurita Pessôa Raja Gabáglia, *O Cardeal Leme, 1882–1942*, ch. 20; Margaret Todaro Williams, "Pastors, Prophets, and Politicians"; João Camilo de Oliveira Torres, *História das idéias religiosas no Brasil*, 182–89; Alceu Amoroso Lima, *Memórias improvisadas*, pp. 95–131.

60. *Jornal do Brasil*, 4 Jan. 1927, p. 6; 28 Dec. 1926, p. 6; 18 May 1927, p. 8; *A Pátria*, late Nov. 1928, passim. Cf. Robert G. Nachman, "Positivism, Modernization, and the Middle Class in Brazil."

61. See the sources cited in Michael L. Conniff, "The Tenentes in Power"; *Jornal do Brasil*, 11 May 1927, p. 5; 18 May 1927, p. 7; *O Globo*, 3 Jan. 1929, pp. 1–2; 7 Jan. 1929, p. 1; 21 Jan. 1929, p. 2.

62. Bertha Lutz, interview, 24 June 1972; Rachel Soihet, "Bertha Lutz e a ascensão da mulher, 1919–1937"; Stepan, *Beginnings of Brazilian Science*, ch. 7; "Bertha Lutz Report," *Internal Affairs of Brazil*, 832.00/622, 12 July 1925; 832.405/-, 26 Dec. 1924; *Jornal do Brasil*, 9 Jan. 1929, p. 9. Cf. June E. Hahner, "Women and Work in Brazil, 1850–1920: A Preliminary Investigation," Alden and Dean, *Socioeconomic History of Brazil*, p. 100.

63. Stanley J. Stein, *The Brazilian Cotton Manufacture*, pp. 124–28; Warren Dean, *The Industrialization of São Paulo, 1880–1945*, pp. 136, 142 ff.; Fishlow, "Import Substitution," pp. 326–27; Brasil, *Anuário 1939/1940*, pp. 1329–31; "The Credit Situation in Brazil," three parts, *Internal Affairs of Brazil*, 832.50/27, 832.50/29, 832.50/31, of 8 June 1926, 10 July 1926, 2 Aug. 1926. Cf. the recent study by Eulália Maria Lahmeyer Lobo, *História do Rio de Janeiro*, 2:532–52.

64. Neuhaus, *História monetária*, pp. 90–95; *Jornal do Brasil*, 10 Feb. 1928, p. 5; *O Jornal*, Nov. 1928, passim; 23 Feb. 1929, p. 1; *Internal Affairs of Brazil*, 832.00/20, 5 June, 1929; Rio de Janeiro, *Sinopse estatístico do Distrito Federal* (Rio: Diretoria de Estatística Municipal, 1937), p. 62.

65. *Retrospecto comercial do Jornal do Comércio*, 1930, pp. 7–25 (quote on p. 25); *Jornal do Brasil*, 22 Jan. 1929, p. 8; 24 Jan. 1929, p. 6.

66. *A Pátria*, 13 Oct. 1928, pp. 4, 6; 24 Oct. 1928, p. 4; 12 Sept. 1928, p. 10; 20 Sept. 1928, p. 1; 5 Oct. 1928, p. 4; *O Jornal*, 2 Dec. 1928, p. 6; *Jornal do Brasil*, 5 Jan. 1929, pp. 9, 17; 13–15 Jan. 1929, passim; 10 Jan. 1929, p. 9; 24 Jan. 1929, p. 18; *O Globo*, 8 Apr. 1929, p. 1; 11 Apr. 1929, p. 2; 29 Jan. 1929, p. 6; 19 Apr. 1929, p. 1; 18 Apr. 1929, p. 8.

Chapter 4: Toward Mass Politics

1. For general background on politics during the Old Republic, see Thomas E. Skidmore, "The Historiography of Brazil, 1889–1945: Part I," 716–43; Carone, *República Velha*, vol. 2; José Maria Bello, *A History of Modern Brazil, 1889–1964;* Herman G. James, *The Constitutional System of Brazil.*

2. For an example of a major issue, see the discussion of a telephone concession to Rio's Canadian-European electric power company, in *O Globo*, Mar. 1929.

3. Alberto Woolf Teixeira, *Estrutura política e direção administrativa do Distrito Federal, resumo histórico;* James, *Constitutional System*, pp. 52–53, 196–202; Lavrador Murillo, *Síntese histórica da Câmara do Distrito Federal;* Artur Santos, *O Senado e os "vetos" do Prefeito do Distrito Federal; Jornal do Brasil*, 10 Dec. 1933, p. 7. For examples cited in the

text, see *Jornal do Brasil,* 24 Dec. 1926, p. 4; 28 Dec. 1926, p. 5; 24 May 1927, p. 5; 4 Nov. 1927, p. 8; 14 Jan. 1928, p. 8; 28 Jan. 1928, p. 5; 28 Dec. 1928, p. 6.

4. *Jornal do Brasil,* 14 Jan. 1928, p. 8; 2 June 1928, pp. 15–18; 7 June 1928, p. 8; 20 June 1928, p. 6; 11 May 1929, p. 5.

5. Dennis John Mahar, "Fiscal Federalism in Brazil," ch. 4; *Jornal do Brasil,* 21 May 1927, p. 7; 26 May 1927, p. 9; 27 May 1927, passim.

6. *Jornal do Brasil,* 16 May 1928, p. 16.

7. Ibid., 25 Dec. 1926, p. 4; 30 July 1927, p. 8; 6 Aug. 1927, p. 9; 13 Aug. 1927, p. 5; *Correio da Manhã,* 25 Dec. 1926, p. 4; *Internal Affairs of Brazil,* 832.00/570, 13 Apr. 1926; 832.00 B/7, 17 Dec. 1928; 832.00 B/8, 8 Nov. 1928; Noel Bergamini, interview, 30 Aug. 1972.

8. Rios Filho, "O Rio," 274: 3–29; *Internal Affairs of Brazil,* 832.911/8, 27 Oct. 1924; 832.911/9, 15–28 Oct. 1924; 832.911/10, 20–25 May 1925; 832.911/11, 4 June 1925; 832.911/12, 22 Feb. 1926. The press itself was a major source of information about newspapers, of course.

9. *Correio da Manhã,* 21 Jan. 1926, p. 2; 31 Jan. 1926, p. 4; John W. F. Dulles, *Anarchists and Communists in Brazil, 1900–1935,* pp. 404–06.

10. *Jornal do Brasil,* 1 Oct. 1926, p. 11; 23 Feb. 1927, p. 8; 19 Mar. 1927, p. 5; 19 May 1927, p. 5; 3 May 1928, p. 21.

11. Martins, *Frontin,* pp. 119–96.

12. *Jornal do Brasil,* 11 Aug. 1926, p. 6. Cf. ibid., 24 Dec. 1926, p. 8; 29 Dec. 1926, p. 6; 5 Jan. 1927, p. 7; 22 Feb. 1927, p. 6; 12 Apr. 1927, p. 8; 4 Nov. 1927, p. 6; 15 Dec. 1927, p. 8; 27 Feb. 1930, p. 6; 16 Feb. 1933, p. 3; *Correio da Manhã,* 12 Jan. 1926, p. 10; 21 Jan. 1926, p. 4; 25 Jan. 1926, p. 4; Henrique Dodsworth, interview, 27 June 1972.

13. João Baptista de Azevedo Lima, *Reminiscências de um carcomido,* pp. 75–85; Fausto, *Trabalho urbano,* p. 43, n. 3; Henrique Dodsworth and Lourenço Mega, interview, 27 June 1972; Roberto Macedo, interview, 12 June 1972; *Jornal do Brasil,* 2 Oct. 1934, p. 23.

14. Irineu was a principal in the *cartas falsas* episode. See Laurita Pessôa Raja Gabáglia, *Epitácio Pessôa (1865–1942),* 2: 29–30. *Jornal do Brasil,* 7 Aug. 1926, p. 6; 28 Dec. 1926, p. 7; 4 Jan. 1927, p. 6; 11 Jan. 1927, p. 7; 5 Feb. 1927, p. 6; 6 Feb. 1927, p. 6; 15 Feb. 1927, p. 7; 26 Feb. 1927, p. 8; 25 May 1927, p. 13; 10 Dec. 1927, p. 8; 28 Dec. 1928, p. 6.

15. *O Combate,* cited in *Diário da Manhã* (Recife), 1 Oct. 1929, p. 1.

16. On the *coronel* system, see Victor Nunes Leal, *Coronelismo: The Municipality and Representative Government in Brazil;* Eul Soo Pang, "The Politics of Coronelismo in Brazil"; Maria Isaura Pereira de Queiroz, "O coronelismo numa interpretação sociológica," *História geral da civilização brasileira,* vol. 3, pt. 1: *O Brasil republicano: estrutura do poder e economia, 1889–1930,* ed. Boris Fausto (São Paulo: DIFEL, 1975), pp. 155–90.

17. Much of the information about the inner workings of *chefe* and *cabo* politics is based on interviews with Dodsworth, Lourenço Mega, Mozart Lago, and the Amaral Peixoto family, listed in the Bibliography.

18. 25 Nov. 1926, p. 8.

19. Olympio de Melo, "Depoimento no Museu da Imagem e Som," Olympio de Melo Papers (hereafter cited as OMP), p. 3; *Jornal do Brasil,* 29 Apr. 1927, p. 9; 3 June 1927, p. 6; 5 June 1927, p. 6; 29 July 1927, p. 7; 7 June 1933, p. 7; 5 Apr. 1934, p. 9. Cesário was also called the St. George of the Triangle, after an important Afro-Catholic personage.

20. See, for example, the preelection line-ups in *A Pátria,* 20 Oct. 1928, p. 1.

21. *Jornal do Brasil,* 14 Jan. 1927, p. 7; 12 Feb. 1928, p. 30; 9 Mar. 1928, p. 22; 10 Mar. 1928, p. 19; 19 May 1928, p. 7; *Correio da Manhã,* 14 Jan. 1926, p. 4; *A Pátria,* 20 Oct. 1928, p. 3. Cf. James, *Constitutional System,* pp. 55–59.

22. Illustrative careers are those of Mozart Lago (interview, 6 June 1972); Nestor Antenor de Paula (Augusto Cavalcanti, *A politicagem no Distrito Federal*); and Adolfo Holanda Cunha (hearings of the Tribunal Especial da Procuradoria do Distrito Federal, Oct. 1931, in Arquivo do Estado do Rio de Janeiro [hereafter cited as AERJ], caixas com documentos classificados, caixa 11).

23. Dodsworth, interview, 11 July 1972. Labor specialist Jorge Street, in *A legislação social*, pp. 10–11, refers to the law as "Dodsworth's calling card to the Carioca electorate." Cf. Roberto Macedo, *Henrique Dodsworth*.

24. Maurício Lacerda, *Segunda República*, pp. 29, 43 and passim; *Evolução legislativa*, preface; Fausto, *Trabalho urbano*, pp. 225–26; Paulo Sérgio Pinheiro, "O proletariado industrial na primeira república," *História geral da civilização brasileira*, vol. 3, pt. 2: *O Brasil republicano: sociedade e instituições (1889–1930)*, ed. Boris Fausto (Rio: DIFEL, 1977), pp. 168–69.

25. Lima, *Reminiscências*, passim; Dulles, *Anarchists and Communists*, pp. 365–67; Ronald H. Chilcote, *The Brazilian Communist Party*, p. 31 and passim.

26. Ernesta von Weber, *Bergamini; Jornal do Brasil*, 10 Mar. 1931, p. 6; 15 Mar. 1931, p. 6; Noel Bergamini, interview, 30 Aug. 1972; Roberto Macedo, interview, 12 June 1972.

27. *Correio da Manhã*, 20 Jan. 1926, p. 2; 3 Feb. 1926, p. 2; 4 Feb. 1926, p. 4; 13 Apr. 1926, p. 2; *Jornal do Brasil*, 15 Oct. 1926, p. 6; 17 Nov. 1926, p. 6; 2 Dec. 1926, p. 7; 10 Dec. 1926, p. 7; 13 Jan. 1927, p. 7; 18 Jan. 1927, p. 8; 19 Jan. 1927, p. 6; 8 Feb. 1927, p. 8; 16 Feb. 1927, p. 8; 19 May 1927, p. 8; 21 May 1927, p. 8; 25 May 1927, p. 8.

28. Rubens do Amaral, cited in Quijano and Weffort, *Populismo*, p. 102.

29. *Correio da Manhã*, 9 Jan. 1926, p. 7; 21 Jan. 1926, p. 4; 26 Jan. 1926, p. 8; 30 Jan. 1926, p. 6; 11 Feb. 1926, p. 4; 25 Feb. 1926, p. 4; 2 Mar. 1926, p. 4. For an overview, see Paulo Sérgio Pinheiro, *Política e trabalho no Brasil (dos anos vinte a 1930)*.

30. *Jornal do Brasil*, 15 May 1926, p. 7; 1 Aug. 1926, p. 14; 29 Aug. 1926, p. 8; 5 Sept. 1926, p. 6; 7 Sept. 1926, p. 6; 19 Oct. 1926, p. 8; 28 Jan. 1927, p. 5; 4 Feb. 1927, p. 7; 11 Feb. 1927, p. 11; 17 Feb. 1927, p. 8. Irineu was elected senator, while Bergamini, Azevedo Lima, and their reform colleagues swept the second district: *Jornal do Brasil*, 5 Apr. 1927, p. 6.

31. *A Pátria*, 27 Oct. 1928, p. 2; *Jornal do Brasil*, 22 July 1927, p. 19; 16 Nov. 1927, p. 7; 13 Jan. 1928, p. 8; 24 Jan. 1928, p. 6; 14 Feb. 1928, p. 8; 2 Aug. 1928, p. 9; 2 May 1928, pp. 5–8; Dulles, *Anarchists and Communists*, 360–62.

32. *A Pátria*, 8 Aug. 1928, p. 8; 2 Sept. 1928, p. 11; 5 Sept. 1928, p. 8; 8 Sept. 1928, p. 8; 12 Sept. 1928, p. 2; 28 Sept. 1928, p. 3; 19 Oct. 1928, p. 4. Cf. the memoirs of a BOC leader from the 1920s, Octávio Brandão, *Combates e batalhas: memórias*, vol. 1 (São Paulo: Editora Alfa-Omega, 1978). Brandão's papers, along with those of other prominent labor leaders, are housed at the Universidade Estadual de Campinas, and a number of studies based on these materials will shortly be published.

33. *Jornal do Brasil*, 18 May 1927, pp. 7–8.

34. Ibid., 25 May 1927, pp. 7–13. The membership of the Democratic party of São Paulo was strikingly different, with 61 percent lawyers, merchants, and farmers, and an assortment of professionals: *Correio da Manhã*, 24 Mar. 1926, p. 2. Cf. also Paulo Nogueira Filho, *Ideais e lutas de um burguês progressista (subsídio para a história do Partido Democrático e da Revolução de 1930)*, 2 vols. (São Paulo: Anhambi, 1958), 1.

35. *Jornal do Brasil*, 16 Aug. 1927, p. 7; 20 May 1927, p. 6; 26 May 1927, p. 8; 25 June 1927, p. 5.

36. Ibid., 17 Aug. 1927, p. 8; 23 Nov. 1927, p. 5.

37. Ibid., 2 May 1927, p. 7. Cf. *A Pátria*, 8 Sept. 1928, p. 2.

38. *A Pátria*, 12 Sept. 1928, p. 10; 25 Oct. 1928, p. 1; 26 Oct. 1928, p. 1; *Jornal do Brasil*, 3 Aug. 1928, p. 8.

39. *O Jornal*, 1 Nov. 1928, p. 18; 20 Nov. 1928, p. 4; *A Pátria*, 29 Oct. 1928, p. 1.

40. *O Jornal*, 16 Nov. 1928, p. 2; *A Pátria*, 21 Oct. 1928, p. 1; 25 Oct. 1928, p. 1.

41. *A Pátria*, 7 Sept. 1928, p. 4.

42. *O Jornal*, 10 Nov. 1928, p. 16; *O Globo*, 4 Jan. 1929, p. 6.

Chapter 5. Election, Revolution, and Depression in Rio

1. The best synthetic treatments of the 1930 revolution are Alexandre José Barbosa Lima Sobrinho, *A verdade sobre a revolução de outubro* (hereafter cited as *Revolução de outubro*), and Jordan M. Young, *The Brazilian Revolution of 1930 and the Aftermath*. Documentary collections with some narrative are Hélio Silva's ongoing *O ciclo de Vargas* (Rio: Civilização Brasileira, 1964–); Edgard Carone, *A Segunda República*, and *A República Nova*. Carone's bibliographies contain most of the relevant secondary and memoir materials.

2. Aliança Liberal, *Documentos da campanha presidencial* (hereafter cited as *Campanha presidencial*), pp. 70–80; Lima Sobrinho, *Revolução de outubro*, pp. 255–57; Hélio Silva, *1926, a grande marcha*, pp. 358–65; Nogueira Filho, *Ideais e lutas*, 2:386–87, 693–98.

3. Américo Palha, *Lindolfo Cóllor: um estadista da revolução*, pp. 9–12.

4. Aliança, *Campanha presidencial*, quote from pp. 99–100; also available in Getúlio Vargas, *A nova política do Brasil* (Rio: Imprensa Nacional, 1938–44), 1:19–54. The issue of Rio autonomy will be more fully discussed in chapter 6. The progovernment *Jornal do Brasil*, 9 Feb. 1930, p. 6, projected a 54 percent majority for Vargas.

5. Silva, *1926*, pp. 358–65. Much of this account is based on newspaper coverage and personal interviews with participants.

6. *Internal Affairs of Brazil*, 832.00 Presidential Campaigns/6, 7 Sept. 1929; *Um grito de alegria ao tumulto da revolução*, by Matos Pimenta, reviewed in *Jornal do Brasil*, 22 Jan. 1932, p. 7; *Diário Carioca*, 19 Jan. 1932, p. 8.

7. Gabaglia, *Epitácio Pessôa*, 2:794–95; Carone, *República Velha*, 2:408–11.

8. *Internal Affairs of Brazil*, 832.00 Presidential Campaigns/10, 18 Dec. 1929; Presidential Campaigns/11, 23 Dec. 1929.

9. Lima, *Reminiscências*, p. 164; Dias, *Lutas sociais*, pp. 170–73.

10. *Internal Affairs of Brazil*, 832.00B/8, 8 Nov. 1929. Cf. Dias, *Lutas sociais*, p. 209.

11. Election returns and much of the analysis are from the *Jornal do Brasil*, whose editor, Barbosa Lima Sobrinho, had been active in politics for years. Cf. Hélio Silva, *1930, a revolução traida*, pt. 1.

12. Besides the ecological fallacy, the values in table 10 are undermined by the fact that socioeconomic characteristics refer to school children rather than to voters. For that reason the data cannot be safely presented as "ecological regression," with the methods suggested in J. Morgan Kousser, "Ecological Regression and the Analysis of Past Politics," *Journal of Interdisciplinary History* 4 (1973): 237–62.

13. *Jornal do Brasil*, 1 May 1930, p. 8.

14. Ibid., 28 May 1930, p. 8.

15. Ibid., 14 June 1930, p. 8.

16. Lima Sobrinho, *Revolução de outubro*, pp. 286–87; Theodore Michael Berson, "A Political Biography of Dr. Oswaldo Aranha of Brazil, 1930–1937" (Ph.D. diss., New York University, 1971), ch. 3.

17. Lima Sobrinho, *Revolução de outubro*, pp. 206–10, 234.

18. *Jornal do Brasil*, 14 Sept. 1930, p. 6.

19. The following account is based largely on interviews with Pedro Ernesto's son Odilon Baptista. His papers left with the family will be cited as PPE. Another good source is Samuel Wainer, "Pedro Ernesto—sua vida de cirurgião e revolucionário."

20. The Casa de Saúde was so well equipped that it was used to perform major surgery on

President Washington Luís in 1928, attended of course by his own doctors, *Internal Affairs of Brazil*, 832.00 Genl. Conds/7, 5 June 1928.

21. Conniff, "Tenentes in Power," provides a full treatment of Pedro Ernesto as head of the Club 3 de Outubro.

22. Virgílio de Melo Franco, *Outubro 1930*, pp. 305–06, 212 ff.; Brasil, Câmara dos Deputados, *Anaes da Câmara dos Deputados 1936* (hereafter cited Câmara, *Anaes 1936*), vol. 8, p. 91; receipt from Pedro Ernesto to José Cuervo, 11 Aug. 1930, and note from Oswaldo Aranha to Pedro Ernesto, 25 Sept. 1930, PPE; *Correio da Manhã*, 30 Sept. 1930, p. 2; 3 Sept. 1930, p. 4; *Jornal do Brasil*, 24 Mar. 1934, p. 7; 6 Apr. 1934, p. 7; 10 Oct. 1930, p. 6; 18 Sept. 1930, p. 13; 27 Sept. 1930, p. 9; Silva, *1930*, pp. 239, 347–52.

23. *Correio da Manhã*, Sept. and Oct. 1930, passim; Weber, *Bergamini*, p. 215; Silva, *1930*, pp. 243, 352.

24. Lima Sobrinho, *Revolução de outubro*, p. 231; Noel Bergamini, interview, 30 Aug. 1972.

25. None of the Junta members' archives have been made available to historians, so the following material is based largely on memoirs and documents in the archive of Bertoldo Klinger (ABK), who helped organize the coup and briefly served as the Junta's chief of police.

26. Tristão de Alencar Araripe, *Tasso Fragoso, um pouco de história do nosso exército*, pp. 544–46; Silva, *1930*, p. 367; Rubey Menezes-Wanderley, *A expiação*, pp. 45–46. This latter, an apology for the Junta, was suppressed at the time, but portions of it are reprinted in Bertoldo Klinger, *Narrativas aotobiográficas*, vol. 5. Pedro Ernesto's claim to have the active support of one hundred army officers appears in hindsight to have been exaggerated: Berson, "Oswaldo Aranha," p. 95.

27. The details of the Junta and its problems are related in the works cited in n. 26 above; Gabáglia, *Cardeal Leme*, pp. 218–26; Cícero Marques, *O último dia de governo do Presidente Washington Luís;* Silva, *1930*, pp. 364–91; and in the daily press.

28. The studies focused on Vargas or his regimes include Alzira Vargas do Amaral Peixoto, *Getúlio Vargas, meu pai;* John W. F. Dulles, *Vargas of Brazil, a Political Biography;* Robert M. Levine, *The Vargas Regime;* Karl Loewenstein, *Brazil Under Vargas;* Richard Bourne, *Getulio Vargas of Brazil;* and John D. Wirth, *The Politics of Brazilian Development, 1930–1954*.

29. Weber, *Bergamini*, pp. 250–64; Noel Bergamini, interview, 30 Aug. 1972; *Jornal do Brasil*, 3 Dec. 1930, p. 6; 7 Dec. 1930, p. 7; 10 Dec. 1930, p. 6.

30. *Jornal do Brasil*, Jan.–Sept. 1931, passim; letter from Bergamini to Henrique Dodsworth, 20 Jan. 1934, in *Anaes da Assembléia Nacional Constituinte* (Rio: Imprensa Nacional, 1934–1935), vol. 7, pp. 136 ff (hereafter cited ANC, *Anaes*).

31. *Jornal do Brasil*, 16 Apr. 1931, p. 6.

32. Simão, *Sindicato e estado*, pp. 85–87, 98; *Jornal do Brasil*, 16 Nov. 1930, p. 8; Evaristo de Moraes Filho, interview, 20 Jan. 1973.

33. Lídia Besouchet, *História da criação do Ministério do Trabalho*, pp. 59–60; *Jornal do Brasil*, 28 Nov. 1930, p. 6; 28 Dec. 1930, p. 5; 20 May 1931, p. 9; 25 Mar. 1931, p. 6; 23 Jan. 1931, p. 6.

34. Decree 19, 482 of 12 Dec. 1930; *Jornal do Brasil*, 14 Dec. 1930, p. 8; 16 Dec. 1930, p. 6; 18 Dec. 1930, p. 10; 16 Nov. 1930, p. 8.

35. Decree 19,497 of 17 Dec. 1930; Moacyr Velloso Cardoso de Oliveira, *A previdência social brasileira*, pp. 24–25; Moraes Filho, interview, 20 Jan. 1973.

36. *Jornal do Brasil*, 30 Nov. 1930, p. 7; 5 Dec. 1930, p. 7; 6 Dec. 1930, p. 8; 7 Dec. 1930, p. 7; 12 Dec. 1930, p. 5; 16 Dec. 1930, p. 7; 24 Dec. 1930, p. 5; 28 Dec. 1930, p. 6; 3 Jan. 1931, p. 7; 11 Jan. 1931, p. 8; 15 Feb. 1931, p. 8; decrees 19,496 and 19,497 of 17 Dec. 1930; and decree 19,735 of 28 Feb. 1931.

37. Peixoto, *Getúlio Vargas*, p. 394; O'Neil, "Brazilian Mass Education," pp. 292–94; Junqueira, "Ministério da Educação, pp. 77–141.

38. Rio, *Sinopse estatística*, p. 62 and passim; *Jornal do Brasil*, 1 Mar. 1931, p. 5; 6 Mar. 1931, p. 11; 4 Sept. 1931, p. 8; 23 Jan. 1931, p. 5.

39. Ibid., 2 Dec. 1930, p. 8; 6 Jan. 1931, p. 13; 11 Feb. 1931, p. 5; *Correio da Manhã*, 12 Sept. 1930, p. 3; Brasil, Departamento Nacional de Saúde Pública, *Boletim mensal de estatística demographo-sanitária da cidade do Rio de Janeiro* 27 (1930): passim.

40. Annibal Villanova Villela and Wilson Suzigan, *Política do governo e crescimento da economia brasileira, 1889–1945*, sections 2.25, 2.26, and p. 431; Fishlow, "Import Substitution," pp. 327–39; *Jornal do Brasil*, 12 Jan. 1934, p. 7. A polemical treatment of the Depression impact is Carlos Manuel Peláez, "A balança comercial, a grande depressão, e a industrialização brasileira."

41. *Jornal do Brasil*, 21 Apr. 1931, p. 6; 5 June 1931, p. 5; *Anuário 1938*, p. 432.

42. *Jornal do Brasil*, 5 Aug. 1930, p. 5; 11 Mar. 1931, p. 6; *New York Times*, 29 Nov. 1931, section 3, p. 8.

43. *Jornal do Brasil*, 21 July 1933, p. 6; *Correio da Manhã*, 11 June 1932, p. 11.

44. *O Globo*, 28 Dec. 1932, p. 1; *New York Times*, 5 Mar. 1933, section 10–11, p. 2; *Jornal do Brasil*, 5 Aug. 1933, p. 6; 29 Aug. 1933, p. 5.

45. *Anuário 1939–1940*, pp. 1326, 1332, 1333, national figures; Douglas Graham and Sérgio Buarque de Holanda Filho, *Migration, Regional and Urban Growth and Development in Brazil* (São Paulo: Instituto de Pesquisas Econômicas, 1971), tables reproduced in Villela and Suzigan, *Política do governo*, section 2.4.2.

46. Decree 19,482 of 12 Dec. 1930; *Jornal do Brasil*, 4 Sept. 1930, p. 21; Anísio S. Teixeira, *O sistema escolar do Rio de Janeiro*, p. 324; Cruz, *Subúrbios cariocas*, p. 34.

47. In addition to the sources cited in ch. 1, nn. 19, 22, see Giorgio Mortara, *Analyses de resultados do censo demográfico*, p. 10.

48. Conniff, "Tenentes in Power," passim.

49. Some of the material on the Bergamini dismissal is contained in Dossier Morro Santo Antônio, Pasta 11: "Interventor do Distrito Federal," Arquivo Nacional, Presidência 2a (hereafter cited as AN, PR–2a); Maurício Lacerda, *A questão do Morro Santo Antônio;* Caixas com documentos classificados, boxes 9–11, AERJ; Adolfo Bergamini, *As syndicâncias na prefeitura, refutação do Sr. Adolfo Bergamini;* Noel Bergamini, interview, 30 Aug. 1972; Lacerda, *Segunda República*, pp. 345–46.

Chapter 6: The Populist Apogee

1. Augusto do Amaral Peixoto, interview, 7 June 1972; Lourival Coutinho, *O General Góes depoe*, p. 163; Peixoto, *Getúlio Vargas*, pp. 118–28, 208.

2. Agildo Barata, *Vida de revolucionário*, p. 161; *Jornal do Brasil*, 4 Oct. 1931, p. 7; *O Globo*, 28 Dec. 1932, p. 5; Adalto Reis, interview, 3 May 1974. The tenentes who took municipal posts were Augusto do Amaral Peixoto, Hugo and Napoleão Alencastro Guimarães, Rui Santiago, and Delso da Fonseca. Reis was one of the *chefes* who collaborated most closely with Pedro Ernesto.

3. *Jornal do Comércio*, 5 Mar. 1933, p. 16; *New York Times*, 26 Mar. 1933, section 4, p. 8.

4. Decree 12,076 of 24 Feb. 1932.

5. Adalto Reis, interview, 3 May 1974; *Jornal do Comércio*, 13 Apr. 1933, p. 11. Cesário and the Triangle vote are described in chapter 4.

6. Olympio de Melo, interviews 13 June and 19 July, 1972, and "Depoimento no MIS;" *Jornal do Comércio*, 13 Apr. 1933, p. 11; 25 Aug. 1931, p. 6; 31 Oct. 1933, p. 10; 2 Nov. 1933, p. 10; 8 June 1933, p. 6; Maciel Filho, interview, 21 June 1972.

7. Berta Lutz, interview, 24 June 1972; *Jornal do Comércio,* 1 Apr. 1933, p. 4; 23 Apr. 1933, p. 7 and passim; *Jornal do Brasil,* 25 Mar. 1934, p. 7.

8. Celson José da Silva, "Marchas e contramarchas do mandonismo local," pp. 23–30; Pang, "Coronelismo in Brazil," pp. 32, 120.

9. José Honório Rodrigues, *Aspirações nacionais,* pp. 21, 62; Adalto Reis, interview, 3 May 1974.

10. *Anuário 1939–1940,* p. 1405; Rio, *Sinopse estatística,* pp. 126–27; Brasil, Serviço de Estatística Econômica e Financeira, *Comércio exterior do Brasil, 1933–1937,* pp. 414–15. Some of the imported receivers were transshipped to other states.

11. Sales Filho to Vargas, 23 Apr. 1934, processo 44,352, and 16 June 1934, processo 44,368, AN, PR–12. The broadcast seems to have been inspired by a similar experiment in Germany, and for a time Sales Filho included German translations in the programming and exchanged tapes with the German government. See Câmara, *Anais 1935,* vol. 5, pp. 342–50.

12. Sales to Vargas, 13 Aug. 1934, processo 46,580, AN, PR–13.

13. Speech by former interventor Bergamini (elected to the ANC in 1933), in Câmara, *Anais 1934,* vol. 4, pp. 122–30, 297–98, and vol. 6, p. 189; Hélio Silva, *1938, terrorismo em campo verde,* pp. 73–74.

14. Vargas to Oswaldo Aranha, 10 May 1935, Arquivo Getúlio Vargas (hereafter cited as AGV).

15. Maurina Pereira Carneiro, interview, 8 Dec. 1972; Louk Box, "Educational Broadcasting in Brazil," pp. 1–3; speech by Carejeiro Ayrosa on Radio Cajuti, 13 Oct. 1934, in PPE. Among the many testimonials to Pedro Ernesto's charisma see that of Delso da Fonseca, in an oral history interview conducted by Aspásia Camargo on behalf of the Centro de Pesquisa e Documentação em História Contemporânea on 9–16 May 1975: "exceptional figure of a doctor . . . great patriot . . . one of the great Brazilian men . . . he had an outlook that was profoundly honest and idealistic."

16. Renato Murce, "50 anos de rádio," *Jornal do Brasil,* 9 Sept. 1972, cad. B, p. 1; *New York Times,* 2 Jan. 1936, p. 10; Levine, *Vargas Regime,* pp. 83, 167–68.

17. Silva, *1926,* p. 386; *Jornal do Brasil,* 10 June 1931, p. 6.

18. *Jornal do Brasil,* 28 Oct. 1933, p. 8; 2 Jan. 1934, p. 5; 4 Jan. 1934, p. 7; 5 Jan. 1934, p. 7; 13 Jan. 1934, p. 7.

19. Ibid., 23 Jan. 1934, p. 8; 26 Jan. 1934, p. 7.

20. Ibid., 11 Mar. 1934, pp. 6, 9; 25 Mar. 1934, p. 7; 26 May 1934, p. 7; 30 May 1934, p. 7; 18 Apr. 1934, p. 8; 6 Apr. 1934, p. 7; 5 Apr. 1934, p. 9; 11 Apr. 1934, p. 7; *Vanguarda,* 13 Sept. 1934, p. 3; Augusto do Amaral Peixoto, interview, 7 June 1972.

21. Adalto Reis, interview, 3 May 1974; Berta Lutz, interview, 24 June 1972.

22. *O Globo,* 23 Nov. 1932, p. 4; 17 Dec. 1932, p. 6; Câmara, *Anaes 1934,* vol. 3, p. 71, vol. 6, p. 332; *Jornal do Brasil,* 13 July 1933, p. 5; 9 Aug. 1933, p. 13; 1 Nov. 1933, p. 5.

23. Ibid., 23 Jan. 1934, p. 11; 25 Jan. 1934, p. 5; 11 Mar. 1934, p. 5; 26 June 1934, p. 6; Odilon Baptista, interview, 11 Apr. 1972; Wainer, "Pedro Ernesto," p. 3; *Time Magazine,* 24 Aug. 1942, clipping in PPE.

24. Some prominent upper-class supporters of the PADF were Henrique Lage, Pereira Carneiro, Guilherme da Silveira, Jorge Bering de Oliveira Matos, Augusto Corsino, Guilherme Guinle, and Antenor Mayrink Veiga.

25. *O Globo,* 12 Nov. 1932, pp. 1–3; Henrique Dodsworth, interview, 12 June 1972. The PE leaders were João Daudt de Oliveira, Pedro Vivaqua, Serafim Valandro, and Francisco Oliveira Passos, all businessmen.

26. Mozart Lago, interview, 6 June 1972; *Jornal do Comércio,* 13 Apr. 1933, p. 4; *Jornal do Brasil,* 30 June 1934, p. 7.

27. *Jornal do Brasil,* 22 June 1933, p. 7.

28. Ibid., 27 July 1933, p. 8. On government chartered unions, see ch. 7.

29. *Jornal do Brasil,* 2 Oct. 1934, p. 9; Barata, *Vida de revolucionário,* p. 226.

30. *Jornal do Comércio,* 20–21 Mar. 1933, p. 4; *O Radical,* 24 Mar. 1933, p. 5; 28 Mar. 1933, p. 5; 3 Apr. 1933, p. 5.

31. Ibid., 25 Apr. 1933, p. 5; 26 Apr. 1933, p. 5; 29 Apr. 1933, p. 6; 3 May 1933, p. 5.

32. *Jornal do Brasil,* 2 May 1933, p. 10; *O Radical,* 5 Mar. 1933, p. 2. This convention was preceded by one in July and was followed by yet another in February 1933.

33. Ibid., 25 June 1933, p. 6; *Jornal do Brasil,* 1 July 1933, p. 8. See also the attempted formation of a national labor coalition party made up of a large number of unions, called the Partido Nacional do Trabalho, reported in *O Globo,* 29 Dec. 1932, p. 4.

34. *Jornal do Brasil,* 20 Apr. 1934, p. 7; *Vanguarda,* 12 Sept. 1934, p. 2; 18 Sept. 1934, p. 2; 22 Sept. 1934, p. 1; Brasil, Supremo Tribunal Eleitoral, *Boletim eleitoral,* 27 Feb. 1935, p. 568.

35. Margaret Todaro Williams, "The Politicization of the Brazilian Catholic Church: The Catholic Electoral League."

36. Alceu Amoroso Lima, *Indicações políticas, da revolução à constituição,* pp. 133–53, and interview, 25 Aug. 1972; *O Globo,* 18 Oct. 1932, p. 1; 9 Nov. 1932, p. 3; 23 Nov. 1932, p. 1; *Jornal do Comércio,* 30 Apr. 1933, p. 9. The LEC program is reprinted in ANC, *Anais,* vol. 3, pp. 318–35, and in the *Jornal do Comércio,* 12 Mar. 1933. pp. 7–8.

37. Gláucio Ary Dillon Soares, *Sociedade e política no Brasil,* pp. 32–33.

38. *Boletim eleitoral,* 1 June–31 Sept. 1934, n=385. The unskilled were industrial and construction workers *(operários)* and store clerks *(comerciários).*

39. Ibid., 27 Feb. 1935, pp. 568–75; Hercolino Sobral Pinto, interview, 6 July 1972.

40. *Jornal do Brasil,* 6 Apr. 1934, p. 7.

41. ANC, *Anaes, annexos,* vol. 4, pp. 77–78.

42. *Jornal do Brasil,* 2 Oct. 1934, p. 9; Mário Bulhões Pedreira, *Razões de defesa do Dr. Pedro Ernesto Baptista,* p. 194.

Chapter 7: Social Planning in the 1930s

1. Conniff, "Tenentes in Power," pp. 71–72.

2. See ch. 5, nn. 19–20.

3. *Jornal do Brasil,* 21 Mar. 1930, p. 5; Leitão da Cunha, speech in ANC, *Anais,* vol. 6, p. 546; *O Globo,* 13 Sept. 1932, p. 2; *Correio da Manhã,* 5 Apr. 1932, p. 3; Cecília Meireles, "Percorrendo as escolas primárias do D. F.," *Diário de Notícias,* Nov.–Dec. 1932. O'Neil, "Brazilian Mass Education," provides an excellent overview of the problem. Hermes Lima's *Anísio Teixeira: estadista da educação* (Rio: Civilização Brasileira, 1978), is admiring but valuable.

4. "Plano regulador das construções escolares, 1932," Interventoria do Distrito Federal, 1930–1933, pasta 11, AN, PR–2A. The Plano was later published in similar form as Nereo de Sampaio, "O Plano Regulador," in Anísio S. Teixeira, *Educação pública, organização e administração.*

5. Letter from E. do Monte to prefecture, n.d., in "Despachos à prefeitura," 307–4–16, Arquivo Histórico do Itamarati (hereafter cited as AHI).

6. Anísio S. Teixeira, "O sistema escolar do Rio de Janeiro, relatório de um ano de administração," pp. 307–08, 324; *Jornal do Comércio,* 23 Apr. 1933, p. 9; 5 Mar. 1933, p. 8.

7. Anísio S. Teixeira, "As diretrizes da escola nova." On the reform in general and Teixeira's philosophy of education, see O'Neil, "Brazilian Mass Education," pp. 252–60, and Wanda Pompeu Geribello, *Anísio Teixeira, análise e sistematização de sua obra,* pp. 62–79, 157–74.

8. Municipal decree 3810 of 1932, in Octacílio Augusto da Silva, *O ensino popular no Distrito Federal (legislação)*, p. 138; Juraci Silveira (President of the ABE), interview, 10 May 1972.

9. *O Globo*, 7 Dec. 1932, p. 1.

10. Silva, *Ensino popular*, decree 5513 of 4 Apr. 1935; instruction no. 1 of 12 June 1935; legislative decree no. 17 of 2 Sept. 1935, on pp. 114, 116–17, 233–36; Teixeira, *Educação pública*, pp. 243–45; Box, "Educational Broadcasting," pp. 1–12.

11. "Processo da Prefeitura," p. 45, PPE; Hélio de Queiroz Duarte, *Escola-classe, escola-parque, uma experiência educacional*, passim.

12. Rio de Janeiro, *Desenvolvimento do sistema escolar do Distrito Federal e sua atual efficiência*, pp. 15–30; Silva, *Ensino popular*, p. 243. While vocational school enrollments did double, Teixeira was forced to retreat from the integrated curriculum because too few students passed the entrance exams.

13. Pedro Ernesto Baptista, "Relatório apresentado ao Dr. Getúlio Vargas," *Jornal do Brasil*, 16 Nov. 1933, p. 8; J. P. Fontenelle, *A saúde pública no Rio de Janeiro, 1935–1936*, passim; Pedro Ernesto, "Perante o julgamento da conciência nacional," in Pedreira, *Razões de defesa*, pp. 247–52, also published in *Correio da Manhã*, 24 Jan. 1937.

14. *Jornal do Brasil*, 6 May 1931, p. 5; Pinto de Aguiar, *As caixas econômicas e o problema das habitações proletárias* (Salvador: Typografia Naval, 1935), p. 11.

15. ANC, *Anais*, vol. 14, pp. 68 ff.

16. *Jornal do Brasil*, 1 Nov. 1933, p. 5; 19 Apr. 1934, p. 11.

17. Ibid., 20 Apr. 1934, p. 11.

18. *Jornal do Brasil*, 27 Apr. 1934, pp. 11–12; ANC, *Anais*, vol. 13, pp. 556–57. The kickbacks, called *luvas* (gloves), were traditional means of evading property taxes.

19. Christiano Hamann, *História da "S.O.S."* (Rio: Alba, 1952?), pp. 1–7; *Jornal do Brasil*, 24 Apr. 1934, p. 5; 27 Apr. 1934, p. 12; Amoroso Lima, interview, 25 Aug. 1972.

20. *Jornal do Brasil*, 9 Feb. 1934, p. 8. Cf. also 15 Nov. 1933, p. 8; 20 Dec. 1933, p. 8.

21. *Jornal do Comércio*, 18 Jan. 1933, p. 4; 26 Jan. 1933, p. 5; 5 Feb. 1933, p. 10; 11 Feb. 1933, p. 3; 12 Feb. 1933, p. 7; 13 Feb. 1933, p. 6; 17 Feb. 1933, p. 7; 22 Feb. 1933, p. 3; 3 Mar. 1933, p. 7; 22 Mar. 1933, pp. 3–4.

22. *Jornal do Brasil*, 16 Nov. 1933, p. 8: 16 May 1933, p. 11.

23. Partido Autonomista do Distrito Federal, *Ao povo carioca e à opinião pública*. 2 vols. (Rio: Imprensa Nacional, 1935), 1:209–14.

24. Richard M. Morse, "The Heritage of Latin America," pp. 169–77.

25. Kenneth Paul Erickson, *The Brazilian Corporative State and Working-Class Politics;* Malloy, *Authoritarianism and Corporatism;* Pike and Stritch, *The New Corporatism;* Schmitter, *Interest Conflict*, pp. 366 ff; and Peter Flynn, *Brazil: A Political Analysis*, chs. 4–5.

26. For a sampling of these views, see Jarbas Medeiros, ed., *Ideologia autoritária no Brasil, 1930–1945* (Rio: Fundação Getúlio Vargas, 1978), and the sources cited in ch. 8, n. 1.

27. Besouchet, *Ministério do Trabalho*, pp. 59–60; Palha, *Lindolfo Collor*, pp. 9–15. Cf. ch. 5, pp. 136–38 above.

28. Joseph L. Love, *Rio Grande do Sul and Brazilian Regionalism, 1882–1930* (Stanford: Stanford University Press, 1971), pp. 220–23; *Jornal do Brasil*, 16 Jan. 1929, p. 5; Berson, "Oswaldo Aranha," pp. 41–46.

29. Alberto Venâncio Filho, *A intervenção do estado no domínio econômico* (Rio: Fundação Getúlio Vargas, 1968), pp. 30–33; José Maria Bello, *A questão social e a solução brasileira;* Paulo L. Berlamaqui, *As associações profissionais* (Rio: Laemmert, 1936), passim.

30. Decree 19,497 of 17 Dec. 1930; Street, *Legislação social*, pp. 10, 26–27; Besouchet, *Ministério do Trabalho*, p. 61. A complete compilation of the labor laws, together with

justifications, is Alfredo João Louzada, *Legislação social-trabalhista: coletânea.* See also the work by Malloy cited in ch. 3, n. 48.

31. Evaristo de Moraes Filho, *O problema do sindicato único no Brasil,* p. 209 and interview, 20 Jan. 1973; Simão, *Sindicato e estado,* ch. 2.

32. Decree 19,770 of 19 Mar. 1931; *Jornal do Brasil,* 25 Mar. 1931, p. 6.

33. ANC, *Anaes,* vol. 9, p. 338.

34. *Jornal do Comércio,* 10 Apr. 1933, p. 3; Affonso Costa, "Leis sociais," *Jornal do Brasil,* 25 Oct. 1933, p. 5; Rodrigues, *Sindicato e desenvolvimento,* pp. 124–29.

35. *Correio da Manhã,* 15 May 1932, p. 1.

36. João Alberto to Getúlio Vargas, 20 Apr. 1933, "Polícia do Distrito Federal," AN, PR–8, pasta 4, 1931–33; reserved report from Artur Hehl Neiva to Police Chief, 22 Aug. 1932, loc. cit.; *Correio da Manhã,* 8 May 1932, p. 1; *Estado de São Paulo,* 13 July 1972.

37. Evaristo de Moraes Filho, interview, 30 Jan. 1973. The 1934 strikes in Rio were: maritime workers in April, July, and December; railroaders in April and September; textile workers in September and October; postal workers in July and December; city clerks in July; furniture workers in August; and a general strike in March to influence the ANC.

38. Emile Durkheim, *De la division due travail social,* 4th ed. (Paris: F. Alcan, 1930), pp. vi–xxxvi; Alberto Tôrres, *A organização nacional* (Rio: Imprensa Nacional, 1914), p. 350; *Correio da Manhã,* 18 June 1932, p. 3; *Jornal do Brasil,* 30 Jan. 1932, p. 7; 31 Jan. 1932, p. 6; Câmara, *Anaes 1935,* vol. 21, p. 75; ANC, *Anais, annexos,* vol. 4 pp. 77–78; José Affonso Mendonçã de Azevedo, *Elaborando a constitução nacional,* p. 335; *Jornal do Comércio,* 12 Apr. 1933, p. 7; Levine, *Vargas Regime,* p. 9; *New York Times,* 3 Dec. 1932, p. 6.

39. *Jornal do Brasil,* 22 July 1933, p. 5; 8 Apr. 1934, p. 5.

40. Rodrigues, *Sindicato e desenvolvimento,* pp. 151–54, and Maciel to Vargas, 4 Apr. 1933, Arquivo Francisco Antunes Maciel Filho (hereafter cited as AFAM).

41. Decree 22,653 of 20 Apr. 1933; *Jornal do Brasil,* 7 July 1933, p. 9.

42. *Jornal do Comércio,* 20–21 Mar. 1933, p. 4; *Jornal do Brasil,* 4 Feb. 1934, p. 5; 11 Feb. 1934, p. 5.

43. *Jornal do Brasil,* 21 July 1933, p. 7; 22 July 1933, p. 7; 16 Mar. 1934, p. 5; 28 Nov. 1933, p. 7; Moraes Filho, interview, 30 Jan. 1973.

44. Gabáglia, *Cardeal Leme,* pp. 289–92; Lima, *Indicações políticas,* pp. 133–35 and interview, 7 June 1972; Della Cava, "Catholicism and Society," passim.

45. Azevedo, *Brazilian Culture,* pp. 451–52.

46. Campos to Vargas, 18 Apr. 1931, AGV. Religious instruction was made optional in the 1934 Constitution and compulsory again in that of 1937, which Campos himself largely wrote. See Hélio Silva, *1934, a Constituinte,* pp. 91–92, 134, 276–78; and Pontes de Miranda, *Comentários à Constitução Federal de 10 de novembro de 1937,* 2 vols. (Rio: Irmãos Pongetti, 1938), 1:19.

47. Brazilian Episcopacy to Vargas, 12 Oct. 1931, AGV; Gabáglia, *Cardeal Leme,* pp. 291–93; Leme to Vargas, 2 May 1932, AGV; Peixoto, *Getúlio Vargas,* p. 164.

48. Howard J. Wiarda, *The Brazilian Catholic Labor Movement,* pp. 14–16; Gabáglia, *Cardeal Leme,* p. 301; Della Cava, "Catholicism and Society," pp. 44 ff.; Thomas C. Bruneau, "Power and Influence: Analysis of the Church in Latin America and the Case of Brazil," pp. 39–40.

49. Loewenstein, *Brazil Under Vargas,* pp. 339–42.

50. Gilbert Byron Siegel, "The Vicissitudes of Governmental Reform in Brazil," ch. 4; Lawrence S. Graham, *Civil Service Reform in Brazil,* pp. 28 ff.; Boris Fausto, *Pequenos ensaios de história da República, 1889–1945,* p. 87 and passim.

51. Cf. Bolívar Lamounier, "Ideologia conservadora e mudanças estruturais," *DADOS* 5 (1968):5–21.

Chapter 8: Macabre Dance: Populism and Authoritarianism

1. The literature of authoritarianism in Latin America is already large. In addition to Malloy, *Authoritarianism and Corporatism*, and Erickson, *Brazilian Corporate State*, see Ronald M. Schneider, *The Political System of Brazil: Emergence of a Modernizing Authoritarian Regime, 1964–1970*, Alfred Stepan, ed., *Authoritarian Brazil: Origins, Policies, and Future*, and Fernando Henrique Cardoso, "On Characterisation of Authoritarian Regimes in Latin America." For a conceptualization similar to the populist-authoritarian counterpoint, see Aspásia Alcántara de Camargo, "Autoritarismo e populismo, bipolaridade no sistema político brasileiro."

2. *Jornal do Brasil*, 20 Feb. 1931, p. 7; 23 May 1931, p. 6; 10 Oct. 1931, passim; 20 Jan. 1932, p. 10; Pantaleão Telles to Vargas, n.d., AOA; Luzardo to Vargas, 3 Mar. 1932, AGV; Dodsworth, interview, 15 Sept. 1972. Statistics on the Military Police appear in *Anuário 1939–1940*, p. 1427. A recent biography treats Luzardo's administration summarily: Glauco Carneiro, *Lusardo: o ultimo caudilho*, vol. 2, *Entre Vargas e Perón* (Rio: Editora Nova Fronteira, 1978).

3. Góes Monteiro to Vargas, 18 July 1932, AGV; *Correio da Manhã*, 28 May 1932, p. 1; DOPS report, 15 Apr. 1932, AGV; Dulles, *Anarchists and Communists*, p. 103; Carone, *República Velha*, 1:362.

4. Tarcísio Hollanda, "Depoimento do Sen. Filinto Muller," *Jornal do Brasil*, 16 Nov. 1969; Augusto do Amaral Peixoto, interview, 19 Mar. 1973; *Jornal do Comércio*, 24 Feb. 1933, p. 5; 29 Apr. 1933, p. 1.

5. *Veja*, 29 Mar. 1972, p. 23; Muller to Vargas, 4 June 1934, processo 47,158, AN, PR–13.

6. Câmara, *Anais 1934*, vol. 3, pp. 72–73; vol. 6, pp. 12–14.

7. Speech by Alvaro Ventura, 24 Oct. 1934, Câmara, *Anais 1934*, vol. 6, pp. 102–4; vol. 4, pp. 317–18, 335–37.

8. Aliança Liberal, *Documentos*, pp. 93–94; *Jornal do Brasil*, 7 Feb. 1931, p. 5; 29 July 1931, p. 6; 4 Dec. 1931, p. 5; 27 Dec. 1931, p. 5; *Correio da Manhã*, 13 Mar. 1932, p. 4; 8 June 1932, p. 2.

9. ANC, *Anais, annexos*, vol. 4, p. 345; ANC, *Anais*, vol. 8, pp. 418–20; vol. 9, p. 420; *Jornal do Brasil*, 1 Jan. 1934, p. 7; 31 Jan. 1934, p. 7; 17 Jan. 1934, p. 7; Levine, *Vargas Regime*, p. 167.

10. The break between Pedro Ernesto and Góes Monteiro is detailed in Conniff, "Tenentes in Power," p. 78.

11. *Jornal do Brasil*, 11 Feb. 1931, p. 5; 25 Feb. 1931, p. 7; Municipal decree 4,790 of 22 May 1934, published in ibid., 17 June 1934, pp. 6–9. The decree was not approved until two weeks before the October election.

12. Dodsworth and Mega, interview, 30 June 1972; Odilon Baptista, interview, 24 April 1972; Adalto Reis, interview, 3 May 1974; Pedreira, *Razões de defesa*, pp. 50–51; telegrams from Júlio Thiers Perisse (president of the Sindicato Sociedade União dos Proprietários de Imóveis) to Vargas, 17 June 1934, processo 44,360, AN, PR–12, and processo 46,975, AN, PR–13; telegram from comandantes da Guarda Noctura to Vargas, 20 Oct. 1934, processo 48,576, AN, PR–14; ANC, *Anais, annexos*, vol. 4, pp. 484 ff.; Câmara, *Anais 1934*, vol. 1, pp. 42–48; vol. 5, pp. 402–6, 470–72.

13. Câmara, *Anais 1935*, vol. 7, pp. 43, 89; vol. 9, pp. 169, 280; vol. 12, p. 101; vol. 13, pp. 272–74; vol. 17, p. 468; vol. 20, pp. 576 ff.

14. *New York Times*, 20 Jan. 1935, p. 5; 5 Apr. 1935, p. 4; Carone, *Segunda República*, pp. 58–64; Levine, *Vargas Regime*, ch. 3; Dulles, *Anarchists and Communists*, p. 515; Hélio Silva, *1935, a revolta vermelha*, passim.

15. Carone, *Segunda República*, pp. 64–66; *O Radical*, 24 Mar. 1935, p. 1; Aranha to Góes, 9 Mar. 1935, AOA.

16. Câmara, *Anais 1935*, vol. 25, pp. 170–71. Velasco was imprisoned in 1936 as a subversive: Levine, *Vargas Regime*, pp. 128–29.

17. *O Radical*, 1 Jan. 1935, p. 1; 2 Jan. 1935, p. 1; 5 Jan. 1935, p. 1; 9 Jan. 1935, p. 1; *New York Times*, 28 Dec. 1934, p. 7; 20 Jan. 1935, p. 5; Odilon Baptista, interview, 24 Apr. 1973.

18. *O Radical*, 23 Mar. 1935, pp. 1–2. Among tenente leaders no longer active were Ari Parreiras, João Alberto, Miguel Costa, Juarez Távora, and Oswaldo Aranha. As will be seen in ch. 9, the analysis did come true when Vargas released Luís Carlos Prestes in exchange for his support and formed the Brazilian Labor party. For the view that Vargas consciously encouraged the ANL, see Affonso Henriques, *Ascensão e queda de Getúlio Vargas*, vol. 3: *Vargas, o maquiavélico*, ch. 15.

19. Termo de Posse do Prefeito do Distrito Federal, 8 Apr. 1935, doc. 48–3–34, AERJ; Partido Autonomista, *Ao povo*, 1:209–14; "Depoimento no MIS," p. 14, OMP; *Correio da Manhã*, 9 Apr. 1935, p. 3.

20. Polícia Civil do Distrito Federal, *A insurreição de 27 de novembro: relatório do Delegado Eurico Bellens Porto* (Rio: Imprensa Nacional, 1936), pp. 78–90; speech of 13 May 1935 and letter from Edmundo Bittencourt to Pedro Ernesto, 7 Aug. 1935, PPE.

21. Speech at chauffeurs' union and telegrams, PPE; Levine, *Vargas Regime*, p. 103; *O Radical*, 16 July 1935, p. 1; Câmara, *Anais 1935*, vol. 7, p. 204; Silva, *1935*, p. 192; Odilon Baptista, interview, 24 Apr. 1972.

22. Unless otherwise noted, the documentation for this case is the two-volume file of the CFCE in processo 257 (563.631), AN, PR–13.

23. *Jornal do Comércio*, 12 Jan. 1933, p. 5; *O Radical*, 3 July 1935, p. 1; Wirth, *Brazilian Development*, pp. 18 ff.

24. Câmara, *Anais 1935*, vol. 13, pp. 272–74; vol. 21, pp. 314–18.

25. CFCE member Euvaldo Lodi supported Bouças's decision but believed the Russian gas proposal should be given more consideration: *Correio da Manhã*, 25 Sept. 1935, p. 5; 26 Sept. 1935, p. 5.

26. Draft legislation, 18 Mar. 1931, AOA, and in pasta Distrito Federal, AN, PR–15; *Jornal do Brasil*, 5 Feb. 1931, p. 6; 2 Sept. 1933, p. 6; 30 Dec. 1933, p. 7; *O Globo*, 29 Nov. 1932, p. 1; Pinto, Inspetor do Jôgo, to Pedro Ernesto, 4 Oct. 1933, pasta 11, AN, PR–2a; Bittencourt to Vargas, 5 Dec. 1932; Távora to Vargas, 16 Nov. 1932, AGV; Câmara, *Anais 1936*, vol. 19, p. 866; vol. 10, pp. 29–37; Câmara, *Anais 1934*, vol. 1, p. 250; vol. 3, pp. 71–72; Senado, *Anais 1935*, vol. 4, pp. 110–13, 118, 140–56; vol. 5, p. 81; Peixoto, *Getúlio Vargas*, p. 278; Câmara, *Anais 1935*, vol. 17, pp. 293–96, 495–503; Ernani do Amaral Peixoto, interview, 19 July 1972; Alvaro Froes da Fonseca, interview, 15 July 1972; Odilon Baptista, interview, 9 Oct. 1973.

27. *Jornal do Brasil*, 22 Dec. 1933, p. 7; 31 May 1934; p. 7; file "ensino religioso," OMP; Frederico Trotta, interview, 16 May 1972; Adalto Reis, interview, 3 May 1974; Amoroso Lima, interview, 7 June 1972. The debate was carried on at a professional level in two journals: *Debates pedagógicos* and *Humanismo pedagógico*.

28. Câmara, *Anais 1936*, vol. 10, pp. 37–38.

29. Câmara, *Anais 1935*, vol. 9, pp. 169–78; vol. 14, pp. 193–94; vol. 20, pp. 417–30; *Anais 1936*, vol. 8, pp. 229 ff., 396–97; vol. 10, pp. 281–82; vol. 13, pp. 239 ff.; *O Radical*, 27 Aug. 1935, p. 1; 23 Aug. 1935, p. 1.

30. Executive decree no. 17, 2 Sept. 1935, doc. 48–3–34A, AERJ, also described in Macedo, *Dodsworth*, pp. 56–59; *Correio da Manhã*, 3 Sept. 1935, p. 32; 10 Sept. 1935, p. 3; *O Radical*, 2 July 1935, p. 1; 5 July 1935, p. 3; 4 Sept. 1935, p. 1; 5 Sept. 1935, p. 1; 10 Sept. 1935, p. 1; Odilon Baptista, interview, 24 Apr. 1972.

31. *O Radical*, 9 July 1935, p. 2; 17 July 1935, p. 1; 27 July 1935, p. 1; 4 Sept. 1935, p. 1; Luís to Oswaldo Aranha, 18 Mar. 1936, AOA; Adalto Reis, interview, 3 May 1974.

32. Frederico Trotta, interview, 16 May 1972; Augusto do Amaral Peixoto, interview, 19 June 1972; "Depoimento no MIS," p. 16, OMP.

33. Levine, *Vargas Regime*, ch. 5; Silva, *1935;* Thomas E. Skidmore, "Failure in Brazil: From Popular Front to Armed Revolt."

34. Levine, *Vargas Regime*, pp. 134–35; *New York Times*, 2 Dec. 1935, p. 11; Pantaleão Pessôa, *Reminiscências e imposições de uma vida, 1885–1965*, p. 212.

35. Ilvo Meirelles to Luís Carlos Prestes, 13 Dec. 1935; 24 Dec. 1935; 25 Dec. 1935; and unsigned undated note, AGV.

36. João Alberto to Aranha, 3 Feb. 1936, AOA; *O Radical*, 8 Mar. 1936, p. 1; 6 Mar. 1936, p. 5; 13 Mar. 1936, p. 1; Luís to Oswaldo Aranha, 18 Mar. 1936, AOA.

37. *O Radical*, 10 Mar. 1936, pp. 1, 5; 11 Mar. 1936, p. 1; 15 Mar. 1936, p. 5; 17 Mar. 1936, p. 1; 19 Mar. 1936, p. 1.

38. Ibid., 21 Mar. 1936, p. 2; Juraci Magalhães to Vargas, 10 Mar. 1936, AGV; *O Globo*, 2–7 Apr. 1936, several editions, passim; Maciel Filho to Timponi, 29 May 1936, and Virgolino Correa to Júlio Novaes, 30 July 1937, PPE.

39. The principal sources of evidence in the case are contained in Pedreira, *Razões de defesa*, and the prosecution briefs by Bellens Porto and Himalaya Vergolino, in PPE. Significant commentary on the case is found in Congresso, *Diário*, 5 May 1936, p. 11,399; 19 June 1936, pp. 12,577–84; Herbert Moses to Pedro Ernesto, 2 May 1936, and bancada da imprensa to Pedro Ernesto, n.d., PPE; Vargas to Aranha, 8 Apr. 1936, AOA; Aranha to Vargas, 7 Apr. 1936, AGV; Câmara, *Anais 1936*, vol. 19, pp. 852–53. A key document is a deposition by Elíecer Magalhães made in 1936, admitting that while director of public hospitals he served as courier for the PCB and unintentionally implicated Pedro Ernesto in the revolution. The document is filed in AGV near other police evidence, and was read into the Câmara, *Anais 1936*, vol. 8, pp. 158–72.

40. Depoimento no MIS," p. 20, OMP; *A Vanguarda*, 7 Apr. 1936, p. 1; 14 Apr. 1936, p. 3; 2 June 1936, p. 1; *O Globo*, 4 Apr. 1936, p. 1; 6 Apr. 1936, p. 3; *O Radical*, 21 July 1936, p. 1.

41. Cesário de Melo to Vargas, 8 Apr. 1936, AGV; *A Vanguarda*, 11 Apr. 1936, p. 3; 30 Apr. 1936, p. 1; Carvalho to Vargas, telegrams of 13 May, 10 July, 6 June 1936, processos 5124, 5761, and 5428 in AN, PR–21; *New York Times*, 4 Sept. 1936, p. 4; Câmara, *Anais 1936*, vol. 4, p. 271; councilmen to Pedro Ernesto, 25 Sept. 1936, in Câmara, *Anais 1936*, vol. 19, p. 853; Novaes to Pedro Ernesto, n.d. PPE; Novaes to Vargas, 25 May 1936 and Vergara to Muller, 26 May 1937, processo 5247, AN, PR–21; Adalto Reis, interview, 3 May 1974.

42. Luís to Oswaldo Aranha, 16 Aug. 1936, AOA; Augusto do Amaral Peixoto, interview, 10 July 1972; Peixoto, *Getúlio Vargas*, pp. 295–99; legislative decree of 7 Dec. 1936, "Depoimento no MIS," pp. 27–29, OMP; Hélio Silva, *1937, todos os golpes se parecem*, pp. 31, 322; decree 1498 of 15 Mar. 1937.

43. Luís Aranha to Vargas, 21 June 1937; Olympio de Melo to Vargas, 21 June 1937; Vargas to Olympio de Melo, 2 July 1937; Sales Filho to Vargas, 15 May 1937, AGV; Silva, *1937*, pp. 366–68; Ernani do Amaral Peixoto, interview, 19 July 1972; Alzira do Amaral Peixoto, interview, 12 Sept. 1972; Olympio de Melo, interviews, 13 June and 19 July 1972; "Depoimento no MIS," p. 46, OMP; *O Radical*, 2 July 1937, p. 1; 6 July 1937, p. 1; 8 July 1937, p. 2.

44. Important published sources covering this period are Levine, *Vargas Regime*, ch. 7; Carone, *República Nova;* Silva, *1937;* José Américo de Almeida, *A palavra e o tempo, 1937–1945–1950;* Benedito Valadares, *Tempos idos e vividos, memórias;* Coutinho, *Góes*

depõe; Dulles, *Vargas of Brazil;* Fausto, *Pequenos ensaios;* and Frank D. McCann, Jr., *The Brazilian American Alliance,* ch. 1.

45. José Américo, interview, 18 Sept. 1974; Juraci Magalhães, interview, 3 Nov. 1974.

46. *O Radical,* 1 Aug. 1937, pp. 1–2, emphasis added; also in Almeida, *Palavra e tempo,* pp. 47–70. He had given two speeches in Minas during June, but they had not attracted much attention: Valadares, *Tempos idos,* pp. 151–52.

47. José Américo, interview, 18 Sept. 1974; Levine, *Vargas Regime,* p. 144; Peixoto, *Getúlio Vargas,* pp. 286–87; Aranha to Vargas, 24 Aug. 1937, AGV.

48. *O Radical,* 22 Aug. 1937, p. 2; 27 Aug. 1937, p. 1; Juraci Magalhães, interview, 13 Nov. 1974.

49. Maciel Filho to Aranha, 16 Sept. 1972; undated leaflet, AGV; Erani do Amaral Peixoto, interview, 19 July 1972; Levine, *Vargas Regime,* p. 144.

50. Peixoto, *Getúlio Vargas,* p. 257; Silva, *1937,* pp. 217–19; *O Radical,* 23 July 1937, pp. 1–4; 15 Aug. 1937, p. 1 and passim.

51. Pedro Ernesto to Jones Rocha, n.d., and offprint of STM verdict, pp. 329–56, PPE; *O Radical,* 14 Sept. 1937, p. 1; Odilon Baptista, interview, 22 April 1972.

52. *O Radical,* 15 Sept. 1937, pp. 1–4; Vicente Rao to Himalaya Vergolino, 2 Aug. 1937, PPE; Antônio Franco, *Anos de resistência* (Rio: Casa do Estudante, 1950), pp. 91–93; Silva, *1937,* p. 219; speech of 14 Aug. 1937, PPE; Adalto Reis, interview, 3 May 1974.

53. Mayrink Veiga to Armando Sales, 27 Sept. 1937, and Flores da Cunha to Pedro Ernesto, 16 Sept. 1937, PPE; Peixoto, *Getúlio Vargas,* p. 257; Adalto Reis, interview, 3 May 1974; Odilon Baptista, interview, 24 Apr. 1972; speech of 29 Sept. 1937, PPE; *O Radical,* 28 Sept. 1937, p. 2; 29 Sept. 1937, p. 2.

54. Maciel Filho to Aranha, 16 Sept. 1937, AGV.

55. Virgílio de Melo Franco to Aranha, 20 Nov. 1937, AGV; Bruno de Almeida Magalhães, *Arthur Bernardes: estadista da República* (Rio: José Olympio, 1973), p. 265; Dulles, *Vargas of Brazil,* p. 163.

56. The Dutra diary has been deposited with Hélio Silva but is not available to researchers. The account Dutra gave Silva in an interview is reproduced in Silva, *1937,* pp. 455–69; Peixoto, *Getúlio Vargas,* pp. 323–33.

57. José Américo, interview, 18 Sept. 1974, and *Palavra e tempo,* pp. 25–33; Silva, *1937,* pp. 455–69.

Chapter 9: Epilogue: Populism During the Estado Novo

1. Information about Dodsworth's selection and administration is from interviews with him and with Vargas's daughter Alzira do Amaral Peixoto.

2. Macedo, *Dodsworth,* p. 43. Cf. Henrique Dodsworth, *Algumas realizações administrativas de caráter cultural e artístico* (Rio: Henrique Dodsworth, 1966).

3. Henrique Dodsworth, *A avenida Presidente Vargas,* pp. 5–6 and passim; Affonso Henriques, *Ascensão e queda de Getúlio Vargas,* vol. 2: *Vargas e o Estado Novo,* pp. 51–59; Edgard Carone, *O Estado Novo, 1937–1945,* pp. 166–69.

4. Maciel Filho to Benjamin Vargas, 5 July 1944, AGV.

5. Peixoto, *Getúlio Vargas,* p. 314; Silva, *1937,* pp. 539–42, and *1938,* p. 15; Pedro Ernesto to Vargas, 17 Dec. 1937, AGV; "Pedro Ernesto Baptista em razões finais," and transcript of the verdict, in PPE; Augusto do Amaral Peixoto, interview, 19 June 1972.

6. Clipping file, "Quando Pedro Ernesto Morreu," PPE; Wainer, "Pedro Ernesto," p. 22; *Time Magazine,* 24 Aug. 1942, p. 24.

7. Report to Getúlio Vargas, 29 Feb. 1936; Plínio Castanhede to Agamemnon Magalhães, July 1938, AAM; Erickson, *Brazilian Corporate State,* ch. 4, passim.

8. Falcão to Vargas, 3 May 1941, AGV; Waldemar Falcão, *O Ministério do Trabalho, realização integral do governo Getúlio Vargas;* Dulles, *Vargas of Brazil*, pp. 247–48.

9. Erickson, *Brazilian Corporate State*, pp. 29–45; *Boletim do Ministério do Trabalho, Indústria, e Comércio*, Feb. 1942, pp. 50–52 and passim. The *Boletim* is a basic source of information on the evolution of labor policy during the entire Vargas period.

10. See, for example, Alexandre Marcondes Filho, *A democracia do Estado Nacional* (Rio: DIP, 1943); *International Labor Review* 50 (1944):352. The inner workings of the cabinet are narrated in Dulles, *Vargas of Brazil*, and McCann, *Brazilian-American Alliance*.

11. Pontes de Miranda to Vargas, 8 Nov. 1942 and 17 Nov. 1941, AGV; *International Labor Review* 44 (1941):493–537. There had been virtually no coverage in previous issues of the *Review*.

12. Vargas, *Nova política*, 10:291. An example of the radio broadcasts is contained in Marcondes Filho to Vargas, 18 Oct. 1943, AGV.

13. Edgard Carone. *A Terceira República, 1937–1945*, p. 48 and *Estado Novo*, pp. 169–72; Henriques, *Getúlio Vargas*, 2: ch. 20.

14. Genolino Amado, interview, 2 July 1977.

15. The DIP published a journal called *Cultura Política*, filled with unsigned articles of a pangloss nature about the regime, Brazilian history, etc. An expert's assessment is Walter R. Sharp, "Methods of Opinion Control in Present-Day Brazil." Fontes's activities from 1942 to 1945 are covered in anon to Berent, 21 May 1941, and Fontes to Vargas, 18 July 1943, 24 July 1943, 28 May 1944, 29 Dec. 1944, AGV. Fontes's successors were Coelho dos Reis (–July 1943) and Amílcar Dutra Menezes (–1945).

16. Genolino Amado, interview, 2 July 1977.

17. Vargas, *Nova política*, 5:311.

18. Ibid., 11:141, emphasis added. Cf. Carone's analysis of Vargas's mystique in *Estado Novo*, pp. 166–69.

19. Vargas, *Nova política*, 10:288; 11:38.

20. Loewenstein, *Brazil Under Vargas*, p. 339.

21. Clovis Guzmão, "As camadas médias brasileiras em face do momento nacional," remitted in Muller to Vargas, 15 Jan. 1940, AGV.

22. On the formation of the PTB, see Carone, *Estado Novo*, pp. 191–93; Hélio Silva, *1945: por que depuseram Vargas*, pp. 171–73.

23. Moraes Filho, *Sindicato único*, pp. 257 and passim; Dulles, *Vargas of Brazil*, pp. 252–56. At least ten intelligence reports are filed in AGV between Sept. 1944 and Jan. 1945.

24. The best account of the army's role in the events of 1945 is Coutinho, *Góes depõe*, pp. 403–69.

25. Marcondes Filho to Vargas, approx. 24 Dec. 1944, AGV.

26. Maciel Filho to Marcondes, 14 Dec. 1944; Maciel Filho to Benjamin Vargas, 5 July 1944; Alzira do Amaral Peixoto to Vargas, 16 Sept. 1944, AGV; Dulles, *Vargas of Brazil*, pp. 268–69.

27. Venâncio Filho, *Intervenção do estado*, pp. 290–91; Henriques, *Getúlio Vargas*, 2:335–38.

28. The best interpretation of the Vargas-Prestes relationship is Francisco C. Weffort, "Origens do sindicalismo populista no Brasil (a conjuntura do após-guerra)." Cf. Dulles, *Vargas of Brazil*, pp. 260–63; Henriques, *Getúlio Vargas*, 2:320–25; Silva, *1945*, pp. 147–49, 188–210; and Chilcote, *Brazilian Communist Party*, pp. 50–51.

29. Henrique Dodsworth, "Depoimento sobre Getúlio Vargas," reprint from *Rio Magazine*, several nos., 1964, passim.

30. The returns are reprinted in Silva, *1945*, pp. 514–17. A good introduction to postwar elections is Charles Daugherty, James Rowe, and Ronald Schneider, eds., *Brazil: Election Factbook Number 2*.

31. Dutra to PTB leaders, 22 Nov. 1945, AGV.

32. Weffort, "Sindicalismo populista," esp. pp. 88–92.

33. Polícia Civil do Distrito Federal, Boletim No. 113, 17 Oct. 1944, AGV; Henriques, *Getúlio Vargas*, 2: chs. 30–31; Mário Beni, *Adhemar*, pp. 173–81; Dulles, *Vargas of Brazil*, pp. 287 and passim.

34. On the shift in Rio politics see Glenn A. Nichols, "Class and Mass in Pre–1964 Brazil: The Case of Rio de Janeiro," pp. 323–37; and Francisco Pedro de Coutto, *O voto e o povo*. On the new labor-based populism, cf. Leôncio Martins Rodrigues, *Trabalhadores, sindicatos, e industrialização*, pp. 91 ff.

35. This is not to say that these roles had not existed before: most were traditional in politics and may be traced to leaders such as Dom Pedro II, Rui Barbosa, Hermes da Fonseca, Floriano Peixoto, and so forth. Their utilization for urban electoral purposes was Pedro Ernesto's innovation.

Chapter 10: Conclusion: City and State in Modern Brazil

1. The most forthright statement of this idea is Philippe C. Schmitter, "The 'Portugalization' of Brazil?" in Stepan, *Authoritarian Brazil*, pp. 179–232.

2. Paul K. Conklin, *The New Deal* (New York: Thomas Y. Crowell Co., 1967), ch. 3.

3. *Recenseamento 1920*, vol. 5, pt. 1: *Indústria*, pp. lx–lxiv; *Recenseamento 1940*, pt. 16: *Distrito Federal*, pp. 236–37, 264–65.

4. Malloy, *Social Security in Brazil*.

5. Nichols, "Class and Mass," passim. On the Negro vote, see Amaury de Souza, "Raça e política no Brasil urbano," *Revista de Administração de Empresas* 11 (1971): 61–70.

6. Joseph L. Love, "Political Participation in Brazil, 1881–1969."

7. For an analysis of the "exclusion" strategy, see Guillermo O'Donnell, *Modernization and Bureaucratic-Authoritarianism*, pp. 53–55.

Bibliography

1. Interviews

(conducted in Rio de Janeiro)

Genolino Amado, 2 July 1977
José Américo de Almeida, 18 Sept. 1974
Odilon Baptista, 28 Mar., 11 and 24 Apr., 2 May, 24 Aug. 1972; 8 Oct. 1973
Noel Bergamini, 30 Aug. 1972
Maurina Dunshee de Abranches Pereira Carneiro, 8 Dec. 1972
Carlos Delgado de Carvalho, 3 Aug. 1972
Othon Costa, 5 July 1972
Henrique Dodsworth, 13, 27, 30 June, 11 July 1972; 15 Sept. 1973; 30 May 1974
Alvaro Fróes da Fonseca, 15 July, 12 Dec. 1972
Mozart Lago, 6 June 1972
Alceu Amoroso Lima, 7 June, 25 Aug. 1972
Hermes Lima, 14 June 1972
Alexandre Barbosa Lima Sobrinho, 12 Dec. 1973
Bertha Lutz, 24 June 1972
Roberto Macedo, 12 June 1972
Juraci Magalhães, 13 Nov. 1974
Evaristo de Moraes Filho, 30 Jan. 1973
José Soares Maciel Filho, 21 June, 10 July 1972
Olympio de Melo, 13 June, 19 July 1972
Alzira Vargas do Amaral Peixoto, 12 Sept. 1972
Augusto do Amaral Peixoto, 7 and 19 June, 7 July 1972; 19 Mar. 1973
Ernani do Amaral Peixoto, 19 July 1972
Pantaleão da Silva Pessôa, 23 June 1972
Hercolino Sobral Pinto, 6 July 1972
Adalto Reis, 3 May 1974
Juraci Silveira, 10 May 1972
Juarez Távora, 18 and 26 June, 1972
Federico Trotta, 16 May 1972

2. Archival Collections

(those marked with an asterisk are now housed in the Centro de Pesquisa e Documentação de História Contemporânea do Brasil, Fundação Getúlio Vargas, Rio de Janeiro)

Arquivo Oswaldo Aranha* (AOA)
Arquivo Lindolfo Color*
Arquivo Histórico do Itamarati (AHI)
Arquivo Bertoldo Klinger* (ABK)
Arquivo Francisco Antunes Maciel* (AFAM)
Arquivo Agamemnon Magalhães* (AAM)
Arquivo Alexandre Marcondes Filho*
Arquivo Nacional, Presidência da República (AN,PR)
Arquivo Getúlio Vargas (AGV)
Assistência a Trabalhadores, Legião Brasileira de Assistência, Rio de Janeiro
Olympio de Melo Papers (OMP)
Papers of Pedro Ernesto Baptista* (PPE)

3. Newspapers

Correio da Manhã, 1926–35
Diário Carioca, 1932
O Estado de São Paulo, 1926–30
O Globo, 1926–32, 1936
O Jornal, 1928
Jornal do Brasil, 1926–37
Jornal do Comércio, 1922, 1925–36
New York Times, 1925–45
A Pátria, 1928
O Radical, 1933, 1935–37
A Vanguarda, 1934–36

4. Government Publications

Brasil. Assembléia Nacional Constituinte. *Anaes da Assembléia Nacional Constituinte*. Rio: Imprensa Nacional, 1934–35.

———. Câmara dos Deputados. *Anaes da Câmara dos Deputados*. 1930–37. Rio: Imprensa Nacional, 1931–38.

———. Congresso. *Diário do Congresso Nacional*. Rio: Imprensa Nacional, 1930–37.

———. IBGE. *Anuário estatístico do Brasil, 1939–40*. Rio: Serviço Gráfico, 1941.

———. IBGE. *Enciclopédia dos municípios brasileiros*. Vol. 23, *Guanabara*. Rio: Serviço Gráfico, 1960.

———. Ministério do Trabalho. *Boletim do Ministério do Trabalho, Indústria e Comércio*. Rio: Imprensa Nacional, 1931–45.

———. Ministério do Trabalho. *Estatística predial. Distrito Federal, 1933*. Rio: Imprensa Nacional, 1935.

———. *Recenseamento do Rio de Janeiro (Distrito Federal) realizado em 20 de setembro de 1906*. Rio: Officina da Estatística, 1907.

———. *Recenseamento do Brasil realizado em 1 de setembro de 1920*. Vol. 2, pt. 1, *População do Distrito Federal*. Rio: Typografia da Estatística. 1923.

———. *Recenseamento do Brasil realizado em 1 de setembro de 1920*. Vol. 2, pt. 3, *Estatística predial e domiciliária*. Rio: Typografia da Estatística, 1925.

———. *Recenseamento do Brasil realizado em 1 de setembro de 1920.* Vol. 5, pt. 1, *Indústria.* Rio: Typografia da Estatística, 1927.

———. *Recenseamento do Brasil realizado em 1 de setembro de 1920.* Vol. 5, pt. 2, *Salários.* Rio: Typografia da Estatística, 1927.

———. *Recenseamento geral do Brasil, 1 de setembro de 1940.* Pt. 16, *Distrito Federal.* Rio: Serviço Grafico do IBGE, 1951.

———. *Recenseamento geral do Brasil, 1950.* Vol. 24, pt. 1, *Distrito Federal, censo demográfico.* Rio: IBGE, 1955.

———. Serviço de Estatística Econômica e Financeira. *Comércio exterior do Brasil, 1933–1937.* Rio: Ministério da Fazenda, 1940.

———. Supremo Tribunal Eleitoral. *Boletim Eleitoral.* 1934–35.

Rio de Janeiro. Prefeitura do Distrito Federal. *Annuário de estatística da cidade do Rio de Janeiro, 1923–1924.* Rio: Imprensa Nacional, 1926.

———. *Annuário estatístico do Distrito Federal 1938.* Rio: Diretoria de Estatística Municipal, 1939.

———. *Desenvolvimento do sistema escolar do Distrito Federal e sua atual efficiência.* Rio: Instituto de Pesquisas Educacionais, 1934.

———.*Rio de Janeiro, Distrito Federal da República dos Estados Unidos do Brasil.* Rio: Diretoria de Estatística Municipal, 1936.

———. *Sinopse estatística do Distrito Federal.* Rio: Diretoria de Estatística Municipal, 1937.

United States. National Archives. *Records of the Department of State Relating to the Internal Affairs of Brazil, 1910–1929.* Washington, D.C.

5. Books, Articles, and Others

Abreu, Sylvio Fróes. *O Distrito Federal e seus recursos naturais.* Rio: Conselho Federal de Geografia, 1957.

Agache, Alfred. *Cidade do Rio de Janeiro: extensão, remodelação, embellezamento.* Paris: Foyer Brésilien, 1930.

Albuquerque, J.S. Huilhon, comp. *Classes médias e política no Brasil.* Rio: Paz e Terra, 1977.

Alden, Dauril, and Dean, Warren, eds. *Essays Concerning the Socieconomic History of Brazil and Portuguese India.* Gainesville: University Presses of Florida, 1977.

Aliança Liberal. *Documentos da campanha presidencial.* Rio: Alba, 1930.

Almeida, Cândido Mendes de. *Beyond Populism.* Albany: State University of New York, 1977.

Almeida, José Américo. *A palavra e o tempo (1937–1945–1950).* Rio: José Olympio, 1965.

Annaes da Associação Comercial do Rio de Janeiro, Relatório . . . 1930. 2 vols. Rio: Jornal do Comércio, 1930.

Araripe, Tristão de Alencar. *Tasso Fragoso, um pouco de história do nosso exército.* Rio: Biblioteca do Exército, 1960.

Azevedo, Fernando de. *Brazilian Culture: An Introduction to the Study of Culture in Brazil.* Translated by William Rex Crawford. New York: Macmillan Co., 1950.

Azevedo, José Affonso Mendonça de. *Elaborando a constitução nacional.* Belo Horizonte: Imprensa Official, 1933.

Backheuser, Everardo. *Habitações populares.* Rio: Imprensa Nacional, 1906.

———. "A planta atormentada da cidade." *Boletim geográfico* 3 (1945):408–10.

Barata, Agildo. *Vida de revolucionário.* Rio: Editora Melso, [1963?].

Bello, José Maria. *A History of Modern Brazil, 1889–1964.* Translated by James L. Taylor. Stanford: Stanford University Press, 1966.

———. *A questão social e a solução brasileira.* Rio: n.p., 1936.

Beni, Mário. *Adhemar.* São Paulo: Grafikor, [1973–74?].

Bergamini, Adolfo. *As syndicâncias na prefeitura, refutação do Sr. Adolfo Bergamini.* Rio: Rodrigues, 1932.

Berger, Eneida, and Berger, Paulo. *Copacabana.* Rio: Prefeitura do D.F., 1959.

Berson, Theodore Michael. "A Political Biography of Dr. Oswaldo Aranha of Brazil, 1930–1937." Ph.D. dissertation, New York University, 1971.

Besouchet, Lídia. *História da criação do Ministério do Trabalho.* Rio: Ministério do Trabalho, [1957?].

Bourne, Richard. *Getulio Vargas of Brazil.* London: C. Knight, 1974.

Box, Louck. "Educational Broadcasting in Brazil." *Boletín de estudios latinoamericanos* 14 (1973):1–12.

Brown, Richard D. "The Emergence of Urban Society in Rural Massachusetts, 1760–1820." *Journal of American History* 61 (1974):29–51.

Bruneau, Thomas C. *The Political Transformation of the Brazilian Catholic Church.* London: Cambridge University Press, 1974.

———. "Power and Influence: Analysis of the Church in Latin America and the Case of Brasil." *Latin American Research Review* 8, 2 (1973):25–51.

Burlamaqui, Paulo L. *As associações profissionais.* Rio: Laemmert, 1936.

Câmara Portugueza de Comércio e Indústria. *Relatório do conselho director.* Rio: Jornal do Comércio, 1912–36.

Camargo, Aspásia Alcântara de. "Autoritarismo e populismo, bipolaridade no sistema político brasileiro." *DADOS* 12 (1976):22–45.

Cardoso, Fernando Henrique. "On the Characterisation of Authoritarian Regimes in Latin America." Mimeographed, Centre of Latin American Studies, University of Cambridge, 1978.

Carneiro, Edison. *A sabedoria popular.* Rio: Instituto Nacional do Livro, 1957.

Carone, Edgard. *O Estado Novo (1937–1945).* Rio: DIFEL, 1977.

———. *A República Nova.* São Paulo: Difusão Européia do Livro, 1975.

———. *A República Velha.* 2 vols. São Paulo: Difusão Européia do Livro, 1970–71.

———. *A Segunda República.* São Paulo: Difusão Européia do Livro, 1973.

———. *A Terceira República (1937–1945).* São Paulo: DIFEL, 1976.

Cavalcanti, Augusto. *A politicagem no Distrito Federal.* Rio: n.p., 1930.

Chalmers, Douglas A. "Parties and Society in Latin America." *Studies in Comparative International Development* 7 (1972): 102–28.

Chilcote, Ronald H. *The Brazilian Communist Party: Conflict and Integration.* New York: Oxford University Press, 1974.

Conniff, Michael L. "The Tenentes in Power: A New Perspective on the Brazilian Revolution of 1930." *Journal of Latin American Studies* 10 (1978):61–82.

———. "Voluntary Associations in Rio de Janeiro, 1870–1945: A New Approach to Urban Social Dynamics." *Journal of Interamerican Studies* 17 (1975):64–81.

Correia, Armando Magalhães. *O sertão carioca.* Rio: Imprensa Nacional, 1936.

Coutinho, Lourival. *O General Góes depõe.* Rio: Coelho Branco, 1955.

Coutto, Francisco Pedro de. *O voto e o povo.* Rio: Civilização Brasileira, 1966.

Cruz, Henrique Dias da. *Os subúrbios cariocas no regime do Estado Novo.* Rio: DIP, 1942.

Daugherty, Charles; Rowe, James; and Schneider, Ronald; eds. *Brazil: Election Factbook Number 2.* Washington, D.C.: Institute for the Comparative Study of Political Systems, 1965.

Dean, Warren. *The Industrialization of São Paulo, 1880–1945*. Austin: University of Texas Press, 1969.

Della Cava, Ralph. "Catholicism and Society in Twentieth-Century Brazil." *Latin American Research Review* 11, 2 (1976):7–50.

Dias, Everardo. *História das lutas sociais no Brasil*. São Paulo: Editora Edaglit, 1962.

Dodsworth, Henrique. *A avenida Presidente Vargas*. Rio: Jornal do Comércio, 1966.

Drake, Paul W. *Socialism and Populism in Chile, 1932–1952*. Urbana: University of Illinois Press, 1978.

Duarte, Hélio de Queiroz. *Escola-classe, escola-parque, uma experiência educacional*. São Paulo: Faculdade de Arquitetura e Urbanismo, 1973.

Dulles, John W. F. *Anarchists and Communists in Brazil, 1900–1935*. Austin: University of Texas Press, 1973.

———. *Vargas of Brazil, a Political Biography*. Austin: University of Texas Press, 1967.

Erickson, Kenneth Paul. *The Brazilian Corporative State and Working-Class Politics*. Berkeley and Los Angeles: University of California Press, 1977.

Estienne, Gustavo Eugênio Leopoldo. *A cidade do Rio de Janeiro, o que falta fazer . . . .* Rio: Co. Nal. de Artes Gráficas, 1927.

Evenson, Norma. *Two Brazilian Capitals: Architecture and Urbanism in Rio de Janeiro and Brasília*. New Haven: Yale University Press, 1973.

Falcão, Waldemar. *O Ministério do Trabalho, realização integral do governo Getúlio Vargas*. Rio: Imprensa Nacional, 1941.

Faoro, Raimundo. *Os donos do poder: formação do patronato político brasileiro*. 2nd ed, rev., 2 vols. Porto Alegre: Globo; Universidade de São Paulo, 1975.

Fausto, Boris. *Pequenos ensaios de história da República, 1889–1945*. São Paulo: CEBRAP, 1972.

———. *Trabalho urbano e conflito social (1890–1920)*. São Paulo: DIFEL, 1976.

Fishlow, Albert. "Origins and Consequences of Import Substitution in Brazil." In *International Economics and Development: Essays in Honor of Raúl Prebisch*, edited by Luis Eugenio di Marc. New York: Academic Press, 1972.

Flynn, Peter. *Brazil: A Political Analysis*. London: Ernest Benn Ltd., 1978.

Fontenelle, J. P. *A saúde pública no Rio de Janeiro, 1935–1936*. Rio: n.p. 1937.

Franco, Alfonso Arinos de Melo. *Rodrigues Alves, apogeu e declínio do presidencialismo*. 2 vols. Rio and São Paulo, 1973.

Franco, Virgílio de Melo. *Outubro 1930*. Rio: Schmidt, 1931.

Freyre, Gilberto. *The Mansions and the Shanties: The Making of Modern Brazil*. Translated by Harriet de Onís. New York: Alfred A. Knopf, 1963.

———. *Order and Progress: Brazil from Monarchy to Republic*. Edited, translated by Rod W. Horton. New York: Alfred A. Knopf, 1970.

Gabáglia, Laurita Pessôa Raja. *O Cardeal Leme (1882–1942)*. Rio: José Olympio, 1962.

———. *Epitácio Pessôa (1865–1942)*. 2 vols. Rio: José Olympio, 1951.

Geribello, Wanda Pompeu. *Anísio Teixeira, análise e sistematização de sua obra*. São Paulo: Atlas, 1977.

Germani, Gino; Di Tella, Torcuato S.; and Ianni, Octávio. *Populismo y contradicciones de clase en Latinoamérica*. Mexico: Ediciones Era, 1973.

Godoy, Armando Augusto de. *A urbs e os seus problemas*. Rio: Jornal do Comércio, 1943.

Góes, Raul de. *A Associação Comercial no Império e na República: antecedentes históricos*. Rio: O Cruzeiro, 1959.

Goldrich, Daniel. "Toward the Comparative Study of Politicization in Latin America." In *Contemporary Cultures and Societies in Latin America*, edited by Dwight B. Heath and Richard N. Adams. New York: Random House, 1965.

Goulart, José Alípio. *Favelas do Distrito Federal.* Rio: Ministério da Agricultura, 1957.

Graham, Lawrence S. *Civil Service Reform in Brazil.* Austin: University of Texas Press, 1968.

Guimarães, Alberto Passos. "As favelas do Distrito Federal." *Revista brasileira de estatística* 14 (1953):250–78.

Henriques, Affonso. *Ascensão e queda de Getúlio Vargas.* 3 vols. Rio: Distribuidora Record, 1966.

História geral da civilização brasileira. Vol. 3, pt. 1, *O Brasil republicano: estrutura do poder e economia (1889–1930).* Edited by Boris Fausto. São Paulo: DIFEL, 1975.

História geral da civilização brasileira. Vol. 3, pt. 2, *O Brasil republicano: sociedade e instituições (1889–1930).* Edited by Boris Fausto. Rio DIFEL, 1977.

International Labor Organization. *International Labor Review.* London: ILO, 1937–45.

Ionescu, Ghiţa, and Gellner, Ernest, eds. *Populism: Its Meaning and National Characteristics.* New York: The Macmillan Co., 1969.

James, Herman G. *The Constitutional System of Brazil.* Washington: Carnegie Institution, 1923.

James, Preston. "Rio de Janeiro and São Paulo." *Geographical Review* 23 (1933):271–98.

Jannuzzi, Antônio. *Escorço histórico do problema da construcção de casas populares.* Rio: Jornal do Comércio, 1927.

Johnson, Graham E. "Voluntary Associations and Social Change: Some Theoretical Issues." *International Journal of Comparative Society* 16 (1975):51–63.

Johnson, John J. *Political Change in Latin America: The Emergence of the Middle Sectors.* Stanford: Stanford University Press, 1958.

Junqueira, Sônia Botelho. "A criação do Ministério da Educação e Saúde Pública." MA thesis, Pontifícia Universidade Católica do Rio de Janeiro, 1977.

Klinger, Bertoldo. *Narrativas aotobiográficas.* Vol. 5, *O coronel.* Rio: Empresa Gráfica O Cruzeiro, 1950.

Kousser, J. Morgan, "Ecological Regression and the Analysis of Past Politics." *Journal of Interdisciplinary History* 4 (1973):236–62.

Lacerda, Maurício de. *Evolução legislativa do direito social brasileiro.* Rio: Ministério do Trabalho, 1960.

———. *A questão do Morro Santo Antônio.* Rio: n.p., 1932.

———. *Segunda República.* 2d ed. Rio: Freitas Bastos, 1931.

Lamounier, Bolivar. "Ideologia conservadora e mudanças estruturais." *DADOS* 5 (1968): 5–21.

Leal, Victor Nunes. *Coronelismo: The Municipality and Representative Government in Brazil.* Translated by June Henfrey. New York: Cambridge University Press, 1977.

Levine, Robert M. *The Vargas Regime: The Critical Years, 1934–1938.* New York: Columbia University Press, 1970.

Lima, Alceu Amoroso. *Indicações políticas: da revolução à constituição.* Rio: Civilização Brasileira, 1936.

———. *Memórias improvisadas.* Petrópolis: Vozes, 1973.

Lima, João Baptista de Azevedo. *Reminiscências de um carcomido.* Rio: Leo Editores, 1958.

Lima Sobrinho, Alexandre José Barbosa. *A verdade sobre a revolução de outubro.* São Paulo: Gráfico-Editora Unitas, 1933.

Loewenstein, Karl. *Brazil Under Vargas.* New York: Macmillan, 1942.

Lopes, Napoleão. *Todas as associações de classe são 'casos de polícia'.* São Paulo: Centro Brasileiro de Publicidade, 1929.

Lobo, Eulália Maria Lahmeyer. *História do Rio de Janeiro: do capital comercial ao capital industrial e financeiro.* 2 vols. Rio: IBIMEC, 1978.

Louzada, Alfredo João. *Legislação social-trabalhista: coletânea.* Rio: Departamento Nacional do Trabalho, 1933.

Love, Joseph L. "Political Participation in Brazil, 1881–1969." *Luso-Brazilian Review* 7 (1970):3–24.

______. *Rio Grande do Sul and Brazilian Regionalism, 1882–1930.* Stanford: Stanford University Press, 1971.

Macedo, Roberto. *Henrique Dodsworth.* Rio: DASP, 1955.

McCann, Frank D., Jr. *The Brazilian American Alliance.* Princeton: Princeton University Press, 1973.

Machado, Neto, A. L. *Estrutura social da república das letras (sociologia da vida intelectual brasileira 1870–1930).* São Paulo: Universidade de São Paulo, Grijalbo, 1973.

Magalhães, Bruno de Almeida. *Arthur Bernardes: estadista da República.* Rio: José Olympio, 1973.

Mahar, Dennis John. "Fiscal Federalism in Brazil." Ph.D. dissertation, University of Florida, 1970.

Malloy, James M., ed. *Authoritarianism and Corporatism in Latin America.* Pittsburgh: University of Pittsburgh Press, 1977.

______. *The Politics of Social Security in Brazil.* Pittsburgh: University of Pittsburgh Press, 1979.

______. "Social Security Policy and the Working Classes in Twentieth Century Brazil." *Journal of Interamerican Studies* 19 (1977):35–60.

Maram, Sheldon L. "Labor and the Left in Brazil, 1890–1920: A Movement Aborted." *Hispanic American Historical Review* 57 (1977):254–72.

Marcondes Filho, Alexandre. *A democracia do Estado Nacional.* Rio: DIP, 1943.

Marques, Cícero. *O último dia de governo do Presidente Washington Luís.* São Paulo: Impresora Paulista, 1931.

Martins, Luiz Dodsworth. *Presença de Paulo de Frontin.* Rio: Livraria Freitas Bastos, 1966.

Menezes-Wanderley, Rubey. *A expiação.* Rio: Schettino, 1931.

Merrick, Thomas W., and Graham, Douglas H. *Population and Economic Development in Brazil: 1800 to the Present.* Baltimore: Johns Hopkins University Press, 1979.

Moraes Filho, Evaristo de. Introduction to *Apontamentos de direito operário*, by Evaristo de Moraes. 2d ed. São Paulo: Universidade de São Paulo, LTr Editora, 1971.

______. *O problema do sindicato único no Brasil.* Rio: A Noite, 1952.

Morales, María Dolores. "La expansión de la ciudad de México en el siglo XIX: el caso de los fraccionamientos." In *Seminario de historia urbana*, edited by Alejandra Moreno Toscano. Mexico: INAN, 1974.

Morris, James O. *Elites, Intellectuals, and Consensus: A Study of the Social Question and the Industrial Relations System of Chile.* Ithaca: Cornell University Press, 1966.

Morse, Richard M. *From Community to Metropolis: A Biography of São Paulo, Brazil.* Gainesville: University of Florida Press, 1958.

______. "The Heritage of Latin America." In *The Founding of New Societies*, Louis Hartz et al. New York: Harcourt, Brace, and World, 1964.

Morse, Richard M., with Conniff, Michael L., and Wibel, John. *The Urban Development of Latin America, 1750–1920.* Stanford: Center for Latin American Studies, 1971.

Mortara, Giorgio. *Analyses de resultados do censo demográfico.* Rio: IBGE, 1944.

Murillo, Lavrador. *Síntese histórica da Câmara do Distrito Federal.* Rio: Secretaria da Câmara, 1950.

Nachman, Robert G. "Positivism, Modernization, and the Middle Class in Brazil." *Hispanic American Historical Review* 57 (1977):1–23.

Nagle, Jorge. *Educação e sociedade na Primeira República.* São Paulo: EPU, Universidade de São Paulo, 1974.

Neuhaus, Paulo. *História monetária do Brasil, 1900–1945.* Rio: IBIMEC, 1975.

Nichols, Glenn A. "Class and Mass in Pre–1964 Brazil: The Case of Rio de Janeiro." *Journal of Interamerican Studies* 18 (1976):323–57.

Nogueira Filho, Paulo. *Ideais e lutas de um burguês progressista (subsídio para a história do Partido Democrático e da Revolução de 1930).* 2 vols. São Paulo: Anhambi, 1958.

O'Donnell, Guillermo. *Modernization and Bureaucratic-Authoritarianism.* Berkeley: Institute of International Studies, 1973.

Oliveira, Moacyr Velloso Cardoso de. *A previdência social brasileira.* Rio: Editora Record, 1961.

O'Neil, Charles Francis. "The Search for Order and Progress: Brazilian Mass Education, 1915–1935." Ph.D. dissertation, University of Texas, 1974.

Palha, Américo. *Lindolfo Côllor, um estadista da revolução.* Rio: Ministério do Trabalho, 1956.

Pang, Eul Soo. "The Politics of Coronelismo in Brazil: The Case of Bahia, 1889–1930." Ph.D. dissertation, University of California, 1969.

Parisse, Luciano. *Favelas do Rio de Janeiro: evolução—sentido.* Rio: Centro Nacional de Pesquisas Habitacionais, 1969.

Partido Autonomista do Distrito Federal. *Ao povo carioca e à opinião pública.* 2 vols. Rio: Imprensa Nacional, 1935.

Pearse, Andrew. "Some Characteristics of Urbanization in the City of Rio de Janeiro." In *Urbanization in Latin America,* edited by Philip Hauser. New York: UNESCO, 1961.

Pedreira, Mário Bulhões. *Razões de defesa do Dr. Pedro Ernesto Baptista.* Rio: n.p., 1937.

Peixoto, Alzira Vargas do Amaral. *Getúlio Vargas, meu pai.* 2d ed. Rio: Editora Globo, 1960.

Peláez, Carlos Manuel. "A balança comercial, a grande depressão, e a industrialização brasileira." *Revista brasileira de economia* 22 (1968):15–47.

Pessôa, Pantaleão. *Reminiscências e imposições de uma vida (1885–1965).* Rio: Pantaleão Pessôa, 1972.

Pike, Federick B., and Stritch, Thomas, eds. *The New Corporatism.* Notre Dame: University of Notre Dame, 1974.

Pimenta, J. A. Matos. *Casas populares: uma solução rápida, segura, e econômica.* Rio: n.p., 1927.

Pinheiro, Paulo Sérgio. *Política e trabalho no Brasil (dos anos vinte a 1930).* Rio: Paz e Terra, 1975.

Pinto, Luís Aguiar Costa. "As classes sociais no Brasil." *Revista brasileira de ciências sociais* 3 (1963):217–37.

Polícia Civil do Distrito Federal. *A insurreição de 27 de novembro: relatório do Delegado Eurico Bellens Porto.* Rio: Imprensa Nacional, 1936.

Quijano, Aníbal, and Weffort, Francisco C. *Populismo, marginalización, y dependencia.* San Jose, Costa Rica: EDUCA, 1973.

Riding, Eugene W. "Interest Groups and Development: The Case of Brazil in the Nineteenth Century." *Journal of Latin American Studies* 9 (1977):225–50.

Rimlinger, Gaston V. *Welfare Policy and Industrialization in Europe, America, and Russia.* New York: John Wiley and Sons, 1971.

Rios Filho, Adolfo Morales de los. "O Rio de Janeiro da Primeira República." *Revista do Instituto Histórico e Geográfico Brasileiro* 272 (1966):3–200; 273 (1966):3–116; 274 (1967):3–86.

Rodrigues, José Albertino. *Sindicato e desenvolvimento no Brasil.* São Paulo: Difusão Européia do Livro, 1968.

Rodrigues, José Honório. *Aspirações nacionais.* São Paulo: Editora Fulgor, 1963.

Rodrigues, Leôncio Martins. *Trabalhadores, sindicatos, e industrialização.* São Paulo: Editora Brasiliense, 1974.

Saes, Décio. *Classe média e política na Primeira República brasileira.* Petrópolis: Editora Vozes, 1975.

Salmen, Lawrence Fulton. "The *Casas de Cômodos* of Rio de Janeiro." Ph.D. dissertation, Columbia University, 1970.

Santos, Artur. *O Senado e os "vetos" do Prefeito do Distrito Federal.* Rio: Imprensa Nacional, 1947.

Santos, Francisco Agenor de Noronha. *As freguesias do Rio antigo.* Edited by Paulo Berger. Rio: Edições O Cruzeiro, 1965.

______. *Os meios de transporte no Rio de Janeiro.* 2 vols. Rio: Jornal do Comércio, 1934.

Sargent, Charles S. *The Spacial Evolution of Greater Buenos Aires, Argentina, 1870–1930.* Tempe: Arizona State University, 1974.

Schmitter, Philippe C. *Interest Conflict and Political Change in Brazil.* Stanford: Stanford University Press, 1971.

Schneider, Ronald M. *The Political System of Brazil: Emergence of a Modernizing Authoritarian State, 1964–1970.* New York: Columbia University Press, 1971.

Scobie, James R. "Buenos Aires as a Commercial-Bureaucratic City, 1880–1910: Characteristics of a City's Orientation." *American Historical Review* 77 (1972):1035–73.

______. *Buenos Aires: From Plaza to Suburb, 1870–1910.* New York: Oxford University Press, 1974.

Sharp, Walter R. "Methods of Opinion Control in Present-Day Brazil." *Public Opinion Quarterly* 5 (1941):3–16.

Siegel, Gilbert Byron. "The Vicissitudes of Governmental Reform in Brazil: A Study of the DASP." Ph.D. dissertation, University of Pittsburgh, 1964.

Silva, Celson José da. "Marchas e contramarchas do mandonismo local." MA thesis, Universidade Federal de Minas Gerais, 1972.

Silva, Fernando Nascimento, comp. *Rio de Janeiro em seus quatrocentos anos.* Rio: Distribuidora Record, 1965.

Silva, Hélio. *1926, a grande marcha.* 2d ed. Rio: Civilização Brasileira, 1971.

______. *1930, a revolução traída.* Rio: Civilização Brasileira, 1966.

______. *1931, os tenentes no poder.* Rio: Civilização Brasileira, 1966.

______. *1933, a crise do tenentismo.* Rio: Civilização Brasileira, 1968.

______. *1934, a Constituinte.* Rio: Civilização Brasileira, 1969.

______. *1935, a revolta vermelha.* Rio: Civilização Brasileira, 1969.

______. *1937, todos os golpes se parecem.* Rio: Civilização Brasileira, 1970.

______. *1938, terrorismo em campo verde.* Rio: Civilização Brasileira, 1971.

______. *1945, por que depuseram Vargas.* Rio: Civilização Brasileira, 1976.

Silva, Octacílio Augusto da. *O ensino popular no Distrito Federal (legislação).* Rio: Secretaria Geral de Educação e Cultura, 1936.

Simão, Azis. *Sindicato e estado: suas relações na formação do proletariado de São Paulo.* São Paulo: Dóminus, Universidade de São Paulo, 1966.

Skidmore, Thomas E. *Black into White: Race and Nationality in Brazilian Thought.* New York: Oxford University Press, 1974.

______. "Failure in Brazil: From Popular Front to Armed Revolt." *Journal of Contemporary History* 5 (1970):137–57.

______. "The Historiography of Brazil, 1889–1930." Parts 1 and 2. *Hispanic American Historical Review* 55 (1975):716–48; 56 (1976):81–109.

______. *Politics in Brazil: An Experiment in Democracy, 1930–1964.* New York: Oxford, 1967.

Soares, Gláucio Ary Dillon. *Sociedade e política no Brasil.* São Paulo: Difusão Européia do Livro, 1973.

Soihet, Rachel. "Bertha Lutz e a ascensão da mulher, 1919–1937." MA thesis, Universidade Federal Fluminense, Niteroi, 1974.

Souza, Amaury de. "Raça e política no Brasil Urbano." *Revista de administração de empresas* 11 (1971):61–70.

Souza, Maria do Carmo Campello. "O processo político-partidário na primeira república." In *Brasil em perspectiva,* edited by Carlos Guilherme Mota. São Paulo: Difusão Européia do Livro, 1973.

Stann, E. Jeffrey. "Transportation and Urbanization in Caracas, 1891–1936." *Journal of Interamerican Studies* 17 (1975): 75–100.

Stein, Stanley J. *The Brazilian Cotton Manufacture: Textile Enterprise in an Underdeveloped Area, 1850–1950.* Cambridge: Harvard University Press, 1957.

Stein, Stephen Jay. "Populism and Mass Politics in Peru: The Political Behavior of the Lima Working Classes in the 1931 Presidential Election." Ph.D. dissertation, Stanford University, 1974.

Stepan, Alfred, ed. *Authoritarian Brazil: Origins, Policies, and Future.* New Haven: Yale University Press, 1973.

Stepan, Nancy. *Beginnings of Brazilian Science.* New York: Science History Publications, 1976.

Street, Jorge. *A legislação social.* São Paulo: Escolas Salesianas, 1934.

Teixeira, Alberto Woolf. *Estrutura política e direção administrativa do Distrito Federal, resumo histórico.* Rio: n.p., 1950.

Teixeira, Anísio S. *Educação pública, organização e administração.* Rio: Departamento de Educação, 1935.

———. "As diretrizes da escola nova." *Revista do ensino* (Belo Horizonte) 6 (1932):5–33.

———. "O sistema escolar do Rio de Janeiro, relatório de um ano de administração." *Boletim de educação pública* 2 (1932):307–70.

———. *O sistema escolar do Rio de Janeiro.* Rio: Departamento de Educação, 1932.

Torres, João Camilo de Oliveira. *Estratificação social no Brasil, suas origens e suas relações com a organização política do Pais.* São Paulo: Difusão Européia do Livro, Centro Latino-americano de Pesquisas em Ciências Sociais, 1965.

———. *História das idéias religiosas no Brasil.* São Paulo: Editorial Grijalbo, 1968.

Valadares, Benedito. *Tempos idos e vividos, memórias.* Rio: Civilização Brasileira, 1966.

Vargas, Getúlio. *Discursos.* Rio: DIP, 1944.

———. *O Estado Novo e o momento brasileiro.* Rio: DNP, 1938.

———. *A nova política do Brasil.* 11 vols. Rio: José Olympio, 1938–44.

———. *A política trabalhista no Brasil.* Rio: José Olympio, 1950.

Venâncio Filho, Alberto. *A intervenção do estado no domínio econômico.* Rio: Fundação Getúlio Vargas, 1968.

Vianna, Luiz Werneck. *Liberalismo e sindicato no Brasil.* Rio: Paz e Terra, 1976.

Villela, Annibal, and Suzigan, Wilson. *Política do governo e crescimento da economia brasileira, 1889–1945.* Rio: IPEA/INPES, 1973.

Wainer, Samuel. "Pedro Ernesto—sua vida de cirurgião e revolucionário." *Diretrizes,* 15 November 1942, pp. 3–22.

Walker, Thomas W. "From Coronelismo to Populism: The Evolution of Politics in a Brazilian Municipality, Ribeirão Preto, São Paulo, 1910–1960." Ph.d. dissertation, University of New Mexico, 1974.

Warner, Sam Bass. *Streetcar Suburbs.* Cambridge: Harvard University Press, 1962.

Weber, Ernesta von. *Bergamini.* Rio: Editora Moderna, 1931.

Weffort, Francisco C. "Origens do sindicalismo populista no Brasil (a conjuntura do após-guerra)." *Estudos CEBRAP* 4 (1973):65–105.

Wiarda, Howard J. *The Brazilian Catholic Labor Movement.* Amherst: University of Massachusetts Labor Relations and Research Center, 1969.

Williams, Margaret Todaro. "Pastors, Prophets, and Politicians: A Study of the Brazilian Catholic Church, 1916–1945." Ph.D. dissertation, Columbia University, 1971.

______. "The Politicization of the Brazilian Catholic Church: The Catholic Electoral League." *Journal of Interamerican Studies* 16 (1974):301–25.

Wirth, John D. *Minas Gerais in the Brazilian Federation, 1889–1937*. Stanford: Stanford University Press, 1977.

______. *The Politics of Brazilian Development, 1930–1954*. Stanford: Stanford University Press, 1971.

Young, Jordan M. *The Brazilian Revolution of 1930 and the Aftermath*. New Brunswick, N.J.: Rutgers University Press, 1967.

Index

PITT LATIN AMERICAN SERIES

PLAS

Cole Blasier, Editor

ARGENTINA IN THE TWENTIETH CENTURY
David Rock, Editor

ARMY POLITICS IN CUBA, 1898–1958
Louis A. Pérez, Jr.

AUTHORITARIANISM AND CORPORATISM IN LATIN AMERICA
James M. Malloy, Editor

BARRIOS IN ARMS: REVOLUTION IN SANTO DOMINGO
José A. Moreno

BEYOND THE REVOLUTION: BOLIVIA SINCE 1952
James M. Malloy and Richard S. Thorn, Editors

CONSTRUCTIVE CHANGE IN LATIN AMERICA
Cole Blasier, Editor

CUBA, CASTRO, AND THE UNITED STATES
Philip W. Bonsal

CUBA IN THE WORLD
Cole Blasier and Carmelo Mesa-Lago, Editors

CUBAN SUGAR POLICY FROM 1963 TO 1970
Heinrich Brunner

ESSAYS ON MEXICAN KINSHIP
Hugo G. Nutini, Pedro Carrasco, and James M. Taggart, Editors.

FEMALE AND MALE IN LATIN AMERICA: ESSAYS
Ann Pescatello, Editor

GAITÁN OF COLOMBIA: A POLITICAL BIOGRAPHY
Richard E. Sharpless

THE HOVERING GIANT: U.S. RESPONSES TO REVOLUTIONARY CHANGE IN LATIN AMERICA
Cole Blasier

ILLUSIONS OF CONFLICT: ANGLO-AMERICAN DIPLOMACY TOWARD LATIN AMERICA, 1865–1896
Joseph Smith

INTERVENTION, REVOLUTION, AND POLITICS IN CUBA, 1913–1921
Louis A. Pérez, Jr.

MY MISSIONS FOR REVOLUTIONARY BOLIVIA, 1944–1962
Víctor Andrade

THE OVERTHROW OF ALLENDE AND THE POLITICS OF CHILE, 1964–1976
Paul E. Sigmund

PANAJACHEL: A GUATEMALAN TOWN IN THIRTY-YEAR PERSPECTIVE
Robert E. Hinshaw

THE POLITICS OF MEXICAN OIL
George W. Grayson

THE POLITICS OF SOCIAL SECURITY IN BRAZIL
James M. Malloy

PUERTO RICO AND THE UNITED STATES, 1917–1933
Truman R. Clark

REVOLUTIONARY CHANGE IN CUBA
Carmelo Mesa-Lago, Editor

SELECTED LATIN AMERICAN ONE-ACT PLAYS
Francesca Colecchia and Julio Matas, Editors and Translators

SOCIAL SECURITY IN LATIN AMERICA: PRESSURE GROUPS, STRATIFICATION, AND INEQUALITY
Carmelo Mesa-Lago

SOCIETY AND EDUCATION IN BRAZIL
Robert J. Havighurst and J. Roberto Moreira

THE UNITED STATES AND CUBA: HEGEMONY AND DEPENDENT DEVELOPMENT, 1880–1934
Jules Robert Benjamin

URBAN POLITICS IN BRAZIL: THE RISE OF POPULISM, 1925–1945
Michael L. Conniff